M000086943

Kingdom Politics

KINGDOM POLITICS

In Search of a New Political Imagination
for Today's Church

Kristopher Norris
and
Sam Speers

CASCADE *Books* · Eugene, Oregon

KINGDOM POLITICS
In Search of a New Political Imagination for Today's Church

Copyright © 2015 Kristopher Norris and Sam Speers. All rights reserved. Except for
brief quotations in critical publications or reviews, no part of this book may be re-
produced in any manner without prior written permission from the publisher. Write:
Permissions, Wipf and Stock Publishers, 199 W. 8th Ave., Suite 3, Eugene, OR 97401.

Cascade Books
An Imprint of Wipf and Stock Publishers
199 W. 8th Ave., Suite 3
Eugene, OR 97401

www.wipfandstock.com

ISBN 13: 978-1-62564-105-2

Cataloguing-in-Publication Data

Norris, Kristopher, and Sam Speers.

    Kingdom politics : in search of a new political imagination for today's church /
Kristopher Norris and Sam Speers.

    xii + 214 p. ; 23 cm. Includes bibliographical references.

    ISBN 13: 978-1-62564-105-2

    1. Christianity and politics. 2. Church. 3. Christianity—Essence, genius, nature. I.
Norris, Kristopher. II. Speers, Sam. III. Title.

BV600.2 K50 2015

Manufactured in the U.S.A.   04/15/2015

For our parents

Contents

Foreword

IN *DEMOCRACY IN AMERICA*, Alexis de Tocqueville famously spoke of religion as "the first of America's political institutions," whose exquisite variety could be appreciated best in relation to the paradox of its never mixing "directly in the government of society." Considerations of Tocqueville's report have typically led to debates on church-state relations—and ended there.

Fortunately, the resourceful writers of the present volume offer fresh and vivid energy to the often vexing conversation on religion and politics among North American Protestants. Equipped with a modest research grant, a cache of questions, and their iPhones (which for so many researchers have replaced the microcassette recorder as the tool of choice in the field), Kris Norris and Sam Speers offer an insightful and multistoried account of religion and politics on the North American Protestant scene—one that moves us beyond church-state discussions and the various strategic debates on "direct politicking" that preoccupy both liberal and conservative Christians.

Friedrich Schleiermacher, the great nineteenth-century cartographer of religious experience, once said that it would be detrimental to the task of theology to forsake interest in "the true condition" of religious communities.[1] To exert any "deliberative influence," he said, theologians must appraise the actual conditions of the church in its historical particularity. This is, I think, an illuminating and paradigm-shifting recommendation for the theological enterprise. Yet modern Protestant theology, as an academic discipline in its liberal and confessional varieties, has tended to ignore the lived, faith-shaped practices of people in real congregations.

---

1. Schleiermacher, *Brief Outline of the Study of Theology*, §96 (Edinburgh: T & T Clark, 1850), 130.

Norris and Speers, while no doubt sympathetic to the ecclesial turn in recent Protestant thought, and grateful for the Barthian revolution that propelled it, do not intone "the church" as some kind of magical ideal that miraculously transforms collections of worshipers into authentically Christian communities. Churches are formed by practices; and while practices are inherently communicative—not only ways of *doing* things, as Wayne Meeks has said, but of *saying* things—they adhere always to particular social settings, and are therefore complex, idiosyncratic, and messy. Theology needs a sense of place and contextual embeddedness, where theory and practice coalesce in concrete life. Lived theology, as exemplified in this volume, reminds us that it is not doctrine, catechism, and confession in abstraction but *the flow of lived experience* that renders Christian truth claims intelligible. By asking how theological convictions shape distinctive ways of *being church,* Norris and Speers emerge as sharp and insightful observers of American religious life and the complex, and tumultuous, interactions between the church and the political order.

If churches are "inherently political," theologians should look to the church's "distinctive speech and practices" to find the kind of political imagination best suited for a faithful Christian witness in the North American context.[2] To make the claim that churches should pursue "not conservative politics, liberal politics, or anti-politics, but kingdom politics"—if we wish to do more than assert an empty slogan—requires ethnographic, sociological, and historical attention to real communities. It requires thoughtful and critical attention to the ways that particular churches understand and practice politics, to the distinctive and concrete visions of the kingdom of God that precede partisan loyalties.

Attention to the political practices of Christian congregations via ethnography and participant-observation alone, however, will not produce the theological perceptions necessary to invigorate the church's witness in the world, or cleanse it of its deceptions. These perceptions must be shaped by the distinctive speech and practices of churches in particular contexts, and in contexts that sometimes clash. In this manner, interpreting and narrating the political habits of Christian communities remains a fundamentally theological task. If church communities are inherently political, then it seems evident that any regard for the integrity of the worldly space called the church must maintain a specifically theological character; which is to say, churches' inherent politics can be best ascertained in theological

2. Karl Barth, *Church Dogmatics*, I.1 (Edinburgh: T & T Clark, 1975).

observation and analysis. Theological tropes lead to embodied and "emplaced" politics, and uncover the world views expressed in communities as built-sacred spaces, which in turn help orient the church's engagement in the political order.[3]

Conversely, theological commitments animate practice and frame courses of action within social contexts, shaping them in distinctive ways. For theological convictions and commitments in their inner logic aspire toward lived expressions, which in turn can be observed, narrated, analyzed, and appropriated (theologically) in the contextual elements and practices of Christian social existence.

I hope that in addition to the rich insights that await the reader of *Kingdom Politics*—and the delight of following these two energetic writers as they map the dense landscape of American religion and politics—the reader will further appreciate a style of theological writing shaped by attention to the patterns and practices of lived faith. We might distinguish this style of *lived theology* in terms of its concern to (1) attend to the lived singularities of Christian existence; (2) explore the intentionality of theological convictions, and doctrinal and confessional commitments, toward particular modes of political behavior and identity; and (3) clarify the lived consequences of theological ideas in ways that help Christians more truthfully communicate and embody the truth of the gospel. While there are no easy formulas for predicting the political consequences of Christian faith and practice, every church community exists as a wellspring of outward-moving conviction and energy. "The dogma is the drama," as Dorothy Sayers wrote.

I realize that my remarks tend to cast *Kingdom Politics* within the parameters of contemporary academic theology. But lived theology, as a distinctive style, method, and pedagogy, is more than anything else an invitation to take theological questions into the field. It invites theologians to include the wisdom, depth, and details of lived experience in this marvelous discipline of thinking about God, which in turn creates the impulse to wander, ask, explore, investigate, and partake in the divine dramas unfolding beyond our academic enclaves. In order to say who "God the Lord is," as Jürgen Moltmann has written, we need to be willing to honestly tell the stories of what people have actually experienced.

3. Manuel Vasquez, *Lived Theology and Civil Courage* (Charlottesville, VA: Project on Lived Theology, 2003).

some with young children, filtered into the building and out of the late May heat with watermelon and popsicles they had picked up near the door.

An array of baguettes and cinnamon raisin bread from a nearby bakery was placed on coffee tables, alongside boxed wine from Trader Joe's—the sacred elements for today's communion. But first, pastor Doug Pagitt wanted to introduce the church to its newest staff member, a facilities manager named Ben. The two sat and talked on stools in the center of the room while the congregation watched comfortably, some finishing their popsicles or checking their iPhones. After asking Ben about his hobbies, his Middle Eastern heritage, and his world travels, Doug put him on the spot.

"Now Ben, I've heard that you have a very special talent, and I think everyone would love for you to share it with us."

Ben laughed and covered his face with his hands, shaking his head in protest as the congregation clapped and shouted encouragement. After much playful prodding, he revealed his talent: he can recite the entire climactic battle speech from the film *Braveheart*, verbatim. The crowd cheered as Ben stood with mock reluctance and asked if anyone had the soundtrack on their iPhone. Within moments, the sound of bagpipes reverberated through the sanctuary. We tried to conceal our look of "What is happening here?!" as Ben began pacing purposefully around the couches. Suddenly inspired, he picked up a communion baguette from a nearby coffee table, and, brandishing it as a sword, began his nearly three-minute performance, complete with Scottish accent and dramatic eye contact with his bemused "soldiers."

This was just our second stop in a series of visits to churches across the country to talk with church leaders about their approaches to politics— and already, the diversity was profound. Just twenty-four hours earlier, we had visited the magnificent Basilica of St. Mary in downtown Minneapolis, where the communion elements are kept locked in an ornate gold box on an altar beneath a fifty-foot, marble-columned baldachin. The sacred elements are handled only by the priest and administered only to bona fide Catholics in a solemn litany of Jesus' betrayal and sacrifice. We watched as, one by one, the congregation came forward in quiet reverence to receive the transubstantiated body and blood, drawn to the altar by the somber notes of a Latin hymn echoing off of the immense vaulted ceiling.

Back at Solomon's Porch, less than five miles away, Ben waved his communion-baguette sword high, pointing at his cheering troops as he cried, "They may take our lives, but they will never take our *freeedommm*!"

With the speech concluded and victory secured, communion proceeded joyfully—even boisterously—with much warm chatter and little structure. We even noticed a few folks pouring themselves a little extra wine to carry them through the remainder of the service.

THE PROBLEM: AVOIDANCE VS. ACCEPTANCE

These two communion experiences point to a vast diversity of styles and traditions within the American church landscape: communion-baguette swords vs. gold-plated altars, Bach chorales vs. rock worship, postservice voter registration vs. sermons condemning the politicizing of the church. Despite the apparent disunity in purpose and practice, all of these churches are proposing answers to the same question: "What is the mission of the church in the world?"

Their answers are as diverse as their communion liturgies. And yet, we realized, nearly all of their answers have something in common: they have separated the pursuit of spiritual formation from the work of social transformation, and therefore struggle to produce disciples who grow in love for both God and neighbor. For some churches the focus is primarily on the individual, on evangelism and developing members' "personal faith," while other churches focus on public issues of social justice and government policy.

Church leaders are struggling to understand what worship has to do with missions, and how the Word becomes the Word made flesh. How are they best integrated into the lives of disciples? How should preaching impact our social vision? How can the way in which we greet and fellowship with each other shape the way we reach out to the "least of these?" What does a church's leadership structure say about how its members should think about citizenship? And conversely, how should a church's cross-cultural witness alter the way it worships and thinks about God? These questions aren't new; in some ways they reflect the same struggle that Paul and James addressed in teaching their communities what faith has to do with works (Eph 2:8–9, Jas 2:14–26).

The same biblical tension persists today. Observers label these often-competing agendas in several ways: priestly and prophetic, faith and action, conversionist and activist, personal piety and social change, worship and missions. Our favorite way to frame this is that many churches worship Jesus the King, but avoid the messiness of working for his kingdom. Others policy change. For example, sociologist James Hunter claims that "Politics has become so central in our time that institutions, groups, and issues are now defined relative to the state, its laws and procedures."[9] Political activism is the "tactic of choice" for churches, Hunter laments, so much so that "the dominant public witness of the Christian churches in America since the early 1980s has been a political witness."[10] In other words, churches now allow the partisan ethos of this vision to overdetermine their own missions and practices.

The problem is that both responses reflect a poor understanding of the political nature of the church, and the type of political action the church is called to. The first response—avoiding politics altogether—ignores the church's responsibility to address important social issues. To avoid talking about significant social (and yes, political) issues that the church has a stake in—such as immigration policy, racial justice, and abortion—is to miss important opportunities to engage with the world on issues of justice. The second option—jumping into partisan politics—often allows the church's practices to be overdetermined by partisan agendas, and limits their political response to those actions with direct policy implications. It risks turning churches into activist organizations with a slightly religious flair. Churches that tend to align themselves too closely with a particular party or overemphasize a particular social or moral issue risk developing a misdirected allegiance to party or issue. This approach restricts the church's imagination about the kinds of political causes it could support, or the kinds of partners it could work with.[11]

One of our professors has written that most churches fail to engage with the world because the only models of public engagement they have encountered are too closely tied to political and partisan agendas.[12] And in both cases outlined above, congregations have forgotten that the church is an inherently political body: a community defined by its allegiance to a new King, its citizenship in a new world, and its call to work alongside others in pursuit of a new way of life. Both responses are incomplete, and limit the power of church practices to form disciples and impact society. Both types of churches have allowed a narrow conception of politics to determine their mission and ministries. This narrow sense of politics, informed by sociologists and political theorists from Machiavelli to Max Weber and onward, limits politics to actions by or for the state—actions necessarily involving coercion, competition, or domination. Operating with this limited sense of politics has "delimited the imaginative horizon through which the church and Christian believers think about engaging the world," prioritizing methods that require "the state, the law, or a political party."[13]

Ignoring deeper political dimensions of what it means to be the church in the world limits the ability of both types of congregations to harness the full formative power of their practices. According to James K. A. Smith, regularly performed practices of worship and mission form our hearts to believe certain things about the nature of God, God's kingdom, and our role in it.[14] But this process is most effective when we *understand* the formative potential of our practices, and intentionally orient them toward a desired end—in this case, a rightly ordered allegiance. "Practices aren't like prescribed medicine that will cure you whether or not you understand how it works," N. T. Wright argues. "Our conscious mind and heart need to understand, ponder, and consciously choose the patterns of life which these practices are supposed to produce in us and through us."[15] Neglecting this formative power hinders not only a church's effectiveness in ministry, but also its faithfulness to God's mission.

OUR CLAIM: KING AND KINGDOM

Churches on both the Left and the Right have accepted a vision of politics based on the strategy of the religious right, which they either mimic by centering their public mission on policy advocacy, or react against by washing their hands of politics altogether. Neither response is particularly compelling, and a new, politically confused generation of Christians is looking for "something deeper and something better."[16] Our primary claim in this book is that the church needs a new political vision, one that takes its cues about the nature of politics from another political reality: the kingdom of God.

Claiming this new political vision requires churches to move beyond a shallow understanding of politics based in American partisanship, and understand that the church is, by definition, a deeply political body called to a particular kind of deeply political activity in the world. The kingdom of God is a political reality, and as a witness to and foretaste of this kingdom, the church's response to an overly partisan public arena should be neither to join a camp nor to abandon its political imagination altogether. Rather, it is to orient its allegiance toward the only kingdom that transcends parties and nations, tribes and tongues, cultures and generations. Remaining faithful to God requires the church to understand itself as a political body within the world, and its political existence is exemplified in its faithfulness to God's calling. The church's political task is not primarily to influence state power or achieve desired electoral results. Rather, the church's political task is to witness before the world to the rule of Christ and the coming kingdom of God.

This new political vision also requires churches to broaden their understanding of what constitutes political activity. Depending on the church, politics might mean introducing communion as a tangible expression of our hope for life in a kingdom without oppression and war; or partnering with local government to end gang violence in local schools; or revamping the church leadership structure to empower and mobilize the membership.

For example—returning to the story with which we began this chapter—in what ways was communion at Solomon's Porch political? Sitting on couches in the round, with the pastor perched on a stool in the center of the congregation rather than an elevated pulpit, reenacting a movie scene before the sacred act of communion, handling the communion elements in a casual (perhaps irreverent) way—this all works to shape the members at Solomon's Porch in important ways. First, it teaches them that the divide between the sacred and secular is blurred. In their presentation and handling of the sacred elements, no effort is made to conceal the fact that they came from aisle six at the local grocery store. If boxed wine and bread from the local bakery can become the elements of worship and means of grace, then everyday objects and practices can become ways of approaching the sacred. And second, by breaking down the typical hierarchy between clergy and laity, members learn that everyone has something to contribute. This structure instills a value for egalitarianism that extends beyond the walls of the church and into their family, workplace, and political lives. These lessons, implicit but powerful, are, in fact, political lessons. They shape the values of the community and help to order its life together. They also impact the way its members relate to those outside that community, connecting their spiritual activities to everyday aspects of their lives.

Piety is Political

How can a new political vision help churches resolve the oft-present tension between King and kingdom? The church's struggle to integrate worship and missions, we believe, is fundamentally a problem of the church forgetting *whose* it is. What appear on the surface to be issues of identity or activity are really questions of *allegiance*—and allegiance is always political.

The church owes its first and ultimate political allegiance to Christ. This ought to determine the ways it engages with society, and especially how it engages with the powers and principalities of this world.[17] True allegiance to Christ as Lord requires both a devotion to Jesus as King over our personal lives and a commitment to the kingdom of God directing our public and social mission. Understanding the church as a deeply political body will link these elements together into one unified mission.

Allegiance binds us to the King, but also calls us to join in God's work in the world in anticipation of God's kingdom coming. Political thinking gives churches the language to talk about these two aspects of their mission and to faithfully consider the relationship between them. In short, allegiance is what enables Christians to balance commitment to God and to neighbor (Matt 22:36–40).

This deeper political imagination, rooted in the politics of the kingdom, helps to integrate the church's commitments to King and kingdom and provides a more holistic and potent understanding of the church's mission. It involves submitting to a different law and ruler, maintaining its own ways of decision-making, defining its own membership and communal identity, carrying out common tasks, demonstrating a distinctive way of life, and effecting social transformation.[18] These commitments—to King and kingdom—are essential and interconnected dimensions of the church's mission, and cannot be separated. When we attempt to separate them, and thus worship from mission, the lack of the one undermines the effectiveness and faithfulness of the other. When we hold them together, each transforms and enhances the other.

Contrary to our original hypothesis, politics was not just the problem—it could also be part of the solution. We propose that a deeper recognition of the church as a political body will help churches to integrate these two functions of their mission, and to recognize that even piety is political.[19] We believe that churches need to broaden their political imagination, to understand that 1) the church is an inherently political community, and 2) ordinary church practices are politically significant. This more biblical understanding of the church will help churches to reintegrate King *and* kingdom by designing practices that more faithfully cultivate holistic followers of Christ—disciples fully devoted to Jesus as Savior and Lord, and committed to continuing Jesus' work to transform the world.

OUR APPROACH

Lived Theology

The topic of church and politics has become very popular in recent years. So why write yet another book about it? While many others have examined the ways churches engage in political activity, most of these treatments have taken the perspective of an academic discipline like sociology or political science, which are limited by their inherently empirical nature.[20] Some recent studies have understated the influence of politics in church because they are only able to locate the political in partisan endorsements or policy advocacy from the pulpit. Not many have examined this through the lens of theology and from the perspective of the local church, with the purpose of helping churches themselves think through this issue more carefully.[21]

But even theological research often focuses too heavily on theoretical assessments made from armchairs, removed from the lived experience of churchgoers. If theology is truly to be in service of the church then it needs to pay attention to what is actually going on in churches.[22] So we decided to actually visit churches, talk with church leaders, participate in church meetings and events, and reflect on our observations with church leaders and with each other. We set out to point to models that churches can use to better navigate their inherently political lives—engaging in public life while remaining faithful to their King. This book models a style of theological research and writing called lived theology, which we discovered at the Project on Lived Theology at the University of Virginia. According to Charles Marsh, lived theology offers "a more disciplined attention to the theological depth and detail of lived experience," in which "the patterns and practices of everyday life are claimed as an essential part of constructive theology."[23] This model takes seriously the practices of church communities, not only as material for sociological study, but also to make important judgments about the ways Christian communities engage in life together, and what kind of witness they offer—judgments that will hopefully lead to a more faithful public witness.[24]

That is why we have written this book not primarily for academic theologians, but for church leaders and those interested in the ways churches think about and engage in politics. This book is for those who are concerned about the ways Christians engage in politics, those wondering if churches can faithfully engage in politics, and those who question what politics has to do with the church in the first place. One famous theologian

What does "lived theology" say about PT?

wrote nearly 200 years ago, "It can only be greatly detrimental on all sides when the leaders of one church community are not acquainted with the true condition of the rest."[25]

The following chapters offer snapshots of what's happening in church and politics right now. If the type of political transformation we have talked about is already occurring, the stories of these congregations will include examples to aspire to, as well as cautionary tales. These five snapshots are meant to be illustrative, not exhaustive. Our stories of visits to these churches highlight the practices of congregations, in their complexity—both when they fall short and when they offer examples for others of the ways churches can be faithfully political, and in doing so, connect their commitment to the King with their work for the kingdom. We hope the stories of these churches will demonstrate ways that churches are inherently political in the deepest and most basic sense, and offer glimpses of the kind of political imagination we need in churches—not conservative politics, liberal politics, or anti-politics, but kingdom Politics.

Formation and Practice

The church practices highlighted in this book are not just illustrative of the ways churches choose to be political; there is more at stake here. So, before we proceed further, we should also let you in on one of our underlying assumptions: ordinary church practices are also deeply formative for congregations—spiritually, socially, even politically. We are convinced that the practices examined in this book work in deep (and often unrecognized) ways to shape the hearts, minds, and actions of the people who attend these churches. The writer of Hebrews talks about a process of Christian formation through repeated practices, of spiritual and moral growth from milk to solid food "for those whose faculties have been trained by practice to distinguish good from evil" (5:14). Therefore, there is a lot at stake in churches recognizing the formative power of their ordinary practices. But why? And how does this work?

We believe that humans are motivated primarily by love. We were created by God with a desire to worship, a desire to love something. We inhabit the world not primarily as thinkers, but as worshipers.[26] In fact, *what* we choose to love defines who we are; it makes us who we are. The object of our ultimate love will determine the type of person we become and the types of behaviors we will engage in. We begin to live in a way that expresses the

means to do so. I still called myself an evangelical, though my friends doubted whether evangelicalism would still claim me. I began pastoring a small evangelical church, but as a minister fresh out of seminary with "radical," perhaps idealistic, notions about the church, I grew impatient with what I perceived as a simple and shallow faith in my congregation, as well as an overt patriotism. Faced with what I perceived to be the only possible choice between deconstructing their theology and reshaping it into one that appreciated the deep political message of Scripture or leaving them to an easy evangelical faith that left them as happy and dedicated Christians, I chose the latter and left the church.

Despite a strong commitment to the mission of the local church, these difficult early years of ministry left me wondering what use there was for the church, and what my role might be within it. I worried that many churches had been co-opted by nationalism, or worse, seduced by politics (both red and blue) to focus on public policy, and failed to offer a distinctively Christian witness to the world. Still, I felt a deep longing for home—for a life in church ministry, and a return to the passion and earnestness of my evangelical roots. In many ways, this project was a personal journey for me, chance to correct for the mistake I made in my pastorate, to help churches identify the deeper political dimensions of their faith and mission and by doing so enrich their work of discipleship. This was also a journey for which I was glad to have some company, as Sam—still ensconced in evangelicalism—helped to guide me on a journey back to a new home.

I (Sam), on the other hand, was more concerned about the watered-down faith I saw in many activist congregations. I grew up in a conservative evangelical church, and while I now questioned some of the theology this church taught, I still thought individual, personal faith was central to the Christian life—the "King" perspective. During college I got involved in a campus ministry that introduced me to a broader vision of Christianity, one that paid attention to issues like poverty and race. But I wondered why so many of the churches that focused on these issues seemed to do so at the expense of training people in their devotional lives and spiritual disciplines. There seemed to be something missing theologically when worship and Scripture were treated as mere jumping-off points for activism.

I agreed to the project hesitantly, a bit reluctant to travel around with this shaggy-haired guy in tattered cargo shorts. (The first time one of my housemates saw Kris, he thought he was a homeless man I had brought in to give some food or money.) I didn't have the same political reading

FOR KING AND KINGDOM

of Scripture, theology, and church practices as Kris, but it intrigued me. I agreed that the way churches were involved in politics was often problematic, having sat uncomfortably through many worship services that conflated faith and national pride, and had not seen many examples of churches talking about politics well. I wanted to discover an expression of the church's political mission that was exciting rather than unsettling.

A Look Ahead

What began as an academic research project by two theology students to examine the political practices of a set of congregations turned into something much broader, deeper, and more personal: a chance to rethink the identity and mission of the church by closely investigating what churches say about themselves and how they engage with the world. We wanted to go deeper, to issues that touch the heart of what it means to be church: What does God call the church to do in the public arena, and what is the public witness of the church? How should the church shape its public witness and the habits and actions of its members in a culture dominated by partisan political discourse? What is the church's role in forming the theological and political identities and behaviors of its members? What practices will help churches to offer a faithful theological vision of hope in Christ to the world, to work missionally to generate transformative change in people's lives, and to remain faithful to their God-given calling and mission? In a culture in which public behaviors and attitudes are largely determined by partisan ideologies, these are ultimately questions of how to witness, how to form disciples, and how to faithfully go about missions within the social and political structures of our society.

It's funny how plans change when you get on the road and see what people are actually doing on the ground. The thesis of this book changed several times over the two years of research and writing (an immense frustration to the more inflexible one of us—that would be Sam—but an exciting challenge for the more laid-back, fun, cooler, and much better-looking one of us). What finally emerged is this: a book that tells the story of our visits to congregations all over the country, the interesting people we met, the problems *and* exemplary practices we encountered, and the ways that we have been changed by these churches. These are stories we want to share with you, stories that churches need to hear.

Our analysis of each church will focus on three primary areas of practice—worship, leadership structure, and missions activities. Each church represents a different model of political engagement. Each one defies easy classification. Still, we think it will be helpful to describe each using strokes broad enough that readers will recognize both similarities to and differences from their own congregations. Within these stories we examine the benefits and drawbacks of each congregation's approach, and highlight practices that can serve as examples for other churches.

Our first stop is Saddleback Church in Orange County, California, the evangelical megachurch home of Rick Warren. At this congregation known for seeker sensitivity, conservatism, and the Purpose Driven movement, we discovered a broad missional agenda with deep political implications. Next we visit Solomon's Porch, one of the first Emergent Church communities, comprised primarily of post-evangelicals in Minneapolis, whose "intentional unintentionality" offers a provocative twist on the formative potential of church practices. Next comes First & Franklin Presbyterian Church, a mainline congregation in Baltimore struggling with declining membership and attempting to reenergize itself through its inclusivity and advocacy for gay rights. Prairie Street Mennonite Church in small-town Elkhart, Indiana is a congregation from the often politically withdrawn Anabaptist tradition that is fully engaged in the life and struggles of its local community. We end with Ebenezer Baptist Church in Atlanta, former home of Martin Luther King Jr., a church that unabashedly wears its political character on its sleeve and engages in overtly political activities like voter registration and protest marches, but embeds these within deep commitments to personal growth in faith and the story of Scripture.

Through exploring these churches and their various models of political engagement in the areas of worship, leadership, and missions, we will argue for the deeply political implications of their everyday practices, identify some pitfalls inherent in each snapshot, and highlight exemplary practices that may serve as models for other congregations.

The conclusions we discover have broad implications for churches across the spectrum. The challenge to politically passive churches is this: understanding worship as politically formative, that it shapes your relationship to the world and not just to God, will enable you to worship in a way that takes advantage of that formative potential. This understanding brings freedom not to shy away from addressing controversial issues that are relevant to the gospel—war, healthcare, immigration, abortion—just because they are political or seem to align with one political party or another. Indeed, wrestling with these issues is part of churches' responsibility to form congregants into disciples.

The challenge to politically active churches is this: for your social activism to be a faithful witness to the kingdom and not just activism, you must ground your practices explicitly in your allegiance to Christ. They must arise out of your worship and faith commitments, and from an understanding that you are activists *for the King,* and not just activists for a particular party or for the sake of activism. This does not mean that you will always change your practices or commitments to particular issues, but that your motivation must always point back to your allegiance to Christ above all.

Each chapter that follows tells the stories of our visit to one of these five congregations. Some parts of each chapter convey our joint thoughts and experiences, and some narrate the perspective or experience of one of us. When the narrator changes, we will always indicate that either by identifying the speaker in parentheses or addressing the other person early in the section. We hope these pages will offer insights into congregational life, help for readers to evaluate the political implications of their own church practices, and suggestions for churches to better integrate their spiritual and social missions through a deeper understanding of the political character of the church.

Chapter 2

Mobilizing the Church to Change the World

Saddleback Church

THE SUN WAS ALREADY fading west as we boarded the plane for our first trip. In five hours we would land in Southern California to begin our visit to Saddleback Church. Saddleback Pastor Rick Warren's "Purpose Driven" ministry philosophy has indelibly altered the landscape of evangelical Christianity in the twenty-first century, and we could think of no better place to begin our research. We looked forward to visiting the renowned home of the pastor known for his acrostic Christian aphorisms, his grand vision for the church, and his trademark Hawaiian shirts—a fashion statement he now claims to have abandoned. (One of us has gone through a similar obsession with tropical shirts—and Sam wants you to know it was not him.)

The now 30,000-member congregation was founded in 1979 by a wide-eyed young pastor named Rick Warren, fresh from Baptist seminary—amazingly, only seven years removed from high school. Warren chose the arid hills of Orange County, California for his new church plant because it had been declared the fastest-growing county in the US during the past decade. Saddleback began humbly as a small Bible study in Warren's home, but soon he and his wife Kay began distributing fliers across the county for their first public worship service, advertised as a church "designed to meet your needs."[1] After hosting over 200 worshippers that first week, within thirty years Saddleback grew into one of the largest and most prominent churches in America. He would achieve international fame as the author of *The Purpose Driven Life*, one of the best-selling religious books of all time with more 30 million copies sold. His previous work, *The Purpose Driven Church*, sold over a million copies, and has been translated into over twenty languages as a how-to guide for church ministers across the globe.[2] Warren and Saddleback have used seventy-nine facilities in fifteen years, from homes to school theaters to canvas tents, finally settling at their massive Lake Forest campus.[3]

Growing up in evangelical, nondenominational churches, and originally from Orange County, California, I (Sam) had spent nearly ten years at an East Coast megachurch that looked to Saddleback as a model. Though I had started to gravitate toward the tight community of smaller evangelical churches in college, I expected Saddleback's size and feel to be comfortable, familiar. However, since playing in worship bands in high school had been the extent of my involvement in church leadership, I was interested in exploring the inner workings of an evangelical megachurch in a way I hadn't done growing up. I was not as skeptical of the megachurch phenomenon as Kris, but wanted to discover the theology and vision behind the church environment that had shaped my faith.

I (Kris) began doing ministry during the "Purpose Driven" craze of the early 2000s. It had been formative for my early years of ministry, until a growing skepticism, a rocky pastorate, and years of academic theology left those beginnings behind and nearly forgotten. In many ways, the Purpose Driven movement seemed to embody what I considered (in my new academic perspective) to be the greatest dangers of contemporary evangelicalism: valorized individualism, ethereal piety at the expense of social action, and shallow discipleship. I assumed the chances of finding an evangelicalism that I could embrace at a megachurch were slim, especially at the birthplace of the Purpose Driven movement.

Our first stop after landing was In-N-Out Burger. Sam, forced to live out his past ten years in In-N-Out-less Virginia, insisted on this immediately upon our arrival. "I really don't get what the big deal is about this place," I told him, just before stuffing myself with a Double-Double Animal Style and a chocolate shake. I quickly learned that anything less than an obsession with In-N-Out was blasphemy among Californians (even former Californians), based on the judgmental glare Sam shot at me.

'IMAGINEERING SADDLEBACK'

On Sunday morning we found the church campus at the edge of the Orange County suburbs, nestled among nondescript office buildings and parking lots at the base of Saddleback Mountain. The massive worship complex sprawled across the hill, looking almost like a theme park. One Saddleback pastor had referred to the church as a "Disneyland of faith," and in fact, Saddleback hired Disneyland "imagineers" to offer advice on landscaping and architectural design.[4] Among the window-tiered main worship center—with stadium seating to house over 3,000 and giant circus-like "tents" for concurrent, themed worship gatherings—the campus spread out in front of us complete with artificial creeks and waterfalls, palm trees, and colorful information kiosks lining winding walkways. Down the hill from the worship center stood a state-of-the-art, eco-friendly youth center called the Refinery, with multiple cafés, a basketball court, a game room, and a sand volleyball court. A life-sized replica of the empty tomb marked the entrance to the nearby children's ministry center. Kris told Sam that he half expected to find a Noah's ark 3D simulator or a "Crossing the Red Sea" water slide.

We finally located our first destination, the Community Resource Center, on the perimeter of the campus, and walked toward the small crowd and smell of frying bacon. The Resource Center was recently constructed to house the church's growing constellation of local ministries: from typical community services like a food pantry and support groups to more complex ministries like career and legal counseling, immigration assistance and ESL classes, with plans for a small medical clinic.[5] Every Sunday morning Saddleback cooks breakfast for members of the Lake Forest homeless population, which totals over 30,000 according to one staff member—a surprising number for one of the nation's most affluent counties.

Our first task was to find our contact, Johnny Montgomery, among the jovial few cooking pancakes and eggs outside. Johnny was a young new minister in charge of Saddleback's internship program (the church employs around fifty college interns every summer). He was delivering the breakfast devotional that morning at the Resource Center, and had invited us to attend. During our many email exchanges prior to our trip, I (Kris) pictured someone with a name like Johnny Montgomery wearing a cowboy hat and spurred boots—someone who always called you "partner" and slapped you on the back. I wished my name were Johnny Montgomery.

When we found Johnny, I quickly noticed no boots or hat. His laid-back SoCal tone did not match the Clint Eastwood aura I imagined—but I bravely concealed my disappointment. The hosts had cooked more than enough food for the number of visitors, so we gratefully accepted the pancakes and coffee offered to us and took our seats at the table. Johnny began his remarks, punctuated by frequent pauses for the Spanish translator—until the Latina visitors departed abruptly, with apology, before he finished. Johnny later admitted his anxiety—this was one of his first speaking assignments as a new minister at Saddleback. We related our own horror stories of leading Bible studies at camps and youth groups, bonding over the awkwardness of the moment.

Making a Positive Identity

After stopping for a free donut from the food truck in the parking lot, we caught a shuttle up to the main sanctuary for the service. Each weekend the Lake Forest campus holds fourteen worship gatherings, many conducted concurrently in the tent-like "venues" located throughout the massive campus. Saddleback offers a flavor for nearly every worship preference: from contemporary worship in the main sanctuary, to rock, contemplative, Spanish-language, and even a "small-church" and hymn service. All this does not include the seven satellite campuses scattered throughout the greater LA area, each with their own worship team and campus pastor, which bring total weekend attendance to over 25,000.

Passing by the splashing waterfalls and swarm of glowing greeters, we settled into seats on the third row of the bleachers. The worship center buzzed as several thousand congregants filled the bright room. The mostly white crowd was still more diverse than we expected—though several pastors admitted that Saddleback's socioeconomic diversity lags behind its racial diversity (Warren targets a specific demographic of young, unchurched, white-collar couples—you reach those you relate to most, he says).[6] As two younger white guys, we had no difficulty blending in—though Sam certainly more easily with his plaid shirt, skinny jeans, and meticulously sculpted hair. (Sam would like to add that this observation comes from someone with a fashion sense so ensconced in the nineties that anything tighter than carpenter jeans is deemed "skinny.")

Percussive tones flooded the sanctuary as the worship band enthusiastically led the congregation in a few contemporary worship anthems.

Every moment was perfectly planned and executed, from opening song to video announcements to transitional prayer. Sam was used to high-energy worship productions, but this was a far cry from the small-town Baptist services that I grew up in, with one organist playing "Just As I Am." I awkwardly shuffled and clapped to the rhythms booming from the stage, and I could have sworn I saw Sam inching away from me.

Following the announcements, Rick Warren emerged, larger than life on the two giant video screens that flanked the stage, to say he was unable to be with us, but that youth pastor Kurt Johnston would continue the sermon series on "Making a Positive Identity." Johnston connected Moses's anxiety about speaking in front of Pharaoh—"Who am I that I should go?"—with his own insecurities about his golf game, height, and ever-encroaching baldness, illustrating his points with a set of golf clubs and an ugly clay vase he had made for his mother as a child. The sermon at Saddleback is presented in a way that "anybody can walk in the doors and understand," a member of the worship team told us, "translated into terms for the unchurched."[7] One pastor called the sermon style at Saddleback "Action-Oriented Preaching"—preaching that gives practical answers to life's questions—and this was a prime example.[8]

As Kurt closed, I worried that the sermon, while rich in practical therapeutic language for those struggling with insecurity, seemed short on theological substance. Kurt had jumped from the Moses story to various "proof texts" for his three cures for insecurity—"Change Your Thinking," "Embrace Your Uniqueness," and "Trust Your Creator"—that could be found on any self-help poster outside a counseling office. Sam says that I always want sermons to include some deep theological insight or prophetic call to action—"to afflict the comfortable" rather than offer comfort. I recalled that other observers of sermons at Saddleback had noted that "it just didn't seem that different from watching Dr. Phil."[9] This approach has led one scholar to suggest that "Warren is willing to obscure his beliefs (at least initially) in an effort to bring more believers to the church."[10]

Sam reminded me that even wealthy Southern Californians need to be taught the comfort and peace offered in Scripture. The Bible does not just demand things of us; it also offers gifts, and part of pastoral care is to remind the congregation of these gifts. While Kurt's trio of insecurity-solvers did not follow the Moses story—God allowed Moses to work with his more eloquent brother rather than fully overcoming his anxiety (Exod 4:1–17)—it did speak to the everyday struggles of the ordinary person, and

22

How do you also do this while also offering comfort to those who need it.

that seemed to be the point. Applying the Bible to everyday life is an important part of preaching, and this conviction was clearly a driving element of the service.

As we would later learn, weekend worship services are designed as the entry point for the Saddleback church community; services contain few elements of Christian formation, but are intended to "expose people to faith,"[11] to be the initial hook that brings people back to church with a desire to become more involved in small groups and specific ministries. According to the Guest Services Pastor, worship services are geared toward seekers and new believers and thus are intended to be, he said with noted reluctance, "a big production."

The Discipleship Funnel

The next morning we parked outside a nondescript office building that looked more like a corporate headquarters than a church office. Johnny met us again—still no cowboy boots, I noted—and guided us down a winding hall to our first meeting with Dave Holden, Saddleback's Purpose Driven Training Director, and the expert on the vision and conceptual organization of the church. Dave leads conferences on the Purpose Driven model of church development for pastors around the globe. For us, he agreed to present the CliffNotes version of his four-hour presentation. We sat down in his small interior office, unprepared for the whirlwind of alliterations, acronyms, and organizational charts about to come our way.

Cramming four hours of information into just one, Dave rapidly explained a Saddleback member's journey from bystander to committed member. A series of concentric circles on a large whiteboard on the wall symbolized increasing levels of commitment: community, crowd, congregation, committed, and core. Saddleback helps members progress through these levels using what Dave calls the "Discipleship Funnel." Taking me back to ninth-grade geometry (that's eighth grade for Sam, who wants you to know he was a bit quicker with math), Dave drew a funnel, sliced horizontally into four segments. Weekend worship services, the mouth of the funnel, are where people are *exposed* to faith. Next are the four membership classes, Saddleback's version of a catechism, where that faith is *explained*.[12] The third level is small group, where faith is *experienced* in a community of Christians. In the final level, the narrow end of the funnel, faith is *expressed* through participation in Saddleback's local and global outreach ministries.

Avoiding Politics

We debriefed our trip down the Discipleship Funnel over fish tacos—I (Sam) couldn't convince Kris to go to In-N-Out two days in a row. Awash in a matrix of acronyms and charts, we began to put the puzzle pieces together. We recalled that less than a week before we were to fly out to Saddleback, we had received an email explaining that the staff was not comfortable with our visit. David Chrzan, Saddleback's Chief of Staff (yes, they have a "Chief of Staff") was concerned about the political language in the research description we sent. Perhaps they thought we were on a covert mission from our liberal university to expose Saddleback as a bastion of the Republican Party! After clarifying that we had no intention of taking down America's most famous congregation, or getting them into trouble with the IRS, and that we were, in fact, interested in the way church practices were political in ways beyond partisan politics, the church leadership conceded. Our initial suspicion was now confirmed, that the church intentionally avoided politics, at least for newcomers to the church, in order to keep the mouth of the Discipleship Funnel as wide as possible.

Rick Warren has been known to dispense politically charged tweets and emails encouraging his congregation to vote based on "nonnegotiable issues" like abortion, gay marriage, and stem-cell research. These forays into electoral politics, however, have often been immediately followed by public backtracking—including twice on *Larry King Live*. In these interviews Warren reversed course, voicing concern over the religious right (much to their chagrin), insisting that he is not an anti-gay marriage pastor, and generally distancing himself from political action by asserting the "limitations of politics."[13]

Warren ventured into the political sphere again in 2008, hosting a presidential debate at Saddleback. However, he considered this "Civil Forum" to be a primarily evangelistic exercise. Warren told his staff that the event was a "bridge for evangelism," to bring people back to church. From the pulpit, especially, Warren and his staff are careful to avoid partisan affairs. Warren titled his sermon for the Sunday after the debate "The Kind of Leader America Needs." But despite the suggestive title, the sermon was nearly apolitical, relating leadership qualities to the daily lives of his congregants rather than discussing political leaders or issues.[14]

As we reflected on our conversations and observations so far, we speculated about the reasons for this aversion to political language.[15] One possible reason, Kris thought, could be a practical concern for public image protection. Saddleback wants to avoid the "political church" stereotype associated with many other evangelical congregations in a world where partisan overtones are generally a turnoff. Thinking more broadly, however, we both understood the church's concern for its image to be rooted in its dedication to outreach. Warren considers evangelism the sole purpose of the worship service.[16] The therapeutic, yet highly passionate worship service, the aesthetic appeal of the church grounds, and the individual and personal-piety orientation of the Discipleship Funnel all seemed to be crafted to tender a warm and inviting face for the congregation, and even evangelicalism.[17] Warren, a staunch pro-lifer, once refused permission to an antiabortion group to set up a display outside the Worship Center, because he did not want it to be a stumbling block to evangelism.[18] Several pastors told us that Saddleback is attempting to reverse the decline of evangelicalism's public image, and become known more for what it stands for than what it stands against.

Kris, however, was unable to shake the feeling that Saddleback's charts and organizational acronyms oversimplified the process of discipleship. He worried that Saddleback promoted a Christianity that was too "user friendly," replete with easy-to-follow steps and rich in personal benefits.[19] In their typically pragmatic style, Saddleback's fresh face is constructed in order to keep people coming back, Kris observed, finishing his last taco and leaning back cynically in his chair. A worship service that doesn't remind congregants of the demands of Christian identity risks promoting the "cheap grace" that worried him at evangelical churches ("cheap grace" being Bonhoeffer's term for grace that is not accompanied by the ethical obedience of discipleship).[20] As merely the "entry point" in the Discipleship Funnel, worship can become solely therapeutic, rather than an experience of the messy social (and, yes, political) dimensions of the gospel. Kris worried that key aspects of formation and discipleship could be lost, especially a sense that worship is political in the way it trains us to be "citizens of another city and subjects of another King."[21]

But we also saw a few positive implications of this approach. During a time when politics is primarily seen as divisive, the church can be a place of relief and refreshment, on multiple levels. By maintaining a friendly posture that rises above the pettiness of partisan rhetoric, Saddleback intentionally increases its appeal to those who arrive skeptical of "political churches," or in need of reprieve from an overpoliticized public arena. In fact, the church leaders seem be aware of the danger of separating evangelistic events from the deeper threads of discipleship formation. Warren laments that too many churches "emphasize the benefits of the Gospel while ignoring the responsibility and cost of following Christ." Attracting seekers is only the first step, he insists, not the driving force of the church. The leaders at Saddleback maintain that even during the weekend worship service, the message is not watered down, only communicated relatably. "Being seeker sensitive does not limit what you say," he claims—only how you say it.[22]

Jesus recognized different levels of commitment, Warren also observes; he began by inviting people to "come and see" (John 1:39), and only after three years did he call the crowd to the ultimate challenge of taking up their cross (Mark 8:34). "Jesus was able to ask for that kind of commitment from the crowd only after demonstrating his love for them and earning their trust," Warren writes.[23] Though, Kris was quick to point out, in other cases, like the rich young ruler and the man who wanted to bury his father, Jesus asked for a full commitment from the start (Mark 10:17–22, Matt 8:21–11). In the case of the rich ruler, perhaps this more demanding calling had to do with the wealth or power of the one called, a notion even more pertinent at an affluent congregation like Saddleback.

Underlying these issues, we think, is a narrow vision of what it means to be political. For Saddleback, politics means partisanship, alliances with politicians and advocacy groups, or pulpit persuasions to vote a certain way—and as it does for many other churches, this means it should be avoided.[24] However, avoiding the political character of the church has the potential to constrain the mission of the church as well, especially in its efforts at evangelism and disciple making. By downplaying the political implications of faith in Christ and alternative political identity of the church in its call to discipleship and outreach to potential believers, Saddleback risks calling people to a shallow conversion consisting of assent to a set of principles rather than a radical change of allegiance (Mark 8:34–35). The church body must be political in order to be truly evangelical.[25]

We suggest that Christianity has an inherent political character, not just at its deepest levels, but *all the way up* the Discipleship Funnel. Even the moment of conversion is deeply political—it is the profession of a new identity, in which the kingdom of God becomes the center of one's political loyalty (Isa 37:16). Though the cultivation of this identity certainly occurs during small groups and church classes, it occurs perhaps most potently and frequently when the entire body is gathered together in worship. By understanding itself as a political body and its practices as politically formative, Saddleback might be able to witness more fully to the allegiance-altering call of Christ.

In any case, it seemed clear that at Saddleback, potentially divisive political conversations are intentionally extracted for the sake of evangelical outreach. The gospel may inform a person's politics, but only because "politics is downstream from culture," as one Saddleback pastor put it.[26] Saddleback works at creating a culture that will help to shape the contours of politics down the road, rather than jumping right into political issues during weekend services.

THE "MISSIONHOOD" OF ALL BELIEVERS

The next morning we arrived back at Saddleback after I helped Kris learn to work the GPS system on his new iPhone. He protested, claiming an acute inner sense of direction, but finally relented after passing the same Golden Spoon yogurt shop three times. (I spend much of my time with Kris helping him overcome his Luddite tendencies—it turns out his claims to innate directionality stem from allegedly winning an eighth-grade geography bee.) After enduring a fifteen-minute lecture on how GPS is precipitating the demise of basic geographical knowledge, I finally saw the street sign for "Purpose Drive."

After greeting a few members of the church staff, we were invited to attend that morning's staff meeting. Expecting a low-key business agenda for the summer, we were surprised to walk into one of the church's worship venues to join a packed crowd of all 300 staff. The entire auditorium was singing worship songs, led by a full band on the stage, with the same energy we had witnessed during Sunday morning services. After a few songs, Warren took the stage and began addressing the expectant audience. He talked about the summer schedule, upcoming guest preachers, and the rules for the summer staff beard-growing contest. Warren addressed everyone with an affectionate tone, from his chief of staff to the keyboard player, modeling the "positive counterculture" that he called his staff to emulate. The staff meeting felt more like a worship service: Warren talked for over forty-five minutes, more about inspiration than agenda, and complete with alliterative mnemonics, of course.

Meeting the Chief

Much of the daily business of coordinating the staff falls to Warren's second-in-command: his chief of staff, David Chrzan (pronounced "shawn"—or "shaaawwwn" if you are Kris and from backwoods North Carolina). Upon first encountering David's intense personality and crushing handshake, we recalled that he was the one initially suspicious of our research intentions. David, with his short-sleeved polo shirt, freshly exercised biceps, and crew-cut hair, gave off a commanding demeanor—fitting for the chief of staff of a 30,000-member institution. Brandishing a Nerf gun left over from a recent youth event, he invited us into his large corner office. We took our seats across from David and Johnny Montgomery on a couch between two giant bookcases, and asked our first questions.

What does it take to keep a 30,000-member church with over 300 staff running smoothly? How does decision-making at Saddleback work? And what exactly does a church "chief of staff" do? These questions seemed to have certain political implications, we thought, and we began asking them (a bit timidly) as David leaned forward in his chair intently, ready to fire back answers.

To our surprise, David told us there is little hierarchy in the church's leadership structure. Warren is the head of the leadership hierarchy as the church's founder and visionary. The rest of the staff are on equal footing, with some pastors serving on a pastoral management team. Saddleback's flat leadership structure is only possible by fostering a culture of trust over suspicion, David said while shooting Johnny with the Nerf gun. Decisions cannot be made in a church of this size without trust between the staff, as well as congregational trust of the pastoral team. Church staff are stuck with one another, he said, and rather than split up every time a conflict occurs, conflict is resolved within the team. David believes prominent evangelicals like Jerry Falwell and Pat Robertson have shrouded evangelicalism in a negative identity—based more on what it stands against than what it stands for—and suggested that the focus on trust between the staff should serve as a model for the trust Christians should gain in the public sphere. Christians need to cultivate an identity as a trustworthy people, not judgmental people who deserve public suspicion. Again, we noted, even the dynamics of conflict resolution among the staff were directed toward a missional and evangelical purpose.

This economy of trust is imperative between staff and congregation, he said, especially in the decision-making process. "So how are big congregational decisions made in this environment of trust?" we asked. Saddleback is not essentially democratic; the staff make most of the administrative decisions. In a church this size there is a logistical need for more centralized government; you can't take a congregational vote on every issue that arises. With this, David stood up and began sketching a diagram on the board. At Saddleback, he told us, drawing a vertical line, there is a distinction between *ministry* decisions (those dealing with outreach or missions to the community) and *administry* decisions (those dealing with internal polity). The staff handle the administry and then empower the members to take charge of the ministry. Those who implement ministry ideas are empowered to make their own decisions about that ministry, and those charged with leading and empowering the members are freed to make all administrative decisions without bringing them before the congregation.[27]

"So if a member has an idea about changing youth curriculum or the need for a new building," we asked, "do you have avenues for congregational input on these internal decisions?" If someone has an idea about some internal matter, he responded, then the staff is certainly open to hearing about it. "There is an avenue for [every member of the congregation] to be involved in ministry," he reiterated, but not the *administry*. "We [the staff] are the administers. They are the ministers. It is not the other way around," he said, citing the distinctions in Ephesians between the various gifts of the body (4:11–12).

Is this merely a pragmatic model, based on the fact that a church of this size can't wait for consensus among its 30,000 members or even take a congregational vote on every decision? David told us that this was certainly part of it: "We can't take a vote on the color of the paint." But the motivation for this model runs deeper. Most churches are bogged down in bureaucracy (much like our national government, he added) because we have imposed an "American form of government" on the church. "It is our Western cultural philosophy that everyone has a right to cast a vote. That's an American democratic idea," he said, growing more animated. "But show me in Scripture where that is. It's just not there." He thinks that democratic structures are more about control than freedom, and, when transplanted into church polity, only impede church growth.

Sitting back down, David pulled out three different smart phones from various pockets, and quickly checked them all, with apologies. Time was running short, so he closed with an illustration. Each year the church holds one congregational business meeting to discuss and vote on the church budget. Last year, out of a church of 30,000 members, "only 73 showed up," he said. "And we've already decided how we are going to spend the money," he said, so the only people in attendance with questions are those who don't trust the leaders. It is not an issue of apathy, he claimed; in today's busy world most people just don't feel the need to be involved in the minutiae of this type of governance. "Most people trust leadership," he concluded.

Mobilizing for Ministry

The ministry structure of the church, however, operates very differently from the *administry*. While the internal, congregational decision-making structure is very top heavy, with minimal input from the folks in the stadium seating, the ministry organization is bottom-up. All ministry ideas arise from members of the congregation, not the staff. And the staff's job is to help empower the members to implement those ideas. Every church leader we spoke with was careful not to call the staff the "ministers," reserving that title for the membership.

Wandering through the maze of offices and cubicles in the deceptively large office building, we finally found Randy Craft, Pastor for Local PEACE, the ministry arm of the church. Randy, Matt Bruce, and a few other Local PEACE pastors explained this ministry vision of the church. The goal of this church is "Every member on mission."[28] And, in fact, it seems to be working here: 10,000 Saddleback members are now involved in 400 local ministries, and the church is preparing to expand its local ministry activity from six neighborhoods to twelve in 2012.

Every member is encouraged to choose or begin a ministry that arises from his or her own passions and gifts. Randy explained that the only requirements are that the member must complete a ministry membership class and have an interview with a staff person to discern her particular gifts. The ministry must, of course, be initiated with a thorough plan and team of volunteers, be compatible with the church's beliefs and values (and here the staff do maintain some regulation and filtering authority, we note), and be self-supporting.

"How does a church of this size operate on a purely lay-led ministry structure?" we asked. "How do you cast a vision that actually energizes this level of sustained involvement?" It all starts with the membership classes, the pastors say. These classes are the most intentional church-wide factor in cultivating the "every member on mission" ethos. They infuse the notion of "living on mission" into the DNA of the members so they know, "yeah, I should do something," as one pastor said. Focusing on the message of Ephesians 2:10—"For we are God's handiwork, created in Christ Jesus to do good works, which God prepared in advance for us to do"—the classes teach that "there are works out there that if you're not doing, they're not getting done," as Matt Bruce put it. Purpose is a great motivator, he suggested, when everyone believes they have a contribution to make. In every activity, from worship to small groups to special events, the vision is repeated.

Everything pivots on the church's missional identity. For example, like many other churches, Saddleback initiated a congregational health program in 2012 called the Daniel Plan, rallying the congregation to lose 250,000 collective pounds in one year and installing a fitness course across the campus. Unlike in many other churches, this program began with diet coaching from television's Dr. Oz and classes from Tae Bo founder Billy Blanks.[29] Warren framed the initiative as a missions effort: a healthier congregation is better equipped to serve God where God calls them. This was one more way for the staff to encourage members to move from spectators to ministers.

Another pastor, in a more pragmatic moment, conceded that beyond convincing people that they have a contribution to make and a responsibility to make it, you must also teach them the personal benefits of Christian work. In this culture, you must answer the question of "what's in it for me," he said, and focus on the benefits of a Christian life, not just its features.[30] The reality is that once people see that Christian growth or mission work is beneficial to them, they are much more likely to participate, even if that becomes less significant after they become involved.

Giving Away the Ministry to the People

After several days of wandering the maze of offices and ferociously copying down acrostics and diagrams, we decided it was time for a break at the beach—we were in Southern California, after all! As we drove down nearby Newport Beach, we discussed Saddleback's complex leadership and ministry organization. Ever the external processor, I (Kris) attempted out loud to reconcile the church's top-down leadership structure with its more democratic ministry model, while simultaneously trying to catch a glimpse of the Pacific *and* find a place to park. Sam nervously motioned for me to pay attention to where I was going, and eventually suggested I just stop talking. Thankfully, his nerves would be calmed by the sun and sand. "You think I could find a job with a church that would allow me to come to the beach every afternoon?" I asked before getting knocked down by a giant wave. Unfortunately our ocean time was cut short by Sam's close encounter with a menacing shark fin—maybe it was a dolphin's, but who has time to investigate when your life is at stake?

Reinvigorated by the pounding waves and surprisingly chilly water, we returned to our conversation about church polity. We had asked David if he saw an inconsistency between such top-down decision-making and the egalitarian, grassroots ministry ethos we encountered in our other conversations. He did not see this as a contradiction. The staff make the big decisions, he said, because of the congregation's trust in them. "Followership" is part of the congregation's participation in Saddleback's mission: "If you have a God-ordained leader [i.e. Rick Warren], then you need to be a God-ordained follower."

I confessed to Sam my concern that confining major church decisions to the pastoral staff limited Saddleback's practice of the priesthood of all believers. It did not seem to apply equally everywhere. Does this model send a mixed message to the congregation? The decoupling of personal ministry from church governance might allow members to abdicate responsibility for decisions involving their community. Only seventy-three members participated in the church budget meeting. While David interpreted this fact as a sign of trust and not apathy, I worried that the two may be linked. Either "trust" could serve as a guise for apathy, or it could slow the development of lay disciples who take responsibility for the life of their church.

Sam was less concerned that Saddleback's centralized decision-making threatened its egalitarian ministry. Paul affirms the idea of different leadership roles in the body of Christ: he writes that God "gave some to be apostles, some to be prophets, some to be evangelists, and some to be pastors and teachers" (Eph 4:11), and even specifically mentions the role of those with "gifts of administration" (1 Cor 12:28). In 1 Timothy, Paul leaves instructions regarding "overseers" and deacons who "take care of God's church," and writes that "elders who direct the affairs of the church well are worthy of double honor" (3:5, 5:17). Not every member of the church needs be involved in every aspect of its operation, and this is the result of the diversity of gifts in the body, not inequality. The logistical challenges of running a 30,000-member ministry should be sufficient to justify a certain amount of control in the hands of those whom God has gifted to be administrators and overseers of the church.

This is not a threat to the priesthood of all believers, Sam insisted. Indeed, every member has a distinctive place, and not all of those places are administrative. The existence of centralized leadership need not communicate diminished congregational participation in the life of the church. Saddleback's member-led ministries actually puts enormous responsibility in the hands of the laity, and seems to be cultivating anything but apathy among the membership.

On another level, we both worried that this process may exclude certain members of the congregation. For a congregation that admits to a lack of diversity, I (Kris) worry that a process of a few (mostly white male) pastors making important decisions fails to affirm and empower marginal voices in the congregation. We noted, especially, that this "egalitarianism" does not always extend to gender roles in church leadership. Saddleback is technically a Southern Baptist congregation, which forbids the ordination of women. At Saddleback, David told us, a woman may hold any office as long as she is under the leadership of a man—"that's what Rick believes Scripture teaches." The only position a woman can never hold is senior pastor. Women do preach and teach at Saddleback; Kay Warren preaches and teaches a systematic theology course.[31] There are twelve to fifteen women in ministerial roles, though none are on the pastoral management team. Despite this rather progressive stance relative to other Southern Baptists, by not allowing women in the highest decision-making positions, the church leadership risks closure to different perspectives and gifts of all parts of the body (1 Cor 12:18–22). It's possible that the community inhibits the work of the Spirit by bracketing certain Spirit-led voices from the conversation.

Still, in a church the size of Saddleback, we were both surprised to find such an egalitarian, ground-up approach to ministry. Most of the church's ministry and mission ideas really are conceived and carried out by members themselves. Neither of us had explored megachurch leadership at such a close proximity, but we had both imagined that a church this size would require more centralized control over its ministries.

"We are giving away the ministry to our people," David told us, which is how Saddleback operates a 30,000-member church with just 300 staff. Saddleback's vision is perhaps more accurately a *"missionhood* of all believers." As one pastor noted, "We firmly believe there is no distinction between staff and volunteers." This is consistent with low-church Baptist tradition—Saddleback is a Southern Baptist congregation after all (though this is an affiliation it "wears lightly").[32]

When practiced within congregations, this grassroots model can cultivate not only participation, but discipleship. And this seemed to be the case at Saddleback. This structure is politically formative even if the church leaders do not use that language to describe it. Members learn that Christians are not just spectators—they are full citizens, ambassadors, colaborers, priests, and apostles drawn into the activity and mission of God in the world. Faith is not merely assent to a set of propositions, but a commitment that requires something of the faithful.

Saddleback's notion of "purposes"—which can often become individualistic—seems to be grafted into a more holistic account of Christian formation and mission. It seemed to us that the purposes take on a communal, theological dimension as the individual Christian discerns not only her own purpose, but also that of the church—how God uses their diverse gifts to renew the world. In a sense, the final purpose, the life of discipleship, culminates in becoming part of God's plan for the world, engaging in God's mission through this collaborative, global effort.

In many ways, we think, this helpfully moves the congregation beyond the limits of a seeker-friendly worship service. An egalitarian, "democratic" ministry ethos engages people at a deeper level of discipleship—teaching them that there is work to be done in the world, and that it is up to them to do it. This mandate incorporates the entire congregation in a communal mission. Everyone is called individually, but everyone is also called to be part of something greater—to participate in God's work in the world.

"PEACE" IS POLITICAL

We passed the palm trees and waterfalls, illuminated in the balmy night air, as we made our way through the campus to one of the worship tents. Kris wanted a picture in front of the empty tomb—"for the book cover," he said—but I hurried us along. We finally intersected a crowd of people and walked into the venue to hear about Saddleback's work in Rwanda. It was Global PEACE Night, an annual event when the congregation gathers to hear stories from the church's PEACE teams serving all over the globe. Rwanda was Saddleback's first global missions initiative, and now serves as a model for the others.

We walked in a bit late to hear the leader of a PEACE team, just back from Rwanda, addressing the problem of land grabbing. The Rwandan government refused to permit pastors to grant civil marriage licenses, and since most married couples did not have the resources to travel to a city court to obtain one, most marriages were never recognized by the state. When husbands died, widows often lost all of their property. The speaker explained that the Saddleback teams persuaded the government to change its policy and then trained local pastors on property rights, court proceedings, and the procedures for granting civil marriages. Saddleback then partnered with the Rwandan Ministry of Justice to ensure that the government continued pastor training in the villages in these areas on an ongoing basis. Another team member noted that this type of government and church partnership could not happen in the US. "The Rwandan government is not fettered by that [separation of church and state] prohibition," she said.

Last year the PEACE Team was called to testify before the US Congress on the effectiveness of their work in Rwanda. "We want to partner deeply with governments," the speaker explained. This is especially true for healthcare and orphan initiatives, major efforts in Rwanda. "We work to mobilize local churches and church members to address their own needs." The PEACE teams trained local church leaders in basic health care skills, creating mini health clinics in villages across the country. They initiated a program to encourage local families in churches to adopt Rwandan children rather than sending them to US families.[33] "Education, business, and government have tried, but the local church is the answer to the healthcare problem," the speaker concluded. As we left that night, we recalled some of Rick's words during his staff meeting: "God's antidote for the world is not politics. It's the church."

From Purpose to PEACE

Most every problem in the world, Warren surmised after a trip to South Africa in 2003, can be traced back to one of five global "giant problems": 1) spiritual emptiness, 2) corrupt leadership, 3) extreme poverty, 4) pandemic disease, and 5) rampant illiteracy. In response, Warren began casting a new missional vision for the church, "so that the whole church cares about the whole gospel in a whole new way—through the local church."[34] Witnessing firsthand the immense need, not only in South Africa, but lingering silently amidst the affluence of Orange County, Warren acknowledged both the "responsibility of influence" of a church as large as Saddleback and the "responsibility of affluence" of one with so many resources. Warren understood it to be Saddleback's task to "to lead the church worldwide to a more focused and effective expression of Jesus' love, forgiveness, and hope."[35]

A year later he launched the PEACE Plan, an attempt to mobilize Saddleback's resources to address the world's problems with five clear points of action, corresponding to the five global "giants" (and, conveniently, the letters of the word PEACE): 1) Promoting reconciliation, 2) Equipping servant leaders, 3) Assisting the poor, 4) Caring for the sick, and 5) Educating the next generation. It consists of many diverse initiatives, including planting twelve new "outpost" churches in key cities, working with persecuted churches, Purpose-Driven training, orphan care, recovery programs, relief work, poverty and hunger initiatives, English classes, basic healthcare training, HIV/AIDS prevention and treatment, sports programs, and clean water initiatives.[36]

For years Saddleback's ministry has pivoted around the "Purpose Driven" concept—the idea that Scripture prescribes five universal purposes for every church and individual (worship, fellowship, discipleship, ministry, mission). And while this still animates much of what Saddleback does, the PEACE Plan is the next step, the "missions strategy of the Purpose model."[37] In a sense, the Purpose Driven idea has been "repurposed" and expanded into a global effort of massive proportions. The PEACE Plan now dominates the thoughts of the staff at Saddleback. Every minister we interviewed took care to narrate its history and outline its basic tenets. The director of the Global PEACE effort is Mike Constanz, who left Campus Crusade in 2003 to join Warren in developing the PEACE Plan. When he first heard Warren explain the vision behind PEACE, he replied, "If you're serious about this, this is the biggest thing I've ever heard in mission."[38]

This ambitious missions philosophy complements the church's grassroots approach to ministry. Missions at Saddleback, Matt Bruce told us, often feel like "building airplanes in the air," constantly tweaking, trashing, and starting over. "We learn, try, do, make mistakes," added another pastor.[39] According to Matt, the bold scope of Saddleback's missions agenda actually compels congregational involvement. "The large goals of the church practically force the congregation to get involved," he says. It sets audacious goals, says Matt, and these goals generate such excitement that people buy into them wholeheartedly.[40]

The Local Church is the Answer

The most recurrent and salient theme in all of our discussions with Saddleback pastors about the PEACE Plan was their confidence in the local church as the vehicle for world change. The church's printed guides to the PEACE Plan explain that "there is no organization or government that can effectively address these giant problems. . . . The church has the world's largest distribution network, the most people ready and willing to serve, and the greatest motivation of all—the love and compassion of Jesus Christ."[41] Government is not the answer, Mike reiterated. The local church is the answer. This strong local-church focus was something Kris had been hoping to see all along, and did not expect at Saddleback. I (Sam) had never heard any of the Evangelical churches I attended, even the megachurches, talk this way either.

Such confidence in the local church's ability to resolve these paralyzing and complex issues could easily come across as a form of church triumphalism or Western Christian imperialism. Mike confirmed Saddleback's awareness of this dark part of Christian history and reiterated their care to avoid entering a situation with prefabricated solutions—or even predetermined perceptions of local problems. He was quick to note that the Rwandan president invited Saddleback to begin working on its PEACE Plan in his country.

We asked Brandon Lyons, an energetic and tattooed young Global PEACE pastor, whether PEACE teams ever experienced any resistance in the mission field. "In some places we had to change the conversation to, 'Here's what we're thinking about doing, what do you think?,'" he told us. "And the truth is, we were probably going to do most of it anyway, but we wanted them to have the opportunity to speak back to us." Once you have gained their trust, he told us, most are completely open to what you have to say. Brandon told us that while occasionally you have to help people understand that they need something, like a town that does not realize it is dying from malaria, most Global PEACE trips start by building relationships. Saddleback leaders contend that both globally and locally, the PEACE Plan is a collaborative effort through and through.

In fact, despite their insistence that government is not the answer, Saddleback's mission program is politically complicated. Its collaborative strategy occasionally involves partnerships with secular and governmental agencies. "The local church is the primary vehicle for social change," Matt Bruce told us, "but if there are local community organizations already on the ground, there may be opportunities for fruitful collaboration." Saddle-back still prefers to partner with other local churches rather than govern-ments or businesses, and it will not engage with them in a way that would appear to endorse a candidate or form of government, Brandon said, add-ing, "Once you get involved with politicians, it gets messy." Saddleback is careful about who it partners with. Other organizations often have agendas at odds with the mission of the church. (This can include groups doing great humanitarian work; Randy Craft cited a recent decision not to partner with Tom's Shoes, for example.) "We won't compromise our beliefs in partner-ships or mission efforts," he asserted. "We have to define the relationship!" According to David Chrzan, "we want to insulate ourselves but not isolate ourselves so that we can live in culture and win people while we live in it."[42]

One of the church's most significant Local PEACE partnerships is with the Orange County District Attorney's office and school district on a col-laborative project called GRIP (Gang Reduction Intervention Partnership). Saddleback approached the DA's office primarily because of the program's effectiveness, and assured them that they would not push an evangelistic agenda.[43] Also, with the addition of the PEACE Resource Center, Saddle-back is now able to offer many alternative social services to locals, including free legal services for immigration issues, family violence issues, divorce issues, and even restraining orders. The newly formed Health Care team assists uninsured patrons in obtaining health coverage, and plans have been made for more comprehensive medical services.[44]

Still trying to wrap our heads around this grand missional vision—a church that thinks it actually has a strategy to solve the world's major social ills—we decided to ask David Chrzan about this audacious confidence in the local church's ability to change the world. We recalled a *Newsweek* article from a few years ago—one of the many forecasting the demise of American religiosity—that cheerfully reported that the proportion of Americans who believed that religion could "answer all or most of today's problems" had dropped from well above 58 percent every year of the '90s and early 2000s to 48 percent in 2009.[45] While this number still closed in on half of all Americans—hardly evidence of impending religious doom—confidence in the church's ability to resolve the world's social ills was admittedly di-minishing. Yet, despite this changing public perception, Saddleback seems resolute in its mission and undeterred in its faith to do just that.

Having gotten a taste of his more pragmatic, realist perspective, we expected David to temper some of the intrepid rhetoric we had heard elsewhere about the local church. But he did not relent; putting it bluntly, he told us that "The church is *the* institution with the resources to solve the world's problems. The church *can* eradicate global poverty." David noted that just 100 years ago, the church ran half of all social institutions; now, he lamented, it has "abdicated" its social ministry and responsibility to the government. For example, the responsibility of healthcare used to belong to the churches, he said. According to David, the problem began when the fundamentalists started overemphasizing personal piety and the mainliners "became society clubs," leaving this work to nonchurch institutions and leaving the church without a social vision. "You have to bring those things back together!" he said, "and ask, 'What can we do that only the church can do?'"

"The more you put social and welfare activities into the hands of the government, the more control you give them over your lives. The question becomes, 'Do you want more government in your life?'" he said looking intently at us and leaving us wondering whether the question was meant to be rhetorical.

Saddleback seems convinced that the church needs a holistic faith and approach to the Christian life, one that understands social needs as integral to the church's mission—not something the church leaves up to others to do with less effectiveness. By mobilizing local churches across the globe, the church can reach people and their needs more effectively. We recalled Brandon Lyons growing animated as he told us, "We've given the UN their shot. We've given education its shot." But the church has over two billion members, he said, asking us if we knew of another organization that had those numbers. "Throughout human history there's only one thing that solves it, and that's the church. There's not enough doctors to cure all the diseases in the world. But if we can train the local church to do it, there's a massive amount of churches in the world. The church can do it." But for Brandon, this goes beyond mere effectiveness. Not only can other organizations not do this as effectively, he said, "We're the only ones with the moral authority to do it."

We concluded our time at the church office by meeting Bill Mugford outside the youth center on a typically paradisal Southern California afternoon. Bill, a denominational vagabond, is an ordained Anglican priest now in charge of Saddleback's HIV/AIDS Initiative. The initiative encourages churches to erase the stigma surrounding the disease and take the lead in ending AIDS through testing, education, and care. It also takes their ministry beyond their city to the state and national levels—Bill had recently met with the director of the Office of National AIDS Policy at the White House to talk about potential joint ventures.

We told him that most of the other pastors we interviewed avoided talking about anything political, but that it seemed his work with HIV advocacy linked the church's ministry with political action. How should the church relate to politics? "The church shouldn't be partisan, but it can't help but be political," he answered. "Its very definition—a *polis*—is essentially people. We are out there and we have to be involved in terms of people." We were caught off guard by Bill's matter-of-fact use of political language. He did not shy away from the term and understood the church to be inherently political. Intrigued, we asked why the church should attempt to affect public policy. Bill seemed convinced that God's mission does not have time for arguments over how political the church should be—the problem is too urgent and the need is too great. "Let's talk about our differences when we have some leisure time," he said.

The Politics of PEACE

This bold vision of the church, manifested through the PEACE Plan on both a local and global level, informs every other activity of the congregation. Saddleback understands itself to be a community that has a particular, Christ-centered mission in the world. It envisions the church—not only its 30,000-member community, but local congregations across the globe—as the institution that will change the world and guide it to redemption from the spiritual and physical ailments that oppress it.

Most pastors at Saddleback prefer not to use political language to describe this vision and its practices. But as we reflected on the whirlwind of conversations over the past days, we concluded that this PEACE vision is nothing if not political, and should be embraced as such. We thought of three reasons it seemed to be politically formative for church members and transformative for the world.

First, the mobilization of local churches to seek the good of people all over the globe is, by its very nature, a political movement, a "revolution." This mission of eradicating poverty and oppression requires the church to understand its mission and identity to be determined by a King who came to rule and renew the whole world. We believe this commitment renders the church's activity as political because it attempts to bring about a new world regime, God's kingdom. By reaching out to the world and continuing Jesus' ministry of healing the sick, helping the poor, and creating a community composed of loyal followers, Saddleback and its local church partners are working to manifest his kingdom in the world.

Second, this PEACE Plan vision is political because it conceives of the church as an alternative political body to the politics of this world. Its pastors speak of the local church as the primary institution called to social responsibility and action, and contrast this with the state, suggesting that churches have abdicated their social responsibility to the government. Churches need to take this responsibility back upon themselves, both because they, collectively, have the resources and ability to mobilize those resources more efficiently than any other institution—including government—and because it is integral to their calling and mission. The church needs, in other words, to operate like a political body.[46] "The Kingdom of God is the greatest cause in the world," Warren writes. "Jesus demands greater allegiance than any dictator that ever lived. The difference is that Jesus has a *right* to it!"[47]

Third, this vision and practice is political because, despite its emphasis on the local church as God's instrument of world transformation, Saddleback still engages with secular organizations, government agencies, and businesses that are already addressing the problems of a local community. The P in the PEACE Plan originally stood for "Planting churches," but Warren later changed it to the more general "Promoting reconciliation." This move from exclusively church-driven language to broader, common-good language opens the door for partnerships with outside, even non-Christian groups. The church, in Saddleback's view, is its own alternative political body, but one that is willing to work alongside other political bodies to negotiate a common life and accomplish the work God calls it to do. It seeks neither to withdraw from the world and its secular agencies nor to resist them. Saddleback's work with government agencies to decrease gang influence in a local Los Angeles neighborhood as well as its work to establish free medical clinics throughout Rwanda constitute political actions—and, like Bill Mugford, we don't believe there is anything wrong with describing them this way.

Still, Saddleback understands that while other groups fix the symptoms of social problems, the church offers a more holistic approach. Through its Christ-centered mission—acting as the presence of Christ in the world—it testifies to the community-creating and world-changing power of God. As

Brandon Lyons told us, "You've got something so small, so simple, yet so massive in your hand when you've got the gospel."

MOBILIZING THE CHURCH TO CHANGE THE WORLD

I (Kris) finally gave in to Sam's persistent attempts to lure me back to In-N-Out. He claimed it was his brotherly duty as a Christian to save me from the purgatory of East Coast fast food—something about "iron sharpening iron." As I watched him devour two Double-Double burgers and a chocolate shake in a matter of seconds, I tried to formulate my thoughts on the barrage of information we had just received.

I had not expected to leave Saddleback with a positive perception of the church. Cynical from past experiences with evangelicalism, I thought it unlikely that an evangelical megachurch could have a strong social vision and commitment to growing discipleship. I had expected to find only a superficial, "cheap" grace and practices that I (perhaps unfairly) associated with megachurches—what one theologian calls a "bar code faith" (once you assent to the right doctrines, God scans your bar code and your debts are paid).[48] The evangelistic zeal of many evangelical congregations is so strong that they dispense a shallow version of faith, not the radical call to discipleship that Jesus proclaimed in the Gospels. And while some of these concerns seemed verified in our initial visits, I came to see and appreciate the costly commitment Saddleback called its members to and the rich vision of church and mission it cultivated. While some misgivings persisted—as they inevitably do for someone who studies the church for a living—this vision of God calling and using the church to concretely and dramatically change the world affirmed my own vision of what the church could be and, even more surprisingly, gave me hope in the church's ability to embody that vision. I confessed to Sam that I had been wrong. He just smiled. I think he knew this would happen all along.

The Church Does It Better

As we reflected on the political dimensions of their mission, we kept returning to the contrasts the church leaders made between church and government: according to Warren, the church operates with a distinction between church and state, but "we do not believe in the separation of faith and politics." The separation is supposed to be one sided: Christians are free to serve

God by serving in government and by influencing social policies, though the church should refrain from endorsing candidates or parties. If God gives you a political platform you are to use that platform to bring glory to God, David told us. But this separation was established to keep the government from infringing on the faithful practices of the church. "The original idea was that the government has no right in the affairs of the church, but your faith has all the right to be in the affairs of the government."

Saddleback believes that God has ordained separate roles for business, government, and church regarding social issues, David said. And the church has resources that neither government nor businesses have: a unique and wider set of volunteers, more distribution points, and a higher motivation. It is uniquely qualified to provide for the social welfare of the world and uniquely called to be God's instrument to transform it. We welcomed this vision of God choosing to use the church to change the world, of the church embodying Christ's ministry and working to bring the kingdom of God to the earth.

Still, we wondered about the rationale behind it. Was it a partisan, socially conservative rationale—based in the libertarian notion that government should not infringe on the freedoms of its citizens in order to create various social welfare programs? Was it pragmatic—based on the idea that nonchurch institutions cannot solve problems as effectively because they do not have the resources or global reach of the church? Or was it theological—based on the conviction that the church is called to do these things whether or not other political bodies attempt them as well?

Based on our experience there, all three motivations are present at Saddleback. David admitted, "Part of [this philosophy] could be *politically* motivated—the fact that we don't want government in our lives. I don't want to pay any more taxes or have some bureaucrat 3,000 miles away deciding what we do here," he said. But another part is *spiritual*, he added. "It is an opportunity to move our members into an intentional discipleship process to say, 'What can we do about the needs around us, as a self-sustaining, ongoing, caring model?'" It is fulfilling the church's calling to "be the hands and feet of Jesus."

But it seems *effectiveness* plays the largest role. "We will come up with a sustainable solution so that government won't have to," David concluded. Nearly every decision in the church seems to pivot on the criterion of its effectiveness. Warren begins the purpose process with the questions: "Are we doing what God intends for us to do?" *and* "How well are we doing it?"

David noted that the purposes are evaluated in terms of measurable results and not just activities. The church is supposed to operate efficiently—and Saddleback does. Because it operates with less bureaucracy than the government, it can do things the government will never be capable of doing. It is simply better equipped, and that is by God's design: God's wisdom will be made manifest in the world *through the church*, they said (Eph 3:10).

For the Sake of the World

Despite its abundance of simplified acronyms and acrostics, Saddleback embodies a complex understanding and practice of politics. It offers a rich witness of political engagement, and a deep understanding of the church as a political body, often positioning itself as a political actor over against government, while at the same time refusing to identify its work as political. This is because, on the one hand, Saddleback understands politics as necessarily divisive, sorting people into opposing camps based on their opinions on particular issues. But we worry that operating with such a thin view of politics causes the church to separate spiritual formation from its mission to address the world's social problems. Separating social transformation from worship may also cause Saddleback to miss opportunities for a worship experience that touches all parts of the Christian life. Withholding the political dimensions of the gospel until further down the Discipleship Funnel risks promoting cheap grace. The broader evangelistic ends Saddleback seeks by avoiding politics in worship are actually hindered by proclaiming a depoliticized view of the gospel, missions, and discipleship. Again, we agree with Oliver O'Donovan: "the church must be political if it is to be truly evangelical."[49]

On the other hand, at its foundational level, Saddleback does engage in a deeply political vision of church through the PEACE Plan—whether it acknowledges this as political or not. In this case, despite some of the superficialities we experienced in their weekend services, we began to understand that Saddleback practices politics without being partisan—a deeper vision of the church political.

After spending time at the church, we came to believe that claiming this vision of changing the world through the local church as a *political* vision would benefit Saddleback. It is possible to understand politics not as primarily divisive, but in terms of allegiance to a common *polis*, which unifies people with differing opinions in pursuit of a common love.

Acknowledging the political character of the church would explicitly connect their spiritual formation to their extensive social and political work, integrating the personal and public—King and kingdom—and offering a more holistic and faithful version of the gospel.

More specifically, it would free them to talk about important social and moral matters during their "seeker-friendly" worship services because it would understand these potentially political issues as integral to the life of discipleship—the Discipleship Funnel is political all the way up. It would allow for more sustained missional partnerships with secular groups without a partisan fear that the government or secular agencies may infringe on the church's territory. And it would provide an accurate and faithful witness of an alternative political imagination for other congregations on how to be an alternative political body that utilizes the politics of the world yet remains distinct from it. Embracing the concept of church as political may help it to harness the full scope and power of its objective—to be faithful to its divine, political King—and encourage it to employ practices, partnerships, and language that advance the kingdom.

In many ways Saddleback does offer this political vision of the church that ultimately refuses to conform, in practice, to a narrow conception of politics that pervades the rhetoric and public image of Saddleback. In a sense, its actions transcend its words. While Bill Mugford was the only pastor willing to employ the language of politics to describe Saddleback's activity, we came to believe that this was the most accurate description of Saddleback's mission. The church does operate as a *polis*: in its ministry and mission practices, Saddleback exemplifies the inherent political dimensions of the church, offering a larger theological vision of the church's mission. Saddleback is a community that imagines the world differently, and crosses worldly political boundaries with its message and mission of hope, love, and justice. It attempts to break through contemporary "dividing walls" that work to prevent faithful ministry and mission (Eph 2:14).

We identified Saddleback's model of political engagement as *mobilizing the local church to change the world*. In light of a growing disillusionment with divisive politics, Saddleback offers a vision of a new form and method of political engagement for evangelicals. Its confidence in the ability and responsibility of the mobilized local church to eradicate the five "global giants" constitutes its "political" vision of the church. By understanding the church as the tangible presence of Christ in the world—a community called to live and work differently in the world under the lordship of a different King while still seeking the welfare of the world alongside worldly political bodies—Saddleback embodies the inherently political identity and mission of God's church. Saddleback also avoids conforming to patterns of narrow, partisan political participation often ascribed to evangelical churches by scholars, that of turning to partisan politics as their primary means of impacting the world.[50] Rather, Saddleback envisions itself, on a deeper political level, as transcending these narrow identifications and practices, and achieves a much more robust practice of political engagement. Through this, it offers the wider church a new vision of faithful political engagement through mobilizing local churches to change the world. This model suggests that churches exist for the sake of the world, in service of God's love for the world. The church is the institution called to extend that gift of grace to a world afflicted with giant, global problems, with the faith that God's grace will overcome.[51]

Several elements of Saddleback's model of ministry and political engagement could serve as models for other churches.

First, intentional exploration of the meaning and purpose of the church will clarify a church's mission and multiply its influence. The practices of a church must arise from the church's purpose, or missional vision—how does the church understand its calling from God and particular resources and gifts?

Second, setting large goals in faith is sometimes the best way to cultivate excitement for and participation in the church's mission. Changing the world through the local church requires casting a vision so audacious and so vested in deep faith that it generates disciples willing to act in faith to achieve those goals.

Third, allowing ministries to emerge from the congregation rather than the staff gives members ownership of and confidence in their role in the church body. This practice generates a membership not of bystanders, but of ministers committed to the mission God has given the church in the world—a "missionhood of believers."

Finally, networking with other congregations is crucial to accomplishing big goals. This bold mandate remains for all churches, regardless of size, wealth, or location. Saddleback's challenge is clear: if one church does not have the resources to accomplish its missional goal, partner with other churches. Don't approach a mission field with pre-prepared answers; learn to identify and participate in the work God is already doing. Above all, act in faith that God desires and is able to bring radical world change through the church.

* * *

As the sun began to set over the coast, we pulled the car off to the side of Highway 1 and walked out onto a rocky cliff at Dana Point. Surfers dotted the foamy coastline below us, and Sam maneuvered between two rocks to try and capture the perfect Instagram. ("I think I can get a good one of the sunset reflecting in your glasses.") Making our way to the edge, we stood and watched as the last rays peeked above the surface of the water.

I told Sam that in moments like this, it feels like God is looking out over us. The world looks so big spread out across the horizon. I know it is not as it should be—giant problems pervade every bit of it. For some reason, it is precisely in moments when I feel so small that I am able to muster the most faith.

As we stood reflecting on our time at Saddleback, we realized that this church had taught us a great deal about faith. We had both encountered a much deeper, more radical understanding of the church than we anticipated. Despite its faults, Saddleback has an earnest faith that God is watching over the world, that God will one day resolve all of these problems—and will use the church to do it.

This faith requires a commitment to Christ beyond any earthly allegiance, and a conviction that God will use the church to usher in the redemption of the world. This vision instills a deep sense of responsibility in the church for God's mission. Warren often points to Ephesians 3:10 as the mantra for their mission: "God's intent is that *through the church*, the manifold wisdom of God should be made known to the rulers and authorities in the heavenly realms."[52] This promise cultivates a radical faith in God as Savior of the world and in God's choice to transform the world through the church. As Warren says, "The only true world 'superpower' is the church—it will last forever."[53]

Chapter 3

Growing an Organic Community
Solomon's Porch Community

OUR ARMS BURNED AS we shoveled mulch in the cold Minneapolis spring rain. This was not the kind of work we signed up for when this project began. But with our flight leaving in a few short hours, moving mulch afforded us one final interview with Doug Pagitt, founding pastor of Solomon's Porch. So we shivered and shoveled and asked our questions between strained bursts of heavy lifting: "So what significance would you say baptism plays in your congregation?"

As the crop of twenty-somethings that started the church thirteen years ago began sprouting children, Solomon's Porch adapted their property to the shifting demographic by constructing a playground. On the morning of our final interview with Doug, the church staff was scrambling to move a small mountain of playground mulch the landscape company had illegally dumped on the street. In typical Solomon's Porch fashion Doug and Ben Younen, the facilities director, recruited anyone that was present and available to help—which on this morning happened to be us!

Solomon's Porch was one of the first congregations to come out of the Emergent Church movement, which was founded in the early 1990s by young, mostly evangelical church leaders who had grown disillusioned with conventional church structures.[1] Doug, an Emergent pioneer, founded this church in 2000 on a deep commitment to inclusive community and transparent, nonhierarchical governance—principles that have uniquely shaped this community over its short life together.

48

The people of Solomon's Porch call themselves a "holistic missional community" rather than a church, and this somewhat granola-y, yuppie community of around 300 is every bit as nontraditional as its name implies. Solomon's Porch effuses a distinctively organic, "intentionally unintentional" culture. They sing only original music, reach out to the local neighborhood through classes in their yoga studio, and decorate the building with rotating local art installations. There is no statement of faith, no creed. Members bristle at anything authoritarian or coercive. Formation occurs from the ground up, shaped by relationships and not by any predetermined spiritual or theological goals.

"Our model of church is like a family or a garden, with the pastor as a gardener," explains worship musician Ben Johnson—introduced to us as the "poet" of the church. And like the community garden that surrounds the church building, the community grows under the light-handed tending of Doug, open and welcoming to anyone who might walk in the door.

I (Kris) was infatuated with the Emerging Church movement during my seminary years, accumulating as many conference and seminar experiences as I could, many of which featured Doug Pagitt and Tony Jones of Solomon's Porch as keynote speakers. I fraternized with Emergent ministers who shared a keen interest in postmodern theology and alternative expressions of the church. Over the years I drifted from that world, guided by a renewed commitment to the institution of the church, but never fully let go of my conviction that the church needs a new vision. I had begun to think that some Emergent pastors went too far in condoning cyber churches, and suspected that many pursued difference simply for difference's sake. Still, at Solomon's Porch I expected to find a church that conformed closely to my understanding of the church and its political mission; a church with practices that formed the community in deeply political ways.

I (Sam) had connections to a church network that many consider part of the Emergent movement. But I had never experienced anything like the ultradeconstructive, postmodern atmosphere of Solomon's Porch. I was interested in exploring new ideas from Emergent pastors about how to do church differently, but wary of what seemed to be an emphasis on postmodern philosophy and culture at the expense of Scripture. I expected to find new and deeply political church practices at Solomon's Porch—and though I hoped some of these practices would challenge and expand my idea of what church should be, I anticipated having strong reservations.[2]

"INTENTIONALLY UNINTENTIONAL"

When we arrived at the church for our first Sunday Gathering, we were surprised to find ourselves directed to a traditional stone sanctuary. I (Sam) quickly pointed out the Solomon's Porch sign to assure Kris that we were in the right place before he could launch into yet another pontification on technological overreliance. (Ever since the GPS directed us to Joe's Garage the auto mechanic in Coon Rapids instead of Joe's Garage the downtown Minneapolis burger joint, these rants had grown steadily worse, now involving dystopian allusions to replicants and Terminators, and the "machines" starting to deceive us).

After relocating several times during its brief history—from the "hip" Linden Hills neighborhood to a sheet metal plant in a low-income area— Solomon's Porch finally settled in the old Hobart United Methodist Church building in the affluent Kingfield neighborhood, surrounded by "super awesome cafes and bakeries," in the words of one member.[3] From the outside this church looked urban and traditional—a "castle on the corner," as Doug calls it disparagingly.[4] And despite his reticence to meet in a traditional church building, Doug led the community to purchase the building in 2012.

Couch Surfing Worshiping

The illusion that this was an ordinary church ended, however, as soon as we stepped inside. The smell of buttered popcorn filled the room. Gone were the rows of wooden pews, altar, and choir loft, all replaced by old couches, coffee tables, and café high-tops arranged in concentric circles around a stool in the center of the room. An eclectic array of original artwork adorned the walls, and a huge paper-mache goose hung delicately overhead. We learned later that it was the Celtic version of the dove, signifying peace, though it appeared to be dive-bombing into the audience. Communion loaves and bottles of wine were scattered among the coffee tables. A giant cross—presumably a remnant from the previous congregation—hung on the back wall where the altar had once been, surrounded by a "directory" of penciled and painted portraits of the congregation: what Doug called, in a rare cheesy moment, "Porchtraits."

Attempting to overcome our "gawker" anxiety (Doug's term for people like us who come to observe or research the church), and unsure of where to sit or what to do, we sank into a floral green couch that appeared to have been salvaged from someone's dingy college apartment. We both glanced nervously at the giant goose dangling precariously above our heads. Meanwhile, the room was abuzz with lively conversation and general disorder. The crowd was noticeably youthful—mostly twenty- and thirty-somethings, some with dreadlocks and beards, others with dark-rimmed glasses and jeans that (to me) appeared a few sizes too small. Many toted infants in their arms, while small children ran excitedly around the couches and tables—we sensed one of the boxes of Trader Joe's wine would soon end up on the floor.

Gradually people settled into their seats as the musicians began playing through a series of songs neither of us had heard before. People freely moved in and out of the sanctuary (or "great room," as they call it) to enjoy popcorn, popsicles, and watermelon from the next room, which we made a point of sampling (for the sake of research, of course). We would later learn that there is no official "order of service"—very little is planned or orchestrated, including the speakers and readers. We noticed many people browsing their iPhones throughout service, during both the music and the sermon, giving the service the feel of a casual coffee shop performance. Tony Jones, the "theologian in residence" at Solomon's Porch, later suggested to us that in most liturgical settings, if something goes wrong, things get awkward. At churches like Saddleback, he said, everything is rehearsed. Here the value is on complete informality—which, he notes, is more in line with our highly participatory "Wikipedia world" in which things go wrong all the time. "We are participatory," Tony told us. "We are egalitarian. Everyone has a voice."

The use of couches in worship is also formative, Tony said, though not "intentional"—since nothing at Solomon's Porch is really intentional. "I can't overestimate the importance of the interior of the church building. I can't tell you how important it is that we sit on couches in concentric circles, that we don't use microphones, that the band is back in the corner," he said, contrasting this layout and its advantages to the stadium setup of Saddleback (the second comparison to Saddleback). "Everything is to convey a posture of equality, where everyone's voice matters, where everyone is literally bodily open to the other."[5] Citing Doug's vision of the church as a place of reconciliation, he concluded, "Think how difficult it is to be reconciled to someone if you are only looking at the back of his head."

51

House Party Style

During another Gathering several months later Doug began the Communion service by reflecting on the upcoming Memorial Day holiday. I could sense Kris tense up next to me, unable to hide his Anabaptist unease with patriotic celebrations in church. We had expected the holiday to go unacknowledged at this church. For this community, Doug quickly added, this is a conflicted moment in which we long for a time when there will be no more Memorial Days—when swords are pounded into plowshares, and valleys and mountains are leveled (Isa 2:4, 40:4). Kris eased back into his seat.

Continuing this theme, Doug infused the practice of Communion with political meaning. The Lord's Supper takes place, he began—spinning on his stool, legs flailing and long body towering above the surrounding couch sitters—within the story of Israel as a nation enslaved by another nation, and eventually liberated by God. When Jesus takes the bread and calls it his body, he foreshadows that he himself will become a victim of the oppressive Roman regime. Communion is a testimony to one who was executed by imperial powers and continually serves as a witness to another, peaceful vision of the world. We take the bread and wine "in remembrance of a victim and in the longing that we would be free from the effects of empire, oppression, and war." Communion is an act of us becoming a part of Christ's story, he concluded, as the crowd recited their Communion Litany (the closest this community comes to a statement of faith):

> We take Communion, by serving and eating bread and wine together, in community with followers of Jesus around the world and throughout all ages. We enter this mystery proclaiming and having the faith of Jesus as the Messiah, whose life, death, burial, resurrection, ascension, and sending show the love of God for the world, free us from sin, and initiate the kingdom of God in our world in new ways, for the benefit and blessing of all the world.

(Our hopes that this litany—surprisingly drenched in orthodoxy—might be a powerful and formative anchor for the church were later dashed when Doug told us that really he is tired of the litany, and maybe it is time to just drop it.)

Doug continued the sermon with a hint of excitement in his voice, inviting everyone to share the communion bread and wine—"house party style!" And in fact, Communion was the most raucous part of the service.

It takes place every Sunday. "There are many things about Solomon's Porch that are leftover evangelical, but other things that are unevangelical, like weekly communion," Tony explained, adding, "with wine!" He suggested that this style of communion deconstructs the way every other Communion is done (another moment when the specter of intentionality seems to emerge). According to Tony, "It is not introduced or served by a clergy person; you don't have to be confirmed or go through a pastor's class. There are no strictures on participation at all. People just keep eating the bread during the service. Even the elements are handled in a very unsacred way."

Like most Protestant services, the meetings pivot on the sermon. Doug remains seated, continually spinning childlike on his stool to address those on the couches around him, with no microphone, no notes, and only a Scripture posted on the screen above. He offers brief (often provocative) reflections, like a pied piper drawing insights and questions out of the congregation. Various people in the crowd read a few verses from the screen, as Doug interjects comments focused mostly on the historical validity of the text and the creative storytelling of the Gospel writers. "The sermon basically consists of me reading [a chapter or two from the Bible] with a running commentary," he says.[6] Occasionally, people interrupt him with their own commentary. Doug often mentions insights from people in the earlier services, always calling them by name, and even noting where they were sitting when they said it.

During the summer months, Doug usually takes a break from preaching as the community listens to "soapbox sermons," which provide an opportunity for anyone in the congregation to "preach" on whatever topic they wish, theological or not. Some are commentaries on films or political issues. Some are more scriptural in nature. According to Tony, "Half the soapbox sermons are absolute shit-shows. And Doug just sits there with a smile on his face, like, 'this is awesome, and if you don't like this, you shouldn't come to this church.'"

Soundtrack of the Congregation

Following the Gathering, we sat down to talk with community musician Ben Johnson on a set of corner couches. The room was still vibrant with folks hanging around to catch up, children running around and playing, and a few people cleaning up communion wine that had spilled on the floor. Raising my voice to be heard above the buzz, I (Sam) asked about the informal nature of the worship service. "We've intentionally embraced a lot of these distractions," Ben said. "We've embraced a theology that all of it is worship. It's the noise, it's the quiet, it's the happy, it's the sad. It's all that jazz."[7] That is why they refuse to call these weekly times together "worship services," or even "worship gatherings"; worship is not limited to these moments on Sunday, but entails all of life.[8]

Ben explained that they sing only original music, written within the Solomon's Porch community—most of it by Ben himself. "Every culture and community has its own music," he explains. "Writing our own music has been huge for how we function. It keeps a soundtrack of our community." The community is acutely aware of the criticisms that accompany such a practice. Most people assume the church has something against music of other churches and generations, Doug says, but that is not true; rather, "Writing our own songs allows us to have an expression of faith that is true to us and our world."[9] Music not only keeps a soundtrack of the community, but also helps to form the way people think and act. This makes it all the more important that lyrics and music are crafted to shape a particular community, he says: "Songs are not just words we sing; they are invitations into a way of life." [10]

Reading the skepticism in our faces, Ben admitted there is something lost in the choice to sing only local music. "But the alternative is to borrow music from another community—like Nashville, for example." This community values context and nuance in their music, not accessibility. By keeping music local, they hope to achieve a depth of expression in worship that is lost with songs produced for mass culture. "I don't know how we are supposed to worship with songs, prayers, and confessions created for other times and places," Doug added.[11]

Reimagining Worship

The weather during our first visit to Minneapolis was surprisingly hot. Actually, it was only sixty-five degrees, but that was enough to lure every Minneapolitan outside. Minnesota is called the land of 10,000 lakes and two of them are located in the heart of the city—a few miles from Solomon's Porch. Kris and I headed out onto the lake the next day to enjoy the sunshine and process our thoughts while paddleboarding. Standing easily on my board, I watched Kris's wavering attempts to climb his, which mostly ended in the water. While waiting for him to catch his breath ("I . . . just need . . . a minute"), we took the opportunity to reflect on the worship experience from the previous evening.

It was unlike any worship gathering either of us had attended. There was certainly a freedom in the worship, both in its openness to all voices and its avoidance of cookie-cutter programs. However, the richness of historic church practices like prayers and responses of faith seemed too easily dismissed in light of the church's commitment to "reimagining" everything. Worship pivoted on the contemporary and local; the use of only original music and the avoidance of creeds or faith statements seemed to overlook the scope and history of the church. At the very least, it illustrated the inherent tension between "starting over" and retaining continuity with the historic church community.

Ben and Doug both insisted that their desire is "not to ignore what's come before us but to be informed and inspired by it"[12]—though Kris and I struggled to see how this was manifest in worship. Doug conceded that he worries less about losing church traditions because the "great risk" of the church is "losing our ability to reimagine."[13] To simply accept the work and interpretations of others as the end of the conversation, as many churches do, is to "outsource" the real and lived theology to those from another time and place.[14] In this way Solomon's Porch offers a helpful reminder that theology and ministry must be contextual and performed within real communities in authentic ways if they are to truly make an impact in the world.

This tension between tradition and reimagination influences the church's relationship not only with the historical church, but with other churches today. In most of our conversations, church leaders described the community in terms of what it is not—primarily an evangelical megachurch. Tony often directly contrasted Solomon's Porch with "what you will see at Saddleback." Most of the people we interviewed referenced some disillusionment or painful experience with the rigid leadership structures of evangelical churches and claimed their affection for this community lay in the fact that it is not one of those.

This may simply reveal the youth of the church; perhaps it has not fully formed an identity beyond that of differentiation. In other ways, as a few leaders admitted, these things are reactions against mainstream Christian culture and language—this church is a "renegade band of misfits."[15] This points to a deeper dimension of its identity. One of the few intentional decisions of the church leadership is to expunge churchy language from the community and create its own: "holistic missional Christian community" rather than church,

"Gathering" instead of worship service, "covenant participants" rather than church members. The traditional terms carry too much baggage, according to Tony. While it may be a violent act against the history of the church, it is necessary to strip away those bad collective memories and say, "We are starting over here." This calls to mind Jesus' warning about pouring new wine into old wineskins (Mark 2:21–22). The new wine of this community may lose all potency if it is contained in what they perceive to be the ruined wineskins of church tradition and language. A reimagined church requires a fresh framework, free from the baggage of collective tradition.

As Kris finally regained his breath atop the paddleboard, he expressed concern that the identity of Solomon's Porch is primarily defined by what the church is *not*, rather than by what it positively stands for.[16] I told him that maybe he is being too negative—perhaps just grumpy from falling into the lake too many times?—and asked him if there might actually be some benefit to distinguishing themselves from other churches. Kris, now paddling swiftly in an effort to gain a head start, yelled back that many of the leaders we spoke with invoked the idea of "healing." One church member suggested that the primary "vision of the church" is to be a place of healing. We all need to be healed from something and "for many of us, Jesus is that healer," she said, adding that the idea of being a "missional Christian holistic community" is to be a place of healing, especially for those who have been hurt by previous church experiences.[17]

But this did not alleviate all of all of our concerns. Solomon's Porch seeks to construct itself into an alternative society, an inherently political act of identity formation. In this case, however, this congregation may serve as an alternative community: not cordoned off from the secular world like many churches, but from the greater church itself. This certainly constitutes a deep political practice, and attempts to bridge the gap between sacred and profane. Still, we worry that such a sectarian character riska missing out on important resources from the wider church tradition, such as its orienting resources—creeds and hymns, rituals and practices—that can serve as important formative markers for the church (even if they need to be nuanced). Our concern is that they may have thrown the baby out with the bathwater. Additionally, sectarianism promotes a posture of inhospitality toward other churches. While embracing the world, a church that partitions itself from other churches hazards a subtle hostility to these communities and misses out on potentially fruitful partnerships with other congregations.[18]

John Donne famously wrote that no man is an island. And just as no Christian can live faithfully as a disciple without others, we are also convinced that no church can faithfully serve God's mission without other churches. Local churches should understand themselves as branches of one living plant, necessarily connected to one another through the vine of Christ (John 15:5–8).[19] Solomon's Porch certainly takes pride in being an island of misfit toys, but we wonder if they want to be misfits just for the sake of being misfits, rather than orienting their identity around a positive theological commitment. This commitment can take many forms—evangelizing the nations, seeking social justice in the name of Christ, spiritually forming its members into faithful disciples of Christ—but is always rooted in a commitment to Christ as Lord and his mission in the world. For Solomon's Porch, however, their identity seems to say more about what the church is *not* than what it *is*. What is it that actually defines this church in a positive, substantive sense?

In one conversation with Doug, we noted that many people in the community described the Porch to us using comparisons to other types of churches. He quickly jumped into philosophy mode and explained that when people are asked to do what he calls "third-level" reflection—that is, to describe their interpretation of their experience to others (for example, how they understand their worship experience at Solomon's Porch)—they will inevitably respond with comparisons. At Solomon's Porch, Doug explained, they try to operate on the first level of genuine experience itself, not make comparisons based on these experiences. This is what makes Solomon's Porch different from "Purpose-Driven" churches, he said.

TRANSCENDING POLITICS

Tony Jones, a Princeton Seminary PhD, prolific author, one-time leader of the Emergent Village network, and now theologian in residence at Solomon's Porch, agreed to meet us for breakfast at a diner that aptly bore some socialist name, like Proletariat Coffee or Marx & Co. Bagels and Soufflé. He walked in a few minutes late wearing thick-rimmed glasses and a gray hoodie, later to be on his way to the lake with his kids.

I (Kris) had first encountered Tony as a speaker at various youth ministry and Emergent church conferences while I was in seminary, and he still seemed like a celebrity to me. He had a flair for the provocative in his blog posts and conference talks, and was known for refusing to pull punches—a posture that often generated controversy in the evangelical community. I stood nervously in line next to him, alternating between looking up and trying to think of something to say and giving up and looking at my shoes. As I waited for the other two to order—Tony, who was happy to accept a free breakfast, and Sam, who never let our meager food budget get in the way of a big meal—I tried to think of the best way to break the ice.

Tony In Residence

When we sat down I opened up my notebook, perused our list of questions, and cleared my throat. "So . . . what's up with your job title?" I started. With a pause and then a chuckle, Tony replied that the title of theologian in residence is really just made up. "Doug had this dream that everyone would be something 'in residence' at the church—lawnmower repairman in residence, whatever."

Tony's PhD work was in ecclesiology, the study of the church. We could tell right away that he understood the basis of our project and was one of the intellectual visionaries behind the unique theology and practices of Solomon's Porch. Sam, too cool to be intimidated himself, jumped in to save me from another awkward question by moving directly to the point—what is the prevalent understanding of politics at Solomon's Porch?

Tony began with an example. "Ninety-eight percent of the people at Solomon's Porch are against the marriage amendment, but we are not going to talk about it in church," he explained about an upcoming state referendum to define traditional marriage. He said that Solomon's Porch strongly values partisan neutrality and avoids "overly politicizing" its worship or events—"in the Republican-versus-Democrat way," he clarified. A politically active person himself, Tony admitted that he has made announcements in church soliciting help for rallies, but claimed that he always explains that the congregation does not have a position and that he is not speaking as a church leader; each announcement requires a long caveat. Similarly, as Ben Johnson suggested to us, "We are a house full of activists, but not all activists for the same thing. We have been intentionally careful to not have any political agenda from the stool [i.e., pulpit]."

Tony recalled a moment when one politically engaged congregation member gave a five-minute rant against the state farm bill during a Gathering. As he finished explaining how the bill would hurt local farmers and was about to sit down, Doug asked him to stand back up for a minute and explain, "If someone were in favor of the farm bill, what would he say?" Taking a sip of coffee, Tony now leaned toward us intently: "I was thinking, Doug just totally fucked with this guy. He deconstructed this entire moment, and sent a shot across the bow of everyone who thinks we are going to be this liberal, lefty, LGBT, every-other-mainline church in this city." He added, "In some ways you would say what Doug did was a political act."

We asked Tony to describe the types of political activity Solomon's Porch members engage in, or perhaps activities the church might encourage. Most people at the Porch, he said, "rather than write their congressman to protest the farm bill, would simply dig up their backyard and plant an organic garden." There is a strong effort to fight human trafficking at the church, he continued, but this takes place mostly through art events to raise awareness or through speakers. The church itself does not try to cultivate any particular political dispositions; "Remember, it's all ad hoc."

"So, even if political formation isn't the goal," Sam asked, "do you think it inevitably happens, or do people come to this church because their political sensibilities already align with the majority of its members?" Sitting back to think for a moment, Tony summarized: "I think, primarily, the Porch reinforces that you can be Christian without being partisan; you can be politically engaged without being partisan." He says people here are more motivated by causes than partisanship—more likely to plant an organic garden than fight the farm bill. "Most people here would say, 'Church is by its nature a different type of institution than other ones we are involved with.'"

Doug in Residence

Despite his best efforts, the centerpiece of the church remains its founding "pastor" (though he doesn't like the word, of course) Doug Pagitt, a post-evangelical celebrity, a regular on the Emergent speaking circuit, and the free spirit to Tony's hard-nosed cynicism. Doug met us at the door of the church office, a space that consists of two small rooms, often shared by five staff members. "He looks like a real Minnesotan," said Kris, who had never been to Minnesota. Tall and lanky, he was sporting an old flannel shirt, faded corduroy pants, and what Kris called "one of those mind-seducing soul patches." ("Everything he says has to be true, Sam, he has a soul patch!") On the drive to the church Kris said that Doug could have been a very successful cult leader—he has all the requisite qualities. "I think

I'd be a member of his cult," Kris mused. I tell him to at least pretend to maintain researcher objectivity.

Doug led us into his small corner office where we took our seats on twin 1970s-style forest-green velvet chairs (does Solomon's Porch steal all of its furniture from abandoned college flats?). Doug sat on the adjacent couch, his legs stretched across the room. Above us a large *pietà* painted by a local "artist in residence" hung directly beside two Bruce Springsteen posters, with a stack of Springsteen books on the shelf below. I also noticed three separate coffee makers, ranging from blue-collar drip to bourgeois French press. After a few moments of small talk—Doug had just run a fifty-mile race the previous week—we jumped right in where we had left off with Tony.

Politics has multiple meanings, Doug began, also anticipating the subtext of our questions. The first type involves "civic political engagement." The second type is more complicated, but means something along the lines of "how humans arrange themselves in power structures and then navigate those power structures."[20] Intrigued, I asked him to explain.

"Here, we do a lot of work and thinking that is political in that second sense: what is the power or organization of how things are accomplished?" In this sense, he said, all organization around power dynamics is political, and so the church can't help but be political. "It's the body choosing to function a certain way, to have a certain kind of life together," he said. "It's the body politic." We pressed for an example as Doug leaned back and crossed his legs. Eating together is really important at Solomon's Porch, he responded, "and our system does not preference thinking things together over eating together." The church offers multiple occasions for shared meals and fellowship each week—a community meal every Wednesday, men's breakfast, open lunch with the staff, and Chipotle after every Sunday evening Gathering. What we choose to value and give meaning to—shared meals rather than teaching opportunities, for example—is a political choice, Doug said. These choices shape the way people interact with one another in this community, and also in the world outside of the church, cultivating a posture of generosity.

Then, what about the first sense of politics at Solomon's Porch, we asked? He quickly echoed Tony: the church does not hold any official political positions. To illustrate he explained that after performing a recent gay marriage ceremony in the church building (gay marriage became legal in Minnesota during the process of our research) someone in the congregation asked him if the church was supportive of gay marriage. Doug replied that Solomon's

Porch has no way to give an answer to that question. "An organization does not have an opinion. It can have a policy, but we don't have those," he said. "Opinions are owned by a person, not an institution." Persons in the community can hold diverse opinions on political issues like this, and they do. He admitted he must continually remind people that it is okay not to agree with everything someone in the church does, even if that someone is the pastor. Because of this open political stance and commitment to partisan neutrality, the congregation ranges from politically conservative people to "full-on anarchists" (though I'm not sure we ever spotted one of these really conservative types during our visit). The nature of partisan issues shifts so frequently, he said, citing the quick turnaround in public acceptance of gay marriage, that we do not concern ourselves with being Left or Right—"Except, I have no time for libertarians!" he added, smiling.

"But you did run for public office, right?" Kris asked, a bit hesitantly. Kris was worried that Doug might take offense to the question and sense the hidden Anabaptist lurking beneath his objective researcher façade. ("Do Anabaptists lurk?" I wondered.) "Do you worry that that could compromise the partisan neutrality of the church?"

"I have no concerns that my Christian commitments will be soiled by my political posture," he said directly, as Kris rustled uncomfortably in his chair. "I have a clear enough distinction between my personal Christian conviction and the role I would play as a state legislator. I don't think it would damage my Christian way." Smiling again, he added, "I lost the election, anyway."

Doug's easy partition between the political self and Christian self fueled a developing concern of ours about the church. I asked him to elaborate on his position. The same person can operate uncompromisingly in both arenas, he insisted. "There is nothing wrong in the political realm that could pollute my Christian commitment." He doesn't worry about church and state issues from the perspective of the church, but only from the state's—that his church commitments may overdetermine his political choices, undermining his role as representative, and rendering him untrustworthy to his constituents. He added that he never felt compelled to make Christian convictions the basis for his political decisions in office—to export them onto everyone else. Rather, he would vote based on the constituents' preferences—the representative quality of government, he believes, tempers the individual politician's personal convictions.

At this point Doug checked his phone and invited us to join him for burgers and beer with a local church planter he was mentoring. Once at the local grill, the conversation moved quickly from the moral ambiguities of philanthropy to shifts in postmodern philosophy to what defines a craft beer ("to me, really, it's a philosophy of brewing . . ."). We alternated rolling our eyes and joining right in. Attempting to interject a few more questions amid the flurry of hip topics, we asked about the mayoral debate Solomon's Porch hosted during the previous election. According to Doug, the civic forum was not the church's idea, but was developed at the request of the local neighborhood association. In fact, not many church members attended, but over 350 people from the community did (though it didn't seem that this event had the same evangelistic intent as the Civil Forum at Saddleback). "Part of our ethic is a willingness to be a neighbor."

We asked how the decision was made to host this event—a potentially controversial event for most churches. He matter-of-factly responded that he and Ben Younen made the decision simply because this type of decision falls within their job responsibilities. "There was not much discussion about it. We are willing to partner with anyone who wants to partner with us," he said. As an example, he recalled that the church hosted a retreat from a conservative Christian college group. "There would be some groups we may not be open to hosting," he admitted, "but they would have to be pretty extreme."

I wondered if this was entirely true. Surely every church has its limits, even one as open and unintentional as Solomon's Porch. If the Minneapolis Tea Party had approached them to host a fundraiser, I asked, would he have also agreed to it? He grinned, "If it was the Tea Party, then yes—though probably not the libertarians!"

Ad Hoc Politics

We left the interview with Doug more confused than when we came, and attempted to clear our minds with gratuitous amounts of ice cream at a highly recommended local joint, Sebastian Joe's. We both agreed the church's approach to political engagement was complex—and slippery. Solomon's Porch resists identification with any party or agenda; Tony proclaimed with joy that they are not going to be just another lefty-mainline church, despite their demographic makeup. The church holds no official position on any controversial political issue, and entertains no official discussions in church about political issues like the marriage amendment—a policy that encumbers their ability to take public and prophetic stances on issues of social importance or justice. Church leaders are determined to dodge partisan rhetoric, going to great lengths to maintain neutrality, and even challenging their members to engage with opposing perspectives.

But neutrality is only one part of the Porch's approach to politics. Their approach is not merely the avoidance of politics, but an attempt to transcend the current cultural obsession with partisan agendas by embracing Doug's second dimension of politics—the deeper sense of church politics that comes close to the vision we explained in chapter one, defined by how a community organizes its life together.[21] And we both are convinced that this deeper dimension of politics is of particular importance for Christians who are called to witness to the kingdom of God by the way we live our life together (Matt 5:14–16, 1 Pet 2:12, Rom 15:5–9). Christianity is inherently political in this second sense, and Solomon's Porch is expressing transcendent politics through a pattern of alternative practices and understandings (like community gardens).

In other words, politics does infiltrate communal life, but in a deeper sense, beyond partisan or electoral identity. At Solomon's Porch, church leaders understand this, and are fashioning an alternative identity through a constellation of deeper political practices that both work for social change from the ground up and witness that another form of politics is possible for Christians.

However, there seems to be a tension in Doug's clean delineation between what he calls "*personal* Christian convictions" and a citizen's *public* political role. He believes individuals can hold political positions, but not institutions like churches, and thus sees a clear separation between his church identity and his political identity (when running for office, for example). In his view, one realm does not corrupt the other, because actions in one (political) are not informed by one's convictions in the other (Christian).[22] At this point his focus seems to shift from competing convictions within organizations to competing convictions within an individual—the moral schizophrenia that results from Martin Luther's idea of an individual acting from both his *Christian* and *secular* person.[23] We agree that individual convictions vary widely within organizations, but we cannot agree they should vary within an individual, representing one position in the church and a differing position in public life.

While some elements of the Porch's deeper political perspective will serve as a positive example for other churches, other elements are more ambiguous. The church does effectively transcend partisan politics, and works to cultivate an alternative political sensibility in its members. But its commitment to remain unintentional, or "ad hoc," precludes it from guiding or directing this alternative imagination, especially when such guidance overlaps partisan issues. It concedes these political judgments to each individual member. As a result, the church seems lodged between competing commitments—to shape its community, and to allow members to shape themselves.

ORGANIC GOVERNANCE

"Does your version have verse 28?" Doug asked me (Kris), referring to the mysterious Mark 15:28 that exists in some translations, but is omitted in others. While this does not seem to be a crucial element in Mark's passion narrative, we spent several minutes of the Tuesday night sermon preparation meeting pondering this puzzle. Each week this meeting is open to anyone wants to join Doug in exploring the text for that Sunday's sermon. The group moves verse by verse, stopping to discuss points that stand out to anyone present, as people pause to investigate answers on their iPads. This evening, Doug seemed fixated on textual variants. We attended to the missing verse 28, the various translations of the liquid offered to Jesus on the cross in verse 36, and the added ending to Mark 16, snake handling and all. The conversation stayed mostly on a scholarly level, rarely dipping into spiritualization or life application. Every person in attendance during our visit had some theological training, and while that is not unusual for this community, Doug wishes more "untrained" members of the community would join in. The conversation is better, more imaginative, if there are more people without formal training, he said.

Doug will use some of these insights and conversations in the sermon on Sunday, giving credit to people for their ideas and drawing further comments from the crowd. He describes his sermons as "drive-by observations for those who have ears to hear," not six points and a poem to try and convince the congregation of some theological point. He makes clear that these are "provisional statements," his thoughts and sometimes those from the sermon prep participants, and cautions that others will read these same texts differently.

Tony calls the sermon the "most potent political act" that takes place at the church because it best exemplifies the noncoercive, nonhierarchical, ad hoc culture of the community. It subverts the traditional place of the sermon as an authoritative monologue, and sends the message that everyone has the authority to interpret (and apply) the Bible.[24] This means that Doug does not make life applications in the sermon.[25] The point is not to apply the message of Scripture to individuals' life situations in particular and practical ways, but to implicate those listening in the story of God in Scripture, he says. He wants the entire congregation to locate themselves in the story of God rather than tell them how other peoples' experiences may apply to their lives. Such applications are better left to each individual, he claims.[26]

Doug believes this approach to preaching takes the priesthood of all believers seriously. His style has several implications. First, the democratic, egalitarian nature of the sermon affirms that everyone is a contributor to the formation of everyone else. Doug hopes it will cultivate a "theological community" that generates new understandings of God together. Second, it eliminates the "dehumanizing effect" of what he calls "speeching"—the traditional monologue sermon—and creates a nonhierarchical relationship between the preacher and the congregation. Though it requires a degree of vulnerability on the part of the preacher, a ceding of control over the full content of what is said during worship meetings, it suggests there is no "one seat of Godly authority." Finally, Doug suggests that this puts the power of the Bible back in the hands of the congregation, transforming the Bible from a static, central authority to a "living member of the community." He contends that this grants more authority to the Bible, as it is opened up to valid interpretation from anyone in the community—though this image of the Bible as a community member (presumably one of many community members) seems to relativize its authority. The image might be more confusing than it is helpful, we think, but Doug really seems to like it.[27]

Central Casting

This democratic, dialogical approach to the sermon reflects a deeper structural sensibility within the church. Janelle Vick, church administrator and volunteer coordinator, calls the governance and decision-making structure "organic," meaning it contains little intentional process and minimal hierarchy.[28] This flat governance structure serves as perhaps the most defining characteristic of the church, and likely its most political.

Janelle was the first person we met at Solomon's Porch. Young and enthusiastic, she welcomed us with freshly baked banana bread and told us to ask anything, even though she was "not quite sure what you are doing here." She is the organizing force behind Doug's ad hoc style, trying to infuse order (budget graphs, organizational charts, minimal policies) while respecting the commitment to nonhierarchy. She relayed the history of the church's leadership structure as we dove into the plate of banana bread. (Hey, we were on a tight food budget!)

The fledgling church began with Doug making most of the decisions, though he quickly sought ways to delegate responsibility. "Solomon's Porch is his baby," Janelle told us, but Doug does not believe that means he has to be involved in everything. "Doug has always pushed for as flat a leadership structure as we could possibly maintain and to empower as many voices in decision-making as possible," she added. Anyone who was passionate about a particular aspect of church life could create a group and facilitate its activities, with no restrictions on who can lead with no training or experience requirements.[29] By 2007, this evolved into a network of "working groups" led by volunteers who were passionate about a particular issue (art, children, Gatherings, etc.) and fully empowered to make decisions in that area. The groups are open to anyone and each designates a nonstaff facilitator to serve as a representative to "Central Casting," the main decision-making body of the church.[30]

At this point in the conversation Janelle took a break and smiled at us as we tried to catch up. An organizational chart—which seems a bit uncharacteristic for the church, but exists nonetheless—helped us wrap our heads around the structure. "So how are decisions made in Central Casting?" I (Sam) asked. "Do you vote on a proposal like typical church committees?"

There is rarely any voting, Janelle replied.[31] Voting should be avoided because you get the opinion of people who don't care about the issue. A bit dramatically, Doug calls it "an act of violence." Solomon's Porch's structure works primarily to empower those who care about specific issues or tasks to make decisions in those particular areas, and trusts others to do the same, in the best interest of the community. At the end of the day, there is no established process for congregational decision-making as long as everybody has a chance to give input and feedback. One member told us, "If you have an idea here it doesn't have to go through layers of review boards and approving. Doug's answer is pretty much, 'That's a good idea, why don't you do that?'"[32] Church member Ben Myrick identifies this as the "antiformula" to traditional church leadership structures. With no standing groups or committees to make decisions—except for Central Casting—all decisions and activities demand the formation of work groups for specific tasks. But "we are not tied to any particular way of doing things," Janelle added. "Doug says if this doesn't work out, then just switch to a new model."

We wondered if there were times when this model did not work well. One member we spoke with later, admitting to being more of an organization freak than most in the right-brained congregation, cited a lack of communication that slows down decisions and activities. Even more significant, "What is sacrificed with the lack of hierarchy is a lack of accountability." A lot of broken people come to the Porch to begin a healing process, "but there are also many times that people just make bad life decisions and sometimes the community could step up more or there could be a sense of accountability for that individual."

"What are the benefits of such a flat structure?" we asked Janelle, peering wistfully into the now empty banana bread plate. The best part, she insisted, is that everyone has the possibility of being a part of decision-making. "I think this is really empowering." She said it feels more organic, like a "collective." Others we interviewed emphasized the "transparency" and "integrity" of this structure. "I've come from personal experiences where leadership is not transparent and very closed door," said Cecka Parks, a working group leader. "I had a very bad taste in my mouth from those experiences. Coming here has been a breath of fresh air to have so much transparency from our leadership." When the community hires someone to be on staff, she trusts them to make decisions on her behalf. "Doug is one of the most inclusive people I've ever met. He doesn't struggle with power or control at all," she insisted. "And that mentality pervades through most of us."

Church Leadership in the "Inventive Age"

For Doug, this organic, democratic form of church governance reflects cultural shifts in the way people view authority today, a cultural paradigm he calls the "Inventive Age." It is not that authority doesn't exist or is always rejected; rather it develops relationally. A leader must first earn trust. Authority is granted from the community, not bestowed externally because of title, position, or tradition. "When you force authority on someone who does not grant it to you, that is an act of violence."[33] In most institutions, but especially in churches, he sees three types of authority frameworks: bounded-set authority, established with doctrinal borders (we believe this and not this, and you are one of us if you do the same); center-set authority, focused on a common theme or experience ("a topic, an issue, a belief, a practice"); and relational-set authority, where the participants are the organization and there are no borders or single unifying belief or practice. Solomon's Porch is not constituted by erecting doctrinal boundaries or focusing on a specific issue, he insists. Instead the community is constituted by the constellation of individuals that make it up—again, an organic community that grows, shifts, and transforms itself. The participants freely choose and direct the organization.[34]

For the community to function within this paradigm, everyone has a specific role. For example, as "pastor," Doug has two specific jobs: Sunday Gatherings and congregational life, with two separate contracts for these two distinct jobs. He is responsible for exercising decision-making authority within these areas only, and is supposed to delegate specific tasks and decisions in other church areas: "our way of divesting the founder's authority." He recognizes that as the pastor, people will ascribe a degree of authority to him and often defer to him—especially those who come from churches with traditional pastors—but he deflects it, insisting on his role as a facilitator and curator.[35]

According to Doug, "every decision should have somebody's name on it." This structure makes decision-making more humanizing and empowering for individuals in the community. "When you are working against powers and principalities," he said with a rare biblical allusion—and a smirk—it is important to empower individual persons. It gives strength to the people who put the effort into it and makes everyone else aware that things don't just magically happen. This governance model generates both power and responsibility, he said, echoing Cecka's sentiments about the integrity and transparency of the framework. It "opens something up so you can see where the power structure is." While insisting on the organic unintentionality of all this in one moment, in the next he alludes to an underlying strategy, explaining that "these practices have created an attitude in our community where people believe they can and should learn from one another."[36]

"A Truer Form of Democracy"

We think this commitment to a flat, inclusive community is the most significant political practice of Solomon's Porch. It is political in a deep sense, affecting the way the church orders and patterns its life together as a community, from education and worship to governance and decision-making. In a sense, this commitment to nonhierarchy is (in ways more intentional than the leaders admit) a prophetic statement about how power ought to be distributed in the church.

The resulting distribution of power is manifest most explicitly in the democratic, egalitarian reconstitution of the sermon. Church members grant each other authority to exegete the Scriptures, and to have their voice heard during the Gathering.[37] Over and over, covenant participants at Solomon's Porch spoke about how empowering this model is for the congregation members. They become a part of the process, from beginning to end. The goal is for everyone to move beyond the role of mere spectator, of soaking up the knowledge of a trained expert and inserting carefully crafted spiritual insights into their daily lives. The pastor is divested of sole authority, and it is dispersed to everyone, equally, regardless of age, theological training, or spiritual maturity. This is a powerful expression of the priesthood of all believers (1 Pet 2:5, 9), and even some not-quite believers.

But the sermon only constitutes one aspect of the church's holistic commitment to openness, empowerment, and egalitarianism. The sermon, sermon preparation meeting, inclusive participation in worship, ad hoc mission efforts, and especially the leadership structure are all ingredient of the church's overarching emphasis on nonauthority in its way of life. In our visits, we observed that a streamlined decision-making process has become a trend for many churches, moving away from the more bureaucratic structures of churches in ages past; and Solomon's Porch is on the leading edge of this development. Here, this commitment serves to give everyone a voice but also works to give a higher degree of power—ultimately final decision-making power—to the one who has taken responsibility for that area of church life. This requires trust in those chosen to make decisions in that area (and in this way Solomon's Porch is actually not that different from Saddleback, despite their efforts to persuade us otherwise!).

Leaning back into the green couch in the corner of his small office, with Jesus and The Boss looking down at us, Doug reflected, "The experience people have within this community is starting to shape their expectations for the way the rest of the world should be." It shows up in people's lives, he claimed, altering how they run their business, teach in their classroom, or interact with coworkers, where they want to live or how they eat, how they raise their kids, or how they approach partnerships or collaboration—even changing their expectations and interactions with political systems. While he does not use the terms "mission" or "witness" to describe this phenomenon, he told us that it is "starting to set the norms for the other areas of their lives."

More than Tony, Doug presents a hopeful account of the social formation that occurs at the Porch. Despite its stated unintentionality, people are formed and shaped to engage in the world in new and fruitful ways, he believes. In some ways we wonder if these are simply the aspirational musings of a founding pastor. When a community holds in tension the values of egalitarian individualism and communal formation, we wonder if one will always undercut the other and hamstring the church's ability to fully embody either value.

As we concluded our interviews for the day, we walked with Ben Myrick back into the Gathering room, now full of vacant couches, dark and dramatic paintings, and the giant goose. Ben began to turn off the overhead lights, and we asked him if he thinks this model really works. "What are the implications of doing church like this?"

He thought for a moment. "You know how ants are really stupid individually but work really well together, or how the brain is just a bunch of synapses firing independently and together they kind of come up with decisions? That's how organic it is here," he said. "Stuff just happens naturally. Change is the only consistent thing here." Ben said this model promotes egalitarianism and empowers the people in the congregation to become more than spectators, to have some stake in what happens here. It is, he said, turning off the lights above the "Porchtraits" surrounding the cross, "a truer form of democracy."

GROWING AN ORGANIC COMMUNITY

The deep, syncopated tones of the upright bass filled the two-story bar, packed closely with small black tables around the stage. As the piano and drums joined in, the trio embarked on an upbeat and impossibly complex Cuban fusion number, with heads bouncing in unison around the room. A couple of members of the church had recommended the Dakota Jazz Club in downtown Minneapolis as the premier jazz venue in the state, and it didn't disappoint.

Jazz has always fascinated me (Sam). The expert jazzman can unravel beautifully improvised melodies from a simple piece, pulling the listener along as he explores new musical terrain, experimenting until something feels just right. Jazz is created in the moment, ad hoc, crafted in real-time response to the audience and the rest of the band. However, the best players know that jazz is a delicate balance of imagination and convention. A great solo is intimately personal, yet constantly indebted to the work of the masters.

Church Improvised

Solomon's Porch, in a sense, is church improvised. It is a church guided by spontaneity and unintentionality, riffing on traditional church elements like communion, proclamation, and mission, with a fresh twist that excites, yet feels vaguely familiar. The leaders claim continuity with early church tradition, but reimagine that tradition with new practices and emphases. They experiment and weave together traditional features of church with something fresh and beautiful, and always open to new possibilities.

The Porch's leaders operate on the assumption that our cultural paradigm has changed—that "church as usual" needs a substantial reworking from the ground up in order to survive. Solomon's Porch's experiment in ecclesial antiauthority offers an image of a church, democratic and improvised, that does indeed appeal to the people of this "Inventive Age." Like Paul in Athens (Acts 17:16–32), the church works with the materials and philosophies of its cultural context (admittedly a mostly white, financially stable, "granola" suburban context) to redirect that culture to be more open to the world and empower the diversity of voices within it. Solomon's Porch's attentiveness and responsiveness to its cultural climate provides an example for any church that needs a new vision for the twenty-first century. The Porch is also a place of healing for those who have been hurt by the church. It gives its members a place to belong and an avenue for self-expression. It serves as a liberating voice for a bunch of souls who feel disenfranchised from a church that failed to welcome, include, and empower them.

We think Ben Myrick is right to call this church structure a "truer form of democracy," implying that it might serve as a model for other polities.[38] In fact, Solomon's Porch seems to run with less bureaucratic meandering than most "democratic" polities. This community models democratic principles, and helps apply these patterns of decision-making to life outside the church.[39] It successfully captures some of the best elements of a democratic ethos: empowering all voices in interpretation and decision-making, offering radical inclusivity of the "other," cultivating the habit of listening, working on both local and global levels, generating participation and responsibility among community members, assigning tasks that align with people's desires and skills.[40] It diffuses temptations to overcentralize authority and teaches people to meet needs with whomever is around to meet them. This ad hoc democratic culture is formative for people in the community, and perhaps for other churches who are taking notice.

However, after our visits and conversations with this community, we left Solomon's Porch wondering if they have actually overcorrected for some of the faults they see in other churches. Does reimagining church as a loosely tied network of organic relationships err too much on the side of improvisation? Has their desire to do something new drifted too far from the original?[41] The aspects of the church examined in this chapter seem to point to two overriding commitments: 1) an ad hoc, unintentional culture, and 2) the cultivation of a set of community values—including openness, cooperation, attention to otherness, individual empowerment, and egalitarianism. These two commitments produce tension between individualism and communalism—between leaving values, judgments, and spiritual and political direction to each individual, and working toward some cohesive community formation.

One the one hand, Doug claims there is a unifying "communal ethic" inherent to Solomon's Porch. Although many people who come tend to be predisposed to the general values of the community noted above, he and Tony insist that people are shaped by being part of this community. In other words, the community is, in fact, formative (they claim)—socially, spiritually, and politically. It animates a new political imagination and sets norms for other areas of members' lives. They believe that the spiritually empowering ethos here offers a witness to the politics of the kingdom. According to Janelle, "People come from all walks of life, some who grew up in the church, some who did not, some who are struggling with their faith, maybe even are agnostic." They are coming because this community means something to them and it changes who they are and how they live their lives, how they treat people.

On the other hand, Doug insists that there is no direction to the community's formation. There are no orienting faith statements, no explicit spiritual goals, no common vision of discipleship. In fact, there seems to be no unifying spiritual, theological, or political purpose at all. The church allows the cares and concerns of the community's members to determine what practices or values are important to the community ("We care a lot about baptism if you care. But if you don't care, we won't care."[42]) "We don't do coercive spirituality," Doug says. "We don't begin with the assumption that there are these qualities or characteristics or outcomes that every person should have and then say, 'We will help you have that in your life.' . . . Instead it begins with a relational dynamic that asks 'What would spirituality look like in your life, for you to live as a whole person?'" That is the guiding question of the community, and the answer varies with every individual.

As we continued to press on this issue, Doug finally admitted that Solomon's Porch *is* intentional, but without desired outcomes. The church is intentional about the process but not about any particular goal or end for the community or community member. This model of using the procedures of democracy while leaving the ends of formation up to each individual member is a deeply political move that influences every area and activity of the church.[43] However, we worry this commitment to unintentionality and individual autonomy hinders spiritual and political formation in the community by leaving the realm of politics, and all political decisions, up to individual church members.[44]

By avoiding most controversial political issues, presenting both angles of a political argument, and understanding church and government as two polities that should not infiltrate or interfere with the other,[45] the church transcends partisan politics but also evades its responsibility to inform or shape the way its members think socially and prophetically. For example, it seems important to us that a church should talk about what Christians should think about issues like gay marriage. That is, Christians should think about social and political matters through a theological and scriptural lens. Solomon's Porch may be missing opportunities to think theologically together and then speak out about issues of political and theological import.[46] Political matters are always theological, and vice versa. However, by disconnecting the realms of church and politics, a church forfeits its public witness to the ways of the kingdom of God here amidst the kingdoms of the earth.

This brings us to the question of the church's self-identity. Doug insists the church operates with a relational-set authority, in which the participants form an organic community that grows without any preestablished borders or purpose. Its identity is framed by the set of individual relationships that make up the community, and by the democratic procedures that empower those voices and relationships. It is less clear whether Solomon's Porch shares the purposes and identities that (on its best days!) define the church universal—a theological and political commitment to submitting and witnessing to the lordship of Jesus Christ. It seems to us that this commitment is what distinguishes churches from any other social organization or community and the cultural norms that guide them. But here, we worry, a unifying allegiance to King and kingdom may be undercut by unintentionality and individualism.

Doug counters that Solomon's Porch doesn't practice a sacred/secular distinction. This community is open to being influenced by yoga or postmodern philosophy. "We are not supposed to be unique," he says. "That is not our goal." We can applaud their efforts to remove the sacred/secular barriers that have damaged the church's public witness and to welcome those who have experienced life as sinners in the hands of an angry church. At the same time, we worry that this commitment to forming the community around a constellation of individual members, their desires and self-prescribed goals, rather than faith in and obedience to Christ as King of their personal lives—even in a way that allows for questioning, wandering, doubting, and discussion—confines the church to doing little more than helping individual members be who they want to be. And then, what is the use of the church? In other words, a church needs both an empowering *procedure* and a kingdom-building, missional *purpose*.[47]

Procedure over Purpose

In the opening monologue to the film *The Departed*, Jack Nicholson's character, mob boss Frank Costello, says, "Years ago we had the church. That was only a way of saying we had each other." Costello refers to a bygone era when the local church was the nexus of his community, but this sentiment also nicely describes the atmosphere at Solomon's Porch. "We are taking care of each other's kids, picking up eggs from each other's houses, sharing professional contacts," Cecka explained. "We are invested in each others' lives." This highlights the Porch's emphasis on building a contextual and relational church. But the force of the word "only" in the quote—is there something more here than a collection of relationships?—also denotes the lack of a unifying substance.

The church's model of political engagement, which we identify as *growing an organic community*, is inwardly focused on building community and embodying an alternative political identity, rather than getting involved in partisan politics or cultivating a public political witness. This growth is organic, allowing individuals to determine their own personal commitments to King and kingdom, with minimal interference or guidance from church leaders. There is no definitive direction for the community, only a definitive procedure—democratic governance dedicated to empowering every voice in the community, but without any unifying constitution. Its attempts to cultivate and model a new political vision may be stunted by its commitment to unintentionality.

"Growing an organic community" is a complex expression of political engagement, and constitutes a deep understanding and practice of the church political. On one hand, by remaining neutral on all partisan issues the church elides many social issues of theological significance, issues on which a community seeking to be faithful to the gospel should take a stand. On the other hand, the Solomon's Porch model avoids partisan entanglements that ensnare many other congregations. The church is an alternative political body that embodies a beneficial, and even faithful, understanding of the political dimensions of gospel faith and life, and there is much in this model that other churches may find helpful.

We conclude this chapter by highlighting four characteristics or practices of Solomon's Porch that we hope can serve as examples for others.

First, most churches are pushing for a flatter leadership structure, and Solomon's Porch is a prime example. Their commitment to empowering every voice and encouraging any person to take responsibility for a mission, workgroup, or project is a great example of missional leadership. Broadening the decision-making process encourages community members to move from spectators to committed participants and even leaders.

Second, the dialogical sermon, formed by community discussion, exemplifies the priesthood of all believers by granting everyone in the community the authority to interpret Scripture. Many churches could benefit by offering weekly sermon discussions to allow a diversity of voices to shape the church's teaching and by encouraging questions during or after the sermon to further the conversation.

Third, one of the defining functions of Solomon's Porch is to be a place of healing—primarily, it seems, for those hurt by previous church experiences. A focus on church as a place where wounds are healed—however or wherever they were received—is a necessary mission within the larger church body. The Porch's attention to people damaged by previous church relationships is an unfortunately necessary mission, and signals an imperative to other churches to be humble and gentle to those who fall into the category of "previously churched" (and to the ministries like Solomon's Porch who reach out to them).

Finally, Solomon's Porch transcends the trap of partisan identification that seduces many churches and leaders. Their approach to political engagement serves as an encouraging model for how other churches can both develop alternative political practices—responding to political issues and crises with community gardens or civic forums—and encourage a deeper political vision of the church in its worship and study by highlighting the political dimensions of Scripture and church practices, like Memorial Day Communion. This points to the church as a deeper political reality and an expression of the true politics of the kingdom of God.

* * *

With rain dripping from our now-filthy clothes, we stood victoriously at the foot of the transported mulch pile like a pair of real Minnesota lumberjacks . . . if only either of us could grow a real beard! We had spent all of this, our last day at Solomon's Porch, with Doug, talking about the church's future and clarifying points from our previous conversations—his comments always accompanied by a joke and a contagious smile.

As with every church we spent time with, our thoughts on Solomon's Porch were complicated. We were drawn to their warm spirit, the way they functioned almost like a family, the way they seriously hoped to be a remedy for the church's multitude of sins. But we also struggled with what seemed like deep ambiguities in their identity and mission.

As Doug thanked us for our help with the mulch and reached for his gym bag, we tried one more time to reconcile these complexities, to frame a question that would give him a chance to fell all of our lingering concerns. But Doug wasn't interested in simplifying the complexity. He gave us a suitably rushed response, then shook our hands with a smile and was off. The rain had stopped and it was time for a run.

Chapter 4

Embracing Public Activism

First & Franklin Presbyterian Church

WE SPOTTED THE TOWERING steeple rising above the low Baltimore skyline several minutes before arriving at the large burgundy stone sanctuary. First & Franklin Presbyterian, a progressive Presbyterian Church (USA) congregation, sits among posh cafes and cozy apartments in the trendy Mount Vernon neighborhood. The 250-year-old church is the oldest in Baltimore and one of the oldest in the country. Construction began on its beautiful Gothic revival sanctuary a decade before the start of the Civil War, and its 273-foot spire, the tallest in the city, can be seen for miles.

But we were interested in more than the age and architecture of the church. First & Franklin boasts a long history of involvement in progressive and social-justice causes—"it just reeks with it," one member says[1]—and is recognized as one of the most politically active congregations in the city. And more than any other church we visited, First & Franklin unabashedly wears its political causes on its sleeve (and on the exterior of its sanctuary), even its stances on controversial issues most other churches avoid. A long row of colored ribbons line the north side of the stone building, a memorial to victims of the wars in Iraq and Afghanistan, and a large rainbow flag declaring "People of Faith for Marriage Equality" hangs directly above the front door.

The church has been heavily involved in LGBT issues for several decades; in 1980, it joined with other dissenting PCUSA congregations in protesting the denomination's ban on the ordination of gay and lesbian ministers. At that time the church employed a gay associate pastor who began an evangelism program in the neighborhood's gay bars, and now more than half the congregation is gay.[2] This commitment to inclusivity has grown into public advocacy for the marriage equality movement in the state of Maryland, especially during the months leading up to the 2012 referendum, held just days after one of our visits. Senior pastor Alison Halsey even appeared in a TV ad supporting gay and lesbian couples' right to obtain state marriage licenses. "The church's identity is one of social action," Alison says.

This visit was a new experience for both of us. Neither of us come from politically active churches, especially regarding issues like marriage equality and gay rights. Kris's Anabaptist background had conditioned him to be wary of any direct political involvement by churches, and none of the theologically conservative churches Sam grew up in would have touched these issues (except perhaps to oppose them). We were both more accustomed to churches avoiding hot-button political issues than campaigning for them. We were interested to see how a church that had so clearly taken a side on a high-profile political issue would understand its own political identity.

The questions of gay civil rights and homosexuality in church are not just political issues for us—they're personal as well. Within the past few years we have each journeyed with close friends as they came to terms with their own sexuality. The question of the treatment, and most often *mistreatment*, of homosexuals in society and the church is not abstract for either of us—it's a struggle we have witnessed up close.

As we continue to struggle with this issue, we have realized that we do not fully agree on it, at least for now. While we both acknowledge the many failures of the church to show Christlike love to homosexual people, we differ on how we believe a church should theologically consider homosexuality, and especially whether a church should marry gay couples or encourage homosexual relationships among gay Christians. We also understand that our readers will fall at many different points on the spectrum of theological and political thought on the matter, and we hope that our exploration of this church can generate reflection, conversation, and respectful disagreement among our readers, as it has for us. Our disagreements have made for great conversations during our long hours on the road—often causing us to miss turns, blame each other, and end up in an even more heated argument about one of us paying attention to where we are going.

We suspected that there was another layer to this church's political character, beneath its controversial political activity. It would be easy to identify First & Franklin's political activity primarily with its involvement in the marriage equality debate, but as with the other churches we visited, we guessed that other practices of the church would be politically significant as well, perhaps in deeper ways.

SANKOFA

The deep tones of the organ welcomed us as we hurriedly stepped into First & Franklin's cavernous main sanctuary. The vaulted ceiling immediately drew our eyes upward to the tall, narrow stained-glass windows and intricate white trim against bright pink walls, a style members describe as "flamboyant Gothic." A massive golden pipe organ filled the back of the room, rising high into the ceiling. The dark wooden pews and balcony seating, enough for several hundred, were arrayed behind the simple altar beneath a large triple arch at the front.

We quickly made our way down the side aisle and took our seats at the end of a pew close to the back as the liturgist offered a few announcements from the pulpit. Our entrance was a bit more conspicuous than we had hoped, since the service had already begun. I (Sam) had spent most the car ride to the church through Baltimore's bumpy streets looking down at my watch as the hands ticked passed 11 a.m. My sense of urgency seemed lost on Kris, who seemed more intent on arguing about C. S. Lewis's natural law theology than getting to church on time. Or was this the argument about which Disney movie has the best soundtrack? Whichever it was, it caused us to be late.

After finally settling into our seats, we took a quick glance around the sanctuary. Perhaps forty congregants sat in a sanctuary constructed for hundreds, a common scenario in older, traditional American churches. The decline of the mainline (white, non-evangelical) church is a common refrain among scholars and pastors. Mainline membership in the US has fallen by more than 25 percent since the height of its influence in the 1950s and '60s.[3] These congregations are struggling to attract younger members: studies show that almost 40 percent of mainline attendees are over sixty years old. Participation in Christian education (Sunday school, Bible studies, or small groups) has declined by 17 percent since 1998, and participation in missions has declined by over 20 percent. Fewer than one out of every ten mainline adults name some aspect of their faith as their highest priority in life.[4]

Finding Their Place

Several of the church members we talked with attributed the waning energy and declining membership of First & Franklin to a disconnect between leadership and laity. "Everything was sort of top-down," one member explained, motioning with his hands. "People up there were determining what was to be done, and we lose the passion down here."[5] The leadership at First & Franklin knew that something had to change. They decided to acknowledge their shortcomings and meet this challenge head on by revamping the leadership structure to infuse more life into the congregation and become more involved in the life of its community.

We sat down with Jeff Watson outside a small deli called Milk & Honey. Jeff was relatively new at First & Franklin. A hospital administrator with a keen eye for organization, he was asked on to the church board within a few months of joining the church, and now leads a team in charge of church resources. Trucks rumbled down the noisy street a few feet from our table, and as we began talking an elderly lady sitting nearby asked if we would watch her yippy, wiry-haired terrier while she went inside to get a drink. With one eye on the terrier and one on Jeff, we asked about the church's decision to shake up its leadership structure.

Declining membership was concerning to everyone, Jeff explained. But numbers weren't the only issue. Most of the church meetings focused on the declining finances that accompanied the slumping membership. Senior pastor Alison Halsey was woefully overworked and often exhausted, and the congregation was losing enthusiasm for community outreach and church involvement. Jeff attributed this loss of energy to a rigid, top-down governance and ministry structure in the church—a relic of Presbyterian polity that no longer made sense for the congregation. The average church attendee felt disconnected from the life of the church, with no voice in major decisions and no direction about how to become involved in the church's ministry. Alison initiated the restructuring process one night through a Bible study she led with the church session (the board of elders in Presbyterian polity). She admitted her exhaustion, and told them, bluntly, that things had to change. For her, this involved two key areas: the church leadership structure needed revision, and the congregation needed to be invited to take greater ownership of the church's ministry. She envisioned First & Franklin as a landmark in their neighborhood, a community called to care for the needs of those right outside their doors and beyond. "More light needs to shine here," she concluded.[6]

Jeff leaned back, lost in his story (and we wondered if that lady was ever coming back for her dog). After meeting with some expert church advisors—including church historian Diana Butler Bass—to strategize, the session invited the entire congregation to have a voice in the process. "We needed to flatten out the structure," Jeff said, "to allow greater opportunity for people to be involved, to create the mechanisms for the pastor to delegate down to people." They needed to get the people most dedicated to the church to participate in discussions about how to change it, to "bring it into the twenty-first century and make it more meaningful and relevant to the community, to the members, and other people, to sustain ourselves and grow, and refresh ourselves." To its members the church had started to feel like a monument to Christendom past—an ancient cathedral towering above the city, empty and quiet, unable to reach a world that had passed it by. As another member put it, First & Franklin was "struggling to find its place."[7] They began their discernment process by asking: "How does the oldest Presbyterian church in the region respond to these revolutionary and evolutionary changes? And who are we serving: the members or the community?"[8]

For First & Franklin, the answer was a two-year self-evaluation and restructuring process they called "Sankofa"—a Ghanaian concept one member described as "looking at the past to discern where you want to go in the future."[9] Church leaders and members gathered to reflect on the history of the church and its impact on the Baltimore community, and discussed how to reclaim the best aspects of that history. "We first asked: What are we about? Then, how do we take the passion and interest and gifts of the congregation and have it boil up to the top?"[10] The energy needed to rise from the bottom, from the passions of those sitting in the pews.

Their first order of business was to address the issues with the leadership structure, as Jeff explained, "to create a structure that would empower people to be more involved and more creative, to let people have more autonomy," and to cultivate "inspired leadership."[11] This required a flatter governing structure that would give the congregation more ownership of the church's mission, and also alleviate some of the leadership burdens on the overworked pastor. Like many pastors, "Alison has a problem with delegation," Jeff joked.

Leadership transitioned to a committee representing five Ministry Teams with a specific ministry focus, Jeff explained. For example, the representative for the Inclusivity Team (how many churches have an entire team dedicated to inclusivity, we thought?) is designated to think about diversity—questions like, "How are we going to plan this concert series to appeal to different kinds of people?" The teams are intentionally fluid: people can "plug in, do your thing, and then unplug, to go somewhere else you are interested in."[12] The staff and committee provide support, training, and leadership; the congregation provides passion, ideas, and discernment. The basic idea is: "If you feel called to do something, grab a friend and go do it."[13]

Jeff stopped and smiled. This change is "reenergizing me," he said. "I find I am recommitting to the church." Jeff believes the process has been successful so far: just two years into the new structure, more people are being given more autonomy, and are getting more done. While most members we spoke with echoed Jeff's enthusiasm about the changes, not everyone was as confident that Sankofa has been a success. One church leader explained that some people have still felt disconnected during the restructuring process due to infrequent communication from the leaders. The church did not witness the immediate surge in participation that they had hoped for, he confessed.

Jeff concluded our conversation—finally sans yippy canine—with a moment of uncharacteristically pietistic language for this church. He hopes that the Sankofa effort will create a "revival." It is happening with him and others. But it's still too early to tell, he says, as his administrative realism kicks in—it will take years to fully understand the results.

Restructure and Renewal

Our reaction to the Sankofa restructuring process was ambivalent. The new leadership structure, streamlined decision-making process, and bottom-up, empowering ministry approach are not generating the significant results the leaders had hoped for. While we agree with Jeff that it is too early to make clear judgments on its effectiveness, we saw a disconnect between the optimism of the church leaders and the sparse Sunday attendance.

While the long-term effectiveness of Sankofa is yet to be seen, we applaud this church's efforts to inspire energy in its congregation. The staff at First & Franklin recognized that the bureaucracy that characterized church leadership in the past had drained the spiritual passion of its congregants, and they chose to involve the entire congregation in finding a solution. In fact, the process itself modeled the bottom-up, inclusive structure they hoped would result. They drew from a rich history of social justice—looking at the past—to lay the tracks to the future. They believed that Sankofa would reconnect them to the neighborhood and to social action.[14]

This seems to us a deeply political move. Upending the internal governance structure and decision-making patterns is a decision intended to cultivate a new political vision—moving members from spectators to participants in kingdom work. It alters the values of the community, allowing leadership to develop from the ground up, and refocuses the community's identity, forming the church and its politics around its ministry. Church leaders hope it connects the personal and social by renewing the spiritual energy of the congregation and infusing it with a passion for community missions. The church's identity becomes more outwardly focused, while empowering the congregation members with more responsibility for and ownership of the church and its mission. This can serve as an example to other shrinking mainline congregations—not as a way to "stay in business" (as if that should be an end in itself),[15] but as a way to expand their missional reach, spiritually strengthen their communities, and cultivate thriving congregations of ministers, even if actual attendance does not increase.[16]

POLITICAL WORSHIP

The call to worship concluded as Sam and I finally settled into our seats. Sam (punctually challenged himself) blamed our late arrival on my sudden urge for another car-ride debate that morning. (He was probably right—but at least I won the argument!) Today was the Sunday before election day 2012. This year's ballot boasted a gamut of contests, from the presidency to important state referendums in Maryland, most notably the marriage equality amendment that would grant marriage rights to same-sex couples. Since we knew this was an important issue at First & Franklin, we were interested to see what role this topic might play in the day's worship service.

I glanced quickly through the Order of Worship handed to us as we entered and pointed out to Sam an announcement soliciting volunteers to greet voters at polling locations on behalf of the group "Marylanders for Marriage Equality." This notice was flanked by an invitation to support global missions through the church's Alternative Christmas Market, a call for volunteers to help with a congregational partnership to set up HIV testing sites across the city, and a reminder about the next concert in the church's "Spire Series," a string ensemble from the Baltimore School of the Arts. Intrigued by this diversity of announcements, my thoughts were abruptly brought back to the worship service by the passing of the peace, which entailed shaking hands with those sitting closest to you and extending the greeting "May the peace of Christ be with you." The congregants were extremely friendly—many flocked to welcome the visitors (I wondered if they have many).

The service followed traditional Presbyterian liturgy, though interspersed with selections from Bach, a Negro spiritual, and an Appalachian folk hymn. Today was All Saints Day, an occasion to remember church members who had passed away that year. The music, litanies, lectionary passages, and sermon focused on these saints, now "a great cloud of witnesses" (Heb 12:1) looking over the congregation. We were surprised that in a church so involved in electoral issues, no direct reference to the election was made until the end. Despite the political accouterments adorning the front door, the liturgical calendar trumped the impending political events during the worship time. Still, as Alison closed the gathering with the benediction, she prayed that "peace and justice will be in those ballot boxes" and concluded with a common and driving proclamation at First & Franklin—"Jesus loves *all* people."

As Alison commissioned us all to service and the worship time came to a close, the pipes of the organ rang through the gothic arches once again. As the postlude began, Sam and I grabbed our coats and walked toward the back door. As we walked into the narthex, we turned around to realize that every single person in attendance had stopped in their pew, turned toward the organ in the balcony, and stood in reverence as classically trained organist Jason Kissel played a lively "Ode to Joy." We exchanged sheepish looks, once more standing conspicuously in front of the entire congregation, until the postlude's climactic conclusion.

Formative Worship Practices

After the service ended, we joined Jason, the organist, for lunch, now more embarrassed about our premature departure than our late arrival—surely an insult to the man whose music everyone turns to admire at the end of every worship service. One of the younger members we had met during our visit, Jason had served as minister of music since 2000, drawn there, he said, because of the social diversity of the congregation and its location in the "cultural hub" of Baltimore. The church values quality music, he said—a point now painfully obvious to both of us.

We decided to begin the interview with a softball, to make up for our rude departure: "Why is music important at First & Franklin?" But in his answer, Jason spoke right to the heart of our research. Music is formative for churches, he said, in the same way that it has been for the great social movements of history, like the powerful Negro spirituals and songs of the civil rights struggle. Worship music, from Bach to spirituals, plays a central role in the life of this congregation, he said, and many people are involved in some form or another. For example, since this congregation values gender inclusivity, Jason will alter the text of some hymns to avoid patriarchy or exclusion, hoping to instill inclusivity in their language both within and outside of the worship context. According to Jason, "Music just has a way of speaking to people that words alone do not." The congregation finds it important as a conduit for worship and vehicle for outreach to the community. He proudly noted that some members began attending the church just to be in the choir.

We asked Jason which other worship practices he thought formed the congregation in social, or even political, ways. He responded by citing the passing of the peace, a war memorial that began during a Pentecost service, and the weekly sermon.

The church initiated the passing of the peace in 1986 in the midst of the HIV/AIDS crisis. First & Franklin had been the first church in the area willing to partner with a local HIV clinic in early 1980s. "The congregation opened the doors," one member recalled, "and said, 'Come, you are welcome.'"[17] This type of outreach to those neglected by most churches became a staple practice at First & Franklin, and the passing of the peace became a way to make this inclusive hospitality a regular and tangible part of the church's worship. "We pass the peace in this church because Pastor Harry Hoefelder said in 1986, 'We are not going to be afraid to touch our neighbors,'" one member told us.[18] There was still fear of the disease spreading through touch in the late '80s, so HIV-positive people essentially became "untouchables." Extending the passing of the peace to everyone who came through the doors gave the "least of these" in the eyes of the world "at least once a week where they knew somebody was going to give them a hug," Alison said. One member we spoke with recalled that "you would have people just come and sit in the back of the church and cry for an hour because they couldn't believe they found a church that would include them."[19] This practice became engrained within the church's identity. "This place is an open door and that is what Jesus taught," another added. "All other limits and expectations are man-made. They are not what Christ said."[20]

Then a few years ago, during a Pentecost service that coincided with Memorial Day weekend, Alison decided it was time for the church to become more outspoken about the wars in Iraq and Afghanistan. Before the service, as people came into the sanctuary, Alison handed each person a list of twenty identified war dead, from both sides of the conflicts. During the service, she had them read their lists simultaneously—an unintelligible yet powerful symphony of names. Several church members and leaders described this as "sounding like Pentecost." Committee chair Jim Schroll explained to us, "you couldn't understand what everyone was saying, but you knew what was going on." Alison concluded the reading with a prayer both for US soldiers and for Iraqi and Afghani civilians. At the end of the service, she led the congregation in tying ribbons to the fence along the outside sanctuary wall. This same public memorial that we saw as we first approached the church contains three rows of ribbons: gold ribbons representing each American life lost and other colors representing civilian deaths. In this way, the memorial serves as a reminder both of fallen soldiers and of the destruction of war, a way to include those in the congregation on all sides of the issue. "Many people saw this clearly as an antiwar statement," Alison explained. "But we never made an actual statement because others saw it as a way of honoring the war dead. If we had tried to make a statement, we would have gotten pushback." Every month the congregation reads off the names of those killed and identified in US conflicts overseas, and prays for an end to all war and violence.

Finally, Jason mentioned Alison's sermons as one of the most socially formative acts of the church. Alison conceives of the sermon as a way to connect the actions of the church back to Scripture, and give some spiritual depth to the social work of the church. She insists that Scripture plays an important formative role in the congregation, though we rarely heard specific references besides general allusions to Jesus loving and accepting everyone. Still, Alison's sermons do seem to inspire a greater awareness for social justice and Christ's call to care for others. Alison mostly avoids addressing political issues in the sermon, Jason noted, though these issues are often discussed on the committee level and sometimes in the "Minute for Missions" part of the service. Occasionally Alison has addressed marriage equality in a sermon, but that rarely happens—and did not during our visit the Sunday before the referendum. "The message that comes from the pulpit is constantly, 'What can we do to help the community?'" said Bill Bridges, who joined the church because of its emphasis on "deed over word." "Alison often quotes Jesus saying, 'As you have done for the least of these [you have done for me].'"

Empty Words or Empty Action

One of the driving convictions of our project is that a politics shaped by the kingdom insists that worship and mission are inseparable; that they enrich, authenticate, and shape each other.[21] Liturgy—by which we simply mean the way a community worships—calls us to praise and confession and edifies us through the proclamation of the word. But it also prepares a congregation for missions work; it inspires us to action, to not only listen to the word but to be "doers of the word" (Jas 1:22–25).[22] The weekly worship service moves beyond words, though still dependent on the word, to form its participants into certain habits. In worshiping, we affirm our allegiance to Christ, and then respond as citizens of the kingdom of God by joining God's mission in the world. In this way, worship practices take on political significance.

At First & Franklin, leaders hope that worship shapes the values of the congregation through repeated actions of sharing peace with one another, recalling the destruction of violence through reading the names of those killed on all sides of the conflicts, and reminding the community of its commitment to serve others. They hope these practices inspire the congregation to take action—to be a church of social activism.[23]

For example, through the passing of the peace, First & Franklin reclaims the significance of physical touch in the life of the church. Churches often focus exclusively on care for souls or intellects, but often fail to recognize the role of the physical body in the social body of Christ.[24] Greeting one another with a word of peace and a touch tangibly reinforces the theological truth that bodies matter—even bodies broken by communicable disease. It affirms that our bodies, together, make up the body of Christ, and witnesses to the promise of our bodily resurrection (1 Cor 12:12–14; 1 Thess 4:16; 1 Cor 15:35–55). This practice expresses Christians' hope that bodily healing will come with the kingdom of God on earth, and witnesses to the embodied reconciliation that is possible with one another right now—that we are physical gifts to one another. It has the potential to reclaim those ostracized at the margins of society as integral parts of the body of Christ. Alison hopes that it forms church members into the type of people who break down the walls of social stigma in all dimensions of life, even outside the walls of the church.

These worship practices can be deeply politically formative for the congregation, generating a new political imagination. They can move a congregation beyond thinking in terms of merely voting or lobbying to the deeply political action of breaking down the categories of friend and enemy through physical touch. Friend and foe are mingled together in worship and share space along the same pew. The untouchables are embraced and blessed with the words of Christ's peace. These are ways the church can reach beyond its borders and witness to an identity distinct from the constructed identities and barriers of the world—clean and unclean, neighbor and enemy. They are deeply political moves that can shape a community and redirect its focus from itself to the injustices of the world—not with the usual set of partisan answers, but with the love and peace of Christ that breaks down the walls that divide us.

However, despite the potential of these practices one church leader worries that First & Franklin becomes involved in important social actions for their own sake and not because this mission is grounded in a love for Christ. He worries that the church focuses on social issues at the expense of worshiping God, rather than as the overflow of its worship.

While the practices examined above have the potential to link worship and missions, spiritual formation and social transformation into a unified political vision, this leader identifies a concern we share: that despite some leaders' intentions, little spiritual formation may actually occur. There seems to be a break between the way the ministry staff talks about these practices and the way the congregation does. The congregation does not seem to always ground them in Scripture, or as a response to what Christ has done for the world. They are performed for legitimate social reasons of compassion, but not explicitly from a deep devotion and ultimate allegiance to Christ.

This leads us to worry that in a church so socially active, it may become easy for social mission to become untethered from the worshiping life of the church, detached from a commitment to Scripture and spiritual growth. In other words, such attention to social missions seems to come at the expense of the significance of spiritual formation and evangelism in the community.

The language of this congregation—focusing on "deeds over words"—began to concern us, because like faith and works, word and deed should be inseparable parts of the Christian life (Eph 2:8–10; Jas 2:17–18, 22). As the Israelite prophet warned, God despises empty words—worship without action (Amos 5:21–24). And as the early church believed, worship is itself a type of "training" in how to live a Christian life in public.[25] Worship inspires mission, we must remember—but this is only half the equation. Worship is also the way we regularly remind ourselves that we are Christians.[26] In it we affirm our identity as the people of God and faith in Christ as Savior and Lord of all areas of our life—social and personal. If these parts become separated, then the ministries of the church become like those of any social agency, and that impacts the way that those ministries are conducted. They are detached from any greater purpose or story about God's desire to redeem the world to God's self, and the work of transformation that entails, and become *empty action*.[27]

As we finished our conversation with Jason over lunch, he told us that as music minister, he envisions his primary task as linking worship and mission so that they become inseparable in the eyes of the congregation. Understanding that music and worship can be socially formative, Jason attempts to shape worship to both inspire people to action and to draw them into communion with God. "I think by leaving Christ at the center of worship, that in and of itself is empowering the congregation to go forth and shaping the way they think." Worship is not just about us and what we do, he said, and this is often the temptation for socially active churches like this one. "Worship at its most basic is people giving praise to God," he explained. "It is the one time of the week that we come together as a body—which itself is very powerful—and it's about that corporate body responding to God. To keep the attention focused on God and not ourselves."

WHAT'S AT STAKE IN THE ELECTION?

The Sunday before election day we joined Alison and a few congregants for a "What's At Stake in the Election?" meeting. When we walked into the church building we were greeted by two older women. Alison had conducted a union ceremony for this couple at First & Franklin, and they told us that this election was especially important to them since they may finally have their marriage recognized by state law.[28] They offered us coffee and donuts (immediately winning Sam over), and asked us how we came to work on this project together. Sam offered some sly comment about me being "so much older" than he is and I bantered back, but things got awkward when we realized that they thought we were a couple as well! I didn't really have the heart to correct them, but I later told Sam that it must have been his skinny jeans and gelled hair that gave them that impression. He said it was my earring.

Having made the conversation sufficiently awkward, we decided to join the others in the parlor for the meeting. The room was elegantly but simply decorated, and had the smell of my grandmother's living room. We took our seats on folding chairs next to two young women, both around our age (there is no such thing as "our" age, Sam still wants you to know), by far the youngest people we had met at this church. The group of about ten, mostly elderly church members, was pensively examining a set of small booklets. One woman handed us a copy of the League of Women Voters' 2012 Voter Guide, and Alison opened the meeting by inviting us to look through the pamphlet and discuss the eight referendum questions on the ballot.

Sam and I were prepared for a new experience—we had never discussed an upcoming election in our home churches. There was a greater sense of electoral concern here than most churches would admit to. The risk of veering into partisanship, or worse, political bickering and division, were enough to keep most churches out of the election discussion. In any case, a "What's At Stake in the Election?" meeting could turn out to be a complete disaster, and we wanted to be there to witness it!

Given the clearly Democratic bent of the church, we wondered how overtly partisan the discussion would become, and how Alison would navigate her roles as both pastor and political informer. As I sat waiting for the meeting to begin, dropping white powder from my donut all over my pants, I tried to shake a growing discomfort. This just seemed too partisan for my

Anabaptist sensibilities. I worried that we might have entered an hour-long Democratic rally.[29]

The discussion began with Alison moving systematically down the list of eight referendum questions on the ballot, outlining the pros and cons of each. She kept the conversation away from discussion of particular candidates, even the presidential candidates. ("Is this because there is no doubt how everyone in the room is voting?" I wondered). The conversation centered on three questions in particular: an immigration reform bill, the marriage rights bill, and gambling. Alison asked someone to read the two opposing positions on each issue printed in the voting guide—several read the more conservative positions with a hint of sarcasm—and asked for responses to these opinions. She explained "what was at stake" with a light hand, drawing out thoughts from the participants, but rarely offering any of her own. The group quickly came to consensus on most of the issues. Some even felt comfortable enough to make a few jokes about the Dream Act and marriage equality votes, indicating that they knew they all stood on the same side.

Alison framed the immigration reform bill in terms of "forgiveness," and another invoked the Greatest Commandments, love God and love your neighbor (Matt 22:37–40)—the only times we recall anyone appealing to Scripture or theology during the meeting. Most of the conversation remained on the practical and political levels. Besides these two comments, you would not have known that we were holding this meeting in a church, and we wondered what role Christian faith would play in the way these members voted.

The meeting closed with few fireworks and no pep rallying. Alison seemed determined to tread lightly on territory where few churches dared tread at all, though the apparent widespread consensus among the church members made this easier. But the fact that a church would hold such a meeting speaks to its political self-understanding. For First & Franklin, voting is an activity important enough for a church discussion, and members understand discussing, advocating, and voting on legislation as a significant part of their Christian life.

Church Politics

We sat down for Sunday brunch at a cramped inner city café with Alison and Pam White, a lay church leader and district judge. Pam and Alison were old high school friends. Having drifted away from the church years ago, Pam walked into First & Franklin one Sunday and was shocked to find Alison in the pulpit. Alison, a quiet but passionate woman, looked and spoke like a college professor, offering her words both freely and carefully with a simple smile. She has been at First & Franklin for more than twelve years, and her husband pastors a church near Annapolis.

The crisp early summer air swept in from the open doors, wafting the smell of pancakes and French toast our way. We jumped right into asking about the church's work on behalf of the upcoming marriage equality referendum, and Alison began by revealing that she had recently appeared in a television ad for the marriage equality campaign.

I did a double take. The notion of a pastor appearing in an election ad shocked me, even at a church so passionate about the issue and so involved in electoral politics. Alison explained this rather nonchalantly, adding that the church marches in the annual gay pride parade in Baltimore and coordinates letter-writing campaigns in support of gay rights legislation. The previous year she had spoken before the Maryland General Assembly in support of marriage equality. It wasn't the first pastoral involvement in electoral politics we had seen; we knew that Rick Warren hosted a Civil Forum and Ebenezer Baptist registered voters after worship services. Still, speaking in front of the state legislature and appearing in campaign ads was the most direct political action we had witnessed yet.[30]

First & Franklin's advocacy does not stop with the senior pastor. As state leaders were considering whether to put the marriage issue to ballot, the church asked Pam to write an amicus brief on behalf of the congregation. The church also released several public statements in support of marriage equality, hung a rainbow banner from their steeple, and now campaigned wholeheartedly for it as the election date drew near. The Sunday before election day we noticed a whiteboard stationed by the sanctuary doorway with the words "I will vote for marriage equality because . . ." written across the top, with markers below for attenders to write down their reasons.

Other members talked about this issue in terms of denominational politics. This was not only a state electoral issue, but an important church issue as well. First & Franklin had been on the cutting edge of the "More Light" movement, a group of Presbyterian churches that welcome and affirm gay members into church leadership. Alison had performed wedding ceremonies for gay couples in the church for several years, conducted in the District of Columbia until the state referendum passed. "I can justify that with the Presbyterian *Book of Order*," she told us. "They deserve that treatment just as much as anyone else in my congregation." This made Alison a bit of a denominational rebel. At the time, the PCUSA did not allow its clergy to perform same-sex weddings, though in 2014 it began permitting them in states in which they were legalized.

"Why has this become such an important issue for this church?" Sam asked, finished with his brunch and now consuming the leftover portions of mine. Alison replied, "I see Jesus all the time reaching out to those who are the outcasts. And I'm thinking, who are those people in our time?" Alison believes the group most often pushed to the margins and ostracized by the church today is the gay community. "And I'm still waiting for someone to show me where Jesus said anything against homosexuality," she added. "I just don't see it."

"Do you worry that these activities blur the lines of separation between church and state?" I asked as we finished the meal. "That's a major tenet of Presbyterianism, isn't it?"

"The separation of church and state has always been a foundational principle of this church," Pam answered. Her legal sensibilities clearly informed her lay work in the church, and her perspective on the church's role in politics. She spoke with the confident tone of a judge, holding court over our small café table as she delivered a history of the congregation. The first pastor, Patrick Allison, was a friend of George Washington and an active proponent of separation of church and state—a controversial stance in his time, since Maryland originally recognized the Church of England as the official state church. Patrick Allison's efforts to have establishment (the recognition of a state church) abolished in the Constitution helped shape the congregation and its perspective on politics. Too often, Pam told us, Christian leaders violate this principle, venturing too far into political matters. She cited the local Catholic bishop's condemnation of the Catholic governor for state-supported abortions as a recent example. (Though just how practically different this is from a pastor appealing to the state legislature to pass gay marriage laws, we are not sure!)

And while we expected the district judge to draw a thick line between church and state, we found that many church members seemed to do the same. "I'm certainly not an advocate of politics in church," church member Bill Bridges told us. He thinks if churches become too involved in political activities, they should lose their tax-exempt status—though he thinks First & Franklin navigates this well. "The church is not there to say vote for this person or that one, or any party. But the church *is* pushing an agenda—not just any agenda, but one that is helping people and [is consistent with] the teachings of the Bible, of course." He told us that when the church sees injustice in the world, it should talk about it and take action. But he frames this as social rather than political action. When we asked him why activities like writing letters to congress are not political, he said the point is simply to do what is good for people.

Worship minister Jason confirmed that most church members prefer to talk about their activities as social rather than political; they too are wary of the stigma of being labeled a political church. First & Franklin joins many other churches in avoiding the language of politics. But this congregation is especially interesting in that they (with the exception of Alison) avoid identifying explicitly electoral activities as political.[31]

Semantics aside, First & Franklin is perhaps more politically involved than any other church we visited. Petitioning Congress to vote for marriage equality legislation, holding political fundraisers,[32] writing amicus briefs, and affirming their pastor's appearance in a television ad are paradigmatic examples of the church engaging in electoral politics. The Peace Committee of the church identifies public advocacy as one of its primary tasks.[33] The group asks the church to take official stands on certain issues, brings in speakers, writes letters to legislators, and organizes marches in D. C.

A few members we spoke with affirm the idea of the church influencing public policy. Jeff Watson told us that he did not think the church is or should be opposed to public policy advocacy, and another member suggested that this is in fact the church's "primary vehicle for social justice" (though still hesitating to call this "political"). Jim Schroll explained that the church simply sees a social justice issue and decides to become involved, to try and help people who need it. The initiatives they engage in to help others may "become viewed as political, but the emphasis behind doing them is what the church feels is right and just."

As Pam concluded her explanation of church and state, I gave Sam a curious look and took a long sip of coffee. I was confused by Pam's strong insistence on the church's commitment to separating church and state when it seemed the church engaged in numerous venues of state politics. So I turned the question to Alison. "How do activities like petitioning Congress and making public statements on political issues not cross this line of separation?"

"I don't tell them they have to do it," she quipped, smiling at us. But out of everyone we spoke with, she was the most willing to describe these practices as political. "I don't have a problem doing that," she told us, leaning back in her chair confidently. "Jesus was fairly political."

The church's other primary mission effort is the Patrick Allison House, which ministers to the large homeless population living outside the trendy cafes and urban apartments of First & Franklin's neighborhood. During the mid-80s, around the same time the church began reaching out to people with HIV/AIDS, they felt compelled to begin a ministry to local homeless residents. They started by serving a free breakfast every Sunday before the church service. "But soon we discovered we were feeding the same people year after year," explained one member. "We needed a new model." After discovering that many of their homeless guests were former inmates with no jobs and nowhere to go, the soup kitchen evolved into a transition house, which helps recently released male inmates struggling with substance abuse get jobs and become productive members of society. The church later added a mentoring and education program, also housed on the church property, which now boasts a 95 percent rate of reintegration into society.[34] Alison explained that there is no state support for released inmates in Baltimore, so many end up right back in prison. This ministry addresses a community need unmet by the government, she explained.

Many members told us that they were initially drawn to First & Franklin because of its reputation for social action—because it was willing to take stands on behalf of what the congregation believes in. Bill Bridges, a lay member active in the church's missions, told us that after feeling disillusioned with church for a while this congregation drew him and his wife back. He admits that he still struggles with all the "religious material," but maintains that he and his wife are "deeds over words people," and have been able to find a home here.

Two Levels of Politics

Although it does not involve advocating policy reform, the church's work through the Patrick Allison house is politically significant. When the church discovered that no government programs existed to help the ex-inmates in their neighborhood, it decided to create one itself. In this way the church acted as its own political body, one with a divine mandate to care for those most neglected by society. It organized itself, partnered with others dedicated to a common cause, and reached out beyond its walls to meet needs in the shadows left by government welfare programs.

The church's work in the area of gay rights provides an interesting case for how a church can operate on multiple registers of politics, even regarding the same issue. With its public advocacy leading up to the election and its project of welcoming homosexual people into its community, the church operates on multiple levels of politics simultaneously.

The practices of public advocacy—speaking to the state legislature, campaigning in television ads, and offering public statements in support of the referendum—are an expression of a church entering into electoral politics. They utilize the resources of state politics to try to change a law that they believe is unjust. They use electoral tools to achieve these political ends just like advocacy or lobby groups. And while we worry that political practices directed solely at electoral ends risk leaving spiritual motivations behind and restricting deeper theological reflection on their motivation and mission, some leaders at First & Franklin recognize that the church enters into this type of politics with a distinctly Christian motivation and vision. (We hope this distinctive vision animates the rest of the congregation, but we cannot be sure.)

First & Franklin's "More Light" stance, on the other hand, is an expression of the church as its own political body. By reaching out to the gay population, welcoming everyone with a hug and the peace of Christ, and engaging those affected by a disease that at the time it primarily plagued the gay population, the church offers a different vision of politics. This type of politics is not confined by partisan division or electoral success, but crosses social barriers to offer a vision of community unencumbered by fears and prejudices of this world. By challenging the denominational policies of the Presbyterian Church and opening up leadership and ministry positions to a group of people whom many churches consider unfit for Christian leadership, First & Franklin embodies an alternative type of political community. This is a structural alternative to state and national politics, ordered around a different set of convictions, a different set of political practices, and ultimately, a different allegiance.

The church engages both dimensions of politics in the "What's at Stake in the Election?" meeting. It seeks to shape the political identities of the congregation through open dialogue and discussion—making brief appeals to Scripture and the Christian life—in a way that sees the church as a distinct political body. But it also aims toward an electoral end, and therefore understands the church as a group that enters into state politics to effect systemic policy change, albeit with a particular vocation and vision for justice.

In the end, both types of political engagement witness to the wider world of a political community that is open and inclusive, as well as engaged and active in its mission and politics. The church participates in the "ministry of reconciliation" to the outcast and oppressed that God instituted it to be (2 Cor 5:18–21). It first enacts this reconciliation within itself, and then spreads it out into the world. While the Christian nature of their activism may not always be at the forefront, most of the church leaders do operate with an underlying sense of the spiritual and even liturgical purpose of their mission. In this way, they offer a model of how churches can operate simultaneously on electoral and deeper political levels, and thus a deeper political imagination than one that jumps directly into policy initiatives. When this model functions at its best, the deep political identity of the church and its allegiance to Christ animates its electoral political efforts. These political actions then become faithful ways of transforming the world in light of the church's commitment to a Savior who wants to redeem the whole world.

EMBRACING PUBLIC ACTIVISM

That night, as we wandered around the Inner Harbor, past the aquarium and old warship and amidst a circus of street performers—sword jugglers, magicians, break-dancing groups—we attempted to reflect on our conversations. I tried to keep Kris focused ("Seriously, Sam, how does that man balance on a skateboard on a bowling ball, juggle three knives, and do the Macarena all at the same time?") as we talked about the way First & Franklin understands its mission, and the political dimensions of this mission. We worry that a community so overtly involved in partisan battles over social issues may turn into just another social agency. What difference does it make that a church is engaging in these practices rather than a social agency? And why do they think it is important for churches to be involved in this type of work?

A Balancing Act

Several answers emerged from our conversations. Churches distinguish themselves by engaging in needs that other organizations, including the government, are not meeting, Jeff Watson told us. First & Franklin does this, especially, with its work at the Patrick Allison House. These notions of the church's mission, understood as a call to engage in work left undone by other groups, reminded us of similar statements we heard at Saddleback. Saddleback talks of "reclaiming" the social mission that originally belonged to the church, work it abdicated to the government (and work the government is not doing as effectively as the church, they add). While First & Franklin did not put this in terms of "reclaiming what is properly our job, and not yours," this juxtaposing of church work and state work marks a thread of continuity in the way these two vastly different churches understand their mission—and politics: the church meets needs that others are not meeting, or are not meeting well. It corrects for faults it sees in the government, and cares for those most neglected by other institutions.

Another lay leader framed the church's work within a biblical mandate to care for others. "We have a command from God to feed the hungry, alleviate those needs, and bring justice," Dorothy Jantzen, chair of the Peace Committee, told us, adding, "This is the church's reason for being. This is what separates us from secular groups." For Dorothy, this biblical motivation trumps others. "When you are working for a cause, whether it is successful or not, if it is one that comes out of Christian teachings, you do it just because it is the right thing to do," she told us. "You have to stand for core principles whether they are winning or not." Unlike Saddleback, Dorothy did not understand First & Franklin's mission to be based in its ability to do the work more effectively than anyone else (i.e., the state or federal government). Effectiveness is not the most important criterion for Christians, but remaining faithful to your principles, she said. "When you stand for peace on a corner, maybe they will laugh at you or maybe they will honk a horn in accord. But what they do doesn't matter, just that you are trying to give a witness for peace."

When we asked Alison these questions, she also cited a biblical foundation, quickly responding that many of these missions efforts actually emerged from the weekly Bible study group. "We ask, 'How can we be the face of Christ in the neighborhood?'" This is the way that they read the Bible, she told us: with a social perspective in mind. "Our specific actions may emulate a YMCA or food shelter program," she admitted, but the motivation is different. "Jesus is still behind this, and I want people to know [that]."

We noted that this was the most scripturally and theologically centered language we had heard at the church. Alison seemed intent on stressing the spiritual underpinnings of the church's mission. Writing letters to congresspersons, marching in the gay pride parade, and mentoring former inmates are not exclusively church activities. Anyone can do them. But the church does them for a different reason, she said. The church has been called to do this work by a different authority. It does them because of Christ.

One church leader offered a different perspective, however. He explained that he was concerned that the church can fall into political activism for its own sake. He believes people come to First & Franklin because it is compatible with their pre-formed political opinions, and was not sure how much new political formation is happening in the congregation. While he was happy about the church's progressive social ministry, he told us: "One danger is that church can become more about social issues than about modeling the love of Christ and worshiping God." For example, he didn't think it was good to be known as "the gay church in Baltimore." This type of identification takes the focus away from God. He worried about this overly social focus, what he called "in-your-face activism," especially during his first few years at the church. "Frequently it felt like we were at a political rally." However, he quickly admitted that at the time, as one of the only "welcoming and affirming" congregations in the area, the church needed to be that way in order to be a sanctuary for the hurting and outcast. But he believes the church has achieved a better balance by connecting the political dimensions of the church's missions to its faith in God through worship. "I think by leaving Christ at the center of worship, that in and of itself, is empowering the congregation to go forth and shaping the way they think."

But with the exception of Dorothy and a few others, these connections of theology and social justice, or faith and activism, remained mostly in the visions of the church leaders. Our conversations with church members revealed that most did not connect the church's social work to specific spiritual or theological underpinnings.[35] Many members seemed reluctant to attribute the church's social activities to anything spiritual—they indeed seemed to be "deed over word people."

Social over Spiritual

Along with this weight given to being a church of "deeds," congregation members often boasted that this is a place of "no judgment." And we both believe this certainly and necessarily corrects for a long history of the church as accuser, judge, and executioner. At a time when polls show that the church is most known for being antigay and judgmental, a church that becomes known as a safe place for the marginalized is a great political witness to the hospitality of the kingdom of God.[36]

But Paul also makes clear to the Corinthians that while it is not their role to judge those outside the church, he considered it a Christian duty to hold accountable those inside (1 Cor 5:12). Checking judgmentalism is a healthy and necessary practice, but when it becomes a church's highest value, the church risks abdicating its authority to call its members to radical obedience. Acceptance and accountability are two sides of the same coin: it is true compassion that calls a fellow Christian back from sin, Dietrich Bonhoeffer once told his seminarians, but the worst cruelty is to abandon him to his sin.[37]

In the end, these two emphases on not judging and on "deeds over words" led to our primary concern. We worry that the political mission of a congregation so active in controversial and partisan issues risks becoming severed from its identity as a worshiping community that offers a witness of Christ to the world. Progressive politics can overdetermine its identity, message, and action, limiting the activities it is willing to engage in and inhibiting it from cultivating a wider vision of its purpose in the world. When spiritual formation takes a back seat to public activism, it often gets lost in the fray.

But a church is called first to be a community of allegiance to and worship of Christ. A church must act publicly and socially out of its faith in Christ and calling from Christ to change the world. If it does not arise out of its worship and devotion to Christ, a church's mission becomes mere ritual.[38]

In short, our worry is that this model of Christian engagement with practical social and political issues may bypass the rich resources of theological thinking, flattening Christian faith into mere activism. A church is meant to be more than simply another social organization reflecting the wider culture's values. When a church risks reducing faith to activism, it is often based on shallow readings of Scripture or deficient understandings of worship that only reinforce political opinions we already have. This leaves the church with little formative and transformative power for its members or for all of society. True social transformation cannot take place if it is not based in a commitment to spiritual formation.

Faithful Politics

Ultimately, our conversations led us to an ambivalence about the political activity at First & Franklin. From our perspective, this congregation is one of the most politically active of the congregations we visited, despite its reticence to use the term. Some seem to avoid it for legal and historical reasons such as the commitment to separation of church and state, and others for reasons of public witness—they do not want their identity to be defined by being the "lefty political church." Others worry that such an extreme focus on politics distracts from other aspects of what it means to be church and restricts the spiritual formation of its congregants.

Fortunately, both Jason and Alison are committed to grounding their mission and political work in their faith. "People tend to come to this church for social action and justice," Alison said, "and part of my job is to reconnect them to a sense of spirituality and the Bible. That is why we do it. Sometimes I worry we just play church. What are we doing to show that we are different, that we are that Acts church, the body of Christ?"

On the other hand, we do believe First & Franklin exemplifies a combination of political practices—both the narrow, electoral kind and the deeper practices of the church as a political body. Their commitment to gay rights and inclusion of homosexuals in the life of the community illustrates how a church can advocate public policy reform while also re-forming the political structures of its own community. Many churches will not ultimately agree with First & Franklin's stance on homosexuality, but the model can apply to other issues as well: for example, advocating for government-regulated healthcare while opening a free clinic, advocating for immigration reform while providing employment and housing for families of undocumented residents, or lobbying for stricter abortion laws while starting a ministry that cares for single teen mothers and their babies. In each of these cases, a church's attempts to change public policy arise out of a deep political conviction in the church as its own locus of politics.

Our visits and conversations with leaders at First & Franklin challenged us on theological and personal levels. I (Sam) knew before we began our visit that First & Franklin would be the furthest theological stretch from the type of church I was used to. Not all my concerns were alleviated—I appreciated the church's emphasis on outreach, but wished their ministries to the poor and unemployed, and their ministry to the LGBT community in their neighborhood, were explained in more explicitly scriptural terms. Church members' work in these areas is clearly motivated (at least in part) by theological convictions, but most expressed these convictions only in broad allusions to Jesus' love—and this is part of the reason why the more conservative half of their denomination finds it difficult to jump on board with their mission. Still, I grew to appreciate First & Franklin's commitment to welcoming groups of people that have so often been ostracized by my evangelical community, particularly the LGBT community. Churches will increasingly be forced to deal with this issue on personal levels—it is not an issue that can be avoided or easily discounted. Other churches can learn from First & Franklin's example of hospitality and care for the marginalized and outcast.

We began this project giving priority to the deeper political practices of church. Kris especially believed that a church that witnessed to an alternative form of politics in its way of life together was sufficiently and faithfully engaged in the affairs of the world. Becoming involved in electoral activities, he repeatedly told me, always risked damaging the church's distinctive witness by intermingling its allegiance to God with allegiance to the state. But these churches, First & Franklin included, began to demonstrate to both of us rich and nuanced ways that churches can engage in efforts to change public policy while still remaining faithful to their God-given mission and distinctive witness.

We don't believe churches should allow electoral or partisan politics to overdetermine their identity, but these congregations were beginning to teach us that there are times when churches need to stand up and declare that a law needs to change or the state needs to better care for its people. First & Franklin believes that in light of urgent needs, the church cannot help but try to influence public policy. It could not remain faithful to its calling, as Martin Luther King wrote, if it continued to "remain silent behind the anesthetizing security of the stained-glass windows."[39] Laws may not bring in the kingdom of God in its full glory, but in the time between the times, they can at least alleviate some earthly suffering and bring comfort to the afflicted—and isn't this part of the church's mission?[40] In the same way that faithful social transformation requires a church first committed to spiritual transformation, faithful political advocacy must be rooted in the church's political allegiance to Christ as King in order to avoid becoming mere partisan activism.

The practices we have highlighted in this chapter frame First & Franklin's model of political engagement—*cultivating public activism*. This congregation believes a church should make a public difference, whether by adding political banners to the sanctuary, embracing a liturgical practice that welcomes the outcast, starting a transition house for former inmates, restructuring its leadership to animate the congregation's passions, or petitioning the state legislature to legalize gay marriage. The church responds to God's call to care for those in need, and it uses whatever means it can to fulfill that mission—even electoral means.

This church helps its members turn their social convictions into actions through both public policy advocacy and local outreach. At the same time, it adapts its inner structures to better facilitate hospitality and participation. Sometimes this happens at the expense of an emphasis on devotional life and spiritual formation. Ultimately, the goal is to weave both together in a healthy balance, so that they mutually influence one another, making worship and mission seamless dimensions of a commitment to a Lord that is, as Alison reminded us, "fairly political."

First & Franklin's political practices can serve as models for other churches.

First, the Sankofa process offers an example for other mainline churches experiencing membership, ministry, and financial struggles. While the verdict is still out on how effective the change will be, efforts to decrease bureaucracy, flatten hierarchy, involve more of the congregation in decision-making, and cultivate a stronger ethos of ministry and activism are welcome changes in churches struggling to "find their place." Dramatic restructuring may be required to reach the world while remaining faithful to the theological roots of mainline tradition.

Second, the church incorporates formative political practices into worship. The "pentecostal" act of reading the names of those who have lost their lives in war and interceding for them in corporate prayer, as well as instituting the passing of the peace to physically welcome a group stigmatized by society, are both examples of the way that worship can form a community to witnesses to another kingdom. While these specific practices may not be appropriate in every congregation, churches should consider how their own worship practices form their community and how these practices can intentionally cultivate its identity as an alternative political body and advance its mission in the world.

Third, the church addresses the underlying structural causes of injustice, rather than seeking Band-Aid, surface solutions. Through its part in founding and partnering with the Patrick Allison House, it moves beyond surface solutions to develop sustainable ministries that offer more permanent benefits to those in need.

Finally, the "What's at Stake in the Election?" meeting shows how churches can form their members to be both better citizens of heaven and, unavoidably, better citizens of earthly communities. Some churches view voting as an important duty and others do not, but regardless, it is important for Christians to be aware of what's going on in the world around them so that they can better meet the needs that exist right outside their doors. Gatherings like this cultivate public awareness and remind us that churches are inherently political bodies that provide a foretaste of the reign of God, whether or not they choose to enter into the world of electoral politics.

* * *

One of our first conversations at First & Franklin was with Phil Adams. A towering figure dressed in a pink and blue flowery shirt, he walked into a small room in the Backus House bursting with energy. Phil had been attending the church for a few years, and now led the worship team and sang in the choir. We began by asking how worship might influence people's social and political behaviors, a topic that we had found important in every congregation we had visited. Since he was team leader for worship, we thought he might give us a helpful outline of the church's thoughts on this. But Phil seemed to be caught off guard by our question. He was not expecting to talk about worship, he said. He seemed surprised that we would connect worship and politics in this way. He told us that he expected us to ask mostly about LGBT issues at the church. Isn't this the type of politics we were interested in?

Phil came from a conservative church background. When he came to terms with his sexuality in his late teens, he became disillusioned with the church, despite his persistent feeling that he still needed it. He attended a gay-friendly congregation in Baltimore but felt like "It wasn't church. It was just gay social hour." When some other area ministers pointed him to First & Franklin, he decided to give church one more try. He was overwhelmed by the welcome he received. "I had arms around my shoulders the first Sunday." He began attending in August and by October was ordained a deacon. He had found a church that embodied both an acceptance of his sexual orientation and the focus on mission that had been missing from other congregations.

"We are all children of God, wondrously made, and loved by God," he said. "Too many people spend too much time looking at the behaviors of other people rather than lifting others up. If all that energy was directed at taking care of one another, we would be much better off." And in many ways, this is the message and mission and politics of First & Franklin. Action and acceptance above all else—and maybe at the expense of all else—define the church's political identity. We remembered how one member summarized the church's witness: "Everyone is welcome. There are no limits, no judgments."

After the interview we wandered back into the cavernous and empty sanctuary. Alison came to see us off. As we thanked her for her time and hospitality, we passed under the massive pipe organ and by the whiteboard in the narthex, now full of reasons church members would be voting for marriage equality that Tuesday. We walked past the towering cathedral back toward our car, and as she locked up the church for the evening, Alison called out to us, "You are welcome anytime."

Chapter 5

Committing to Community
Prairie Street Mennonite Church

WE SAT IN SILENCE as we sped down I-90 toward O'Hare airport, as if on autopilot. My (Kris's) stomach was churning. All we could do now was make it back to Virginia with what little we had left and figure out where to go from there.

The men who broke into our car that morning had taken everything—phones, computers, clothes, IDs, wallets. We had just finished our final interview at Prairie Street Mennonite Church in Elkhart, Indiana. With several hours to kill before our flight from Chicago, we decided to kayak down the Chicago River beneath the skyscrapers and gothic bridges. While we huddled in the kayak shop to escape a brief rainstorm, two men broke into our car and stole, along with everything else, all of our research from Prairie Street—hours of interviews and handwritten notes.

I stepped outside just in time to see them speeding away. There might have been a brief moment in which I could have called for help, tried to stop them, or at least chased after them, but I froze. The police said there was nothing they could do—most stolen property quickly disappears into a network of black markets and dirty pawn transactions. We left messages on our phones promising the thieves that we would not press charges—we just wanted our stuff, and especially our research, back. For me, the worst part was the stinging feeling that this was my fault. I had left the car keys in my pants pocket on the front seat of the car, and the car unlocked.

We approached the airport in silence. Sam often jokes about how difficult it is to get me to shut up—but on this ride, I had nothing to say. We moved like zombies through the airport. In addition to all of our work at the church, Sam had lost several very personal items, like a childhood Bible. I just hoped he didn't hate me.

At the time we thought we had lost the story of this congregation, one that offered a unique approach to politics, identity, and mission. I first encountered Anabaptist theology and ethics during seminary and resonated with much in the Mennonite church. Anabaptism, which traces back to the Radical Reformation, includes groups like Mennonites and Amish. It emphasizes a strict biblicism, communitarian decision-making and scriptural interpretation, a general skepticism of secular politics, and a commitment to nonviolence. Sam had only recently been introduced to Anabaptism, mostly through my persistent attempts to convert him to Christian pacifism. While he agreed with much of Anabaptist theology, he worried that it focused too much on ethics at the expense of worship. He also thought their strong skepticism of state politics may limit the Anabaptists' effectiveness in advocating for social justice. However, we both suspected that this church might offer a model of social engagement that transcended the social and political withdrawal Anabaptist congregations are often charged of.[1]

WE HEART ELKHART

Prairie Street sits in the middle of Indiana Mennonite country—meaning, it's kind of in the middle of nowhere. The land is monotonously flat, covered by cornfields, and cut across by wide roads bearing the cracks of many icy winters. Nearby sits one of only three denominational seminaries in the US, an office of the Mennonite Mission Network, and the Anabaptist-founded Goshen College. Prairie Street has been a leader in denominational politics and missions, instrumental in establishing the Missions Network and the Mennonite Central Committee (the public policy arm of the denomination), and in sending out the first international Mennonite missionaries in the 1890s.[2] Over the years the congregation has also planted a number of churches in the Elkhart area, several that outgrew this one—whose membership, like so many other US churches, is simultaneously aging and shrinking.

Even more "exciting" (at least for one of us), Prairie Street was the home church of America's most famous Anabaptist theologian, John Howard Yoder. Kris was entirely too giddy about visiting Yoder's church—some sort of misdirected pilgrimage, I (Sam) think, in which he expected to pay homage to a stately monument or at least a marble bust. I subtly recalled the story of Aaron and the golden calf on our way to the church, but Kris was still disappointed by the lack of relics available for adoration.[3]

The church, founded almost 150 years ago, occupies a small nondescript brick building constructed in the 1930s. What makes the church stand out, however, is the neighborhood that surrounds it. Prairie Street lies in what locals affectionately call "South Central Elkhart" (Elkhart is a city of only about 50,000 people, with a welcome sign that proclaims it the "RV Capital of the World"). This section of town was severely impacted by "white flight" in the late 1970s and '80s, and was recently rocked by the recession in 2008, leaving small ragged homes and abandoned buildings in its wake. The local newspaper identifies it as one of the neediest neighborhoods in the city, with over 20 percent of its residents unemployed.[4] The local population now consists primarily of ethnic minorities, with a rapidly growing Hispanic community, up to 30% in 2010.[5]

In the late 1990s the church considered moving to the "suburbs" to be closer to most of its members. A large endowment made it easy to purchase land and construct a new building in greener pastures, quite literally. But the pastor at the time, Andrew Kreider, threatened resignation if they chose to relocate. This not only convinced the congregation to stay put, but began to cultivate a deep commitment to the local neighborhood and its people. "At a time when they could have moved out, they remained committed to the neighborhood," said Alan Kreider, Andrew's father. Due to Andrew's stand, Prairie Street grew to care about Elkhart, especially South Central Elkhart, and this commitment came to drive its decisions, witness, and mission.

Jubilee

We joined the congregation one Sunday afternoon for a community picnic at a local park on the bank of the Elkhart River, packed with long tables and midwestern hospitality in the form of casseroles and pies. The entire congregation seemed to turn up to share and celebrate the work of the Jubilee House, an intentional community of Mennonite Voluntary Service members (MVSers) sponsored by Prairie Street. MVS, which began as an alternative to the Selective Service during World War II, places Mennonite students in church-sponsored, community justice-related jobs across the US for one- to two-year stints. After the picnic, we visited the Jubilee House, a three-story Victorian home with a small community garden in the back. Nick, a resident who runs a bike repair shop out of the garage, was chopping zucchini and onions in the kitchen, sporting a braided ponytail and dirty flannel shirt. Katie, a young MVSer from Virginia, welcomed us and led us into a small living room, furnished with donated couches, stacked books, and old carpet.

Prairie Street established the Jubilee House in 2006. Most residents are active in worship services and events at Prairie Street, and according to Katie the church views the house as its primary outreach arm: "We are doing full-time what people at the church with jobs can't necessarily do. Their support of the house is a way for them to be involved in the community."

Four MVSers live in the house for up to two years, cultivating intentional community through weekly meals and devotionals while also hosting weekly potluck dinners for the neighborhood and working forty hours per week in a local community justice ministry. Katie serves in the "Seed to Feed" program of the Church Community Services (a local ecumenical service organization), which supplies food pantries across the county with fresh produce and healthy foods. Other MVSers spend their days working at CSA farms, community organizing and legal jobs, community gardening, the denominational office, and the local Center for Community Justice. Katie offered us drinks as she explained that "cold, gray Elkhart" was not her first choice for an MVS assignment, but that she has grown to love the city. Like the church, she now feels committed to it. As another member put it, "Elkhart has a way of growing on you."[6]

Mega Missions

We met Prairie Street's pastor, Nelson Kraybill, at the seminary shortly after his return from leading a group of students to the Holy Land. Nelson is a commanding presence with a warm smile. The author of several books, he speaks like a professor, but with the compassion of a pastor, especially when explaining the church's work in the local community. He served as president of the seminary for twelve years before leaving academic life in 2010 for the pastorate at Prairie Street. In the ivory tower of academia, it is "easy to lose touch with the grassroots" of ministry, he explained. He was "just itching" to get back into ministry and was drawn to Prairie Street, a "multicultural, multilingual church in a struggling part of the city."

When we asked about local missions and the church's commitment to the neighborhood, Nelson focused on two community organizing efforts that defined Prairie Street's approach to missions—and politics. About five years earlier, the Elkhart school board and city council decided to demolish an old school building a few blocks from the church. Many local residents had attended or taught at the Roosevelt School, and at one time up to thirty Prairie Street members were involved in the school through teaching, tutoring, mentoring, or teacher support groups.[7] It was no surprise then, Nelson recalled, that the council's declaration immediately instigated "organic efforts in the community" to stop the demolition of this community landmark. Because of their continued involvement, leaders at Prairie Street understood the importance of the school to the community and decided to get involved.

Pastor Kreider and Rev. Lafate Owens, pastor of a local African American church, joined forces and mobilized their congregations. Together they led the community effort to stop the demolition by attending school board and city council meetings, writing articles for the local newspaper, and organizing public meetings—the first of which was held at Prairie Street.

Art Stoltzfus, a lay leader on the missions team, spoke about how difficult it can be to successfully advocate change through local politics. At one point he recalled several board members physically turning their backs on the two pastors during their presentation to the school board. If these two eloquent men were begin ignored, Art asked, "What must it be like for a single mother who is working two jobs to try and navigate some of these systems?" Concern for those in the community who did not have a voice, who remained unrepresented by the political system, mobilized the churches to speak up, and together they saved the building. The historic building was soon converted into affordable housing units, a gym, and a cafeteria, as well as space for an alternative school—now a blessing to the community rather than a sign of its demise.

Around the same time, the church also became involved in community efforts to shut down what they call the "mega shredder" (which is neither a Transformer nor a *Ninja Turtles* villain, to Kris's disappointment). A demolition firm had constructed this massive machine to crush automobiles for recycling, and it caused enough vibrations to shake the entire community. Vibrations destroyed the foundations of houses and created significant noise pollution, added Art, who said he could feel and hear it at his home over a mile away. More importantly, the company had placed the mega shredder in the middle of a low-income neighborhood, near South Central, which lacked the political power to oppose it.

Recognizing the injustice, Prairie Street member Darrin Belousek organized neighborhood associations and other church groups and educated himself on zoning codes and public law. He and others from the church then brought a series of photos, research, and graphs to city council meetings and the mayor's office. Pastor Nelson called Darrin "the persistent gadfly on the flank of the municipal horse in Elkhart. He was always there," Nelson told us, sitting back, amused by his own metaphor, "with just a little bit of bite, a little bit of prophetic sting, calling the municipality to justice." The company was fined by the city multiple times until it eventually went out of business.

Like Solomon's Porch, this church takes an ad hoc approach to missions, rallying around community issues as they arise. Unlike Saddleback, missions at Prairie Street focus almost exclusively on partnering with outside (often secular) groups to support existing initiatives, rather than launching church programs. Prairie Street isn't concerned about who owns the initiative, but only that it is effective as an agent of social transformation.

Most members of the church are already involved in various local community efforts, so rather than developing its own programs—like after-school tutoring at Solomon's Porch or the Patrick Alison House at First & Franklin—Prairie Street supports members in their own various missions. "The congregation joins in ministries that are active in the community," Art said. "That may mean joining a tutoring program already active in the schools or joining the Church Community Services program."

According to Alan Kreider, the missions team simply recognized its own limitations. Most members are older and tired, and the younger ones are working too hard. There just isn't enough energy to get new initiatives going. "We're pretty weak," Alan admitted. "We don't talk much about doing our own thing." Partnering is the best strategy for now, Alan continued, considering their limited resources. The church begins by "looking at what is already there and figuring out how they can plug into or partner with things that are already established."[8] Each month during worship Nelson interviews one member about the mission work he or she does as a way of endorsing projects and inspiring others to become involved. As a result, members get connected to missions and to neighborhood groups—some

Christian, some secular, some governmental—that are already doing good work.

Reconciling Missions

When we left the seminary and drove around the neighborhood, I (Kris) pointed out the boarded-up shops and neglected homes as we talked about Prairie Street's approach to missions. Sam noted that commitment to the *local* community seemed to be the top priority for church missions. While the fruits of being a good neighbor were apparent, he wondered if the church addressed local needs at the expense of a global commitment. Leaders we spoke with all acknowledged this tension. While the church had been involved in global missionary efforts from its inception, it began to focus locally in the 1960s as congregation members became involved in the civil rights movement.

Art Stoltzfus expanded on this history. The church budget allocates money for both local and global ministries. However, when the budget dropped as the congregation began to age, the church discussed where they were already involved and where they wanted to focus. The decision to prioritize local missions was based both on limited resources and the fact that most members were already committed to local ministries. Katie Jantzen, still relatively new to the church, ventured a more theological explanation. "The church is aware that there are a lot of problems in Elkhart, and particularly in South Central Elkhart," she told us. "It is good to be aware of what is going on out in the world and what the needs are, but if you do that at the expense of your neighbors, you are missing the point."

We were also struck by the church's decision to support existing community programs rather than creating programs of its own. This approach relies on partnerships, and requires the church to give up substantial control over a program's priorities and methods. I told Sam that I worried about the implications of leaving all missions up to the control of outside groups who inevitably will have other agendas—potentially driven by a different set of values. Can the church maintain the specificity of its message and witness while partnering with secular groups? Isn't there something essential about a church taking charge of this work, something distinctive that only a church body can provide? I admitted that I had been swayed by the church-centered focus of Saddleback.

Most church members we talked with spoke positively about Pairie Street's missional model. Katie suggested that it simply makes sense considering "all of the good community development, social organizations, and community organizing that is already happening here." Another member told us that many outside groups are "doing kingdom stuff that is very impressive." There are finite resources available, both in the congregational budget and in the community as a whole, to support important ministries. Therefore, "we don't want to duplicate things that are already going on," Art said. "Let's see where these resources align." Speaking practically, Katie explained, "A lot of the congregation is older, so starting a group that goes out and builds homes for people wouldn't really fit who we are as a congregation. How we can plug individuals and small groups and their particular talents and resources into things that are already happening?" In other words, the church is intentional about not reinventing the wheel. This is not only a practical value, we reasoned, but a theological one as well. Faithfulness consists both in the wise use of the individual talents and resources of church members, and in openness to the work of non-church groups.

Some members, like Alan Kreider, wish the church was doing some things "that were distinctively ours," though he doesn't know what those would be. Nelson admitted that the Jubilee House, the church's only sustained local missions effort, created a temptation for the congregation to outsource its missions work to the MVSers.

Another disadvantage to this model, Alan added, is its effect on evangelism. Partnering with outside groups in order to do the gospel work of justice does not always allow for the gospel work of evangelism. Alan believes the church should be a visible presence that people are drawn to, but "we are not doing well at evangelism." The church ought to be better at inviting the people they serve to church services, Alan said. He attributes this to Mennonite culture: Mennonites are really good at expressing faith through service, he said, but not verbally. Eleanor Kreider, Alan's wife and a longtime church leader, added that Mennonites have an "exceedingly reticent piety" that often constrains their evangelism.

While we have some concerns about this approach (more on that later), we do agree with these church leaders about the importance of the body being sent into the world to work for the kingdom of God, and then gathered together to celebrate what God is doing (Luke 10:1–2). In typical Anabaptist fashion, this model cedes power to control the world and efforts to fix it,[9] and mingles itself within the messy and complicated structures of justice. It breaks down sacred and secular divisions, and cultivates a faith that God works beyond the walls of the church. We don't have to try and control how and where kingdom work gets done, but God calls us to discern where God is working—even if it is a state-run tutoring program, or ecumenical justice center—and to simply join in, as the church.

Finally, Prairie Street's missions approach is deeply political. Anabaptists have often been viewed as apolitical and sectarian, withdrawing from the messiness of the world to their own enclaves of purity. They believe the church should influence society solely through the witness of its faithful life together, not by engaging in secular political mechanisms.[10]

But at Prairie Street, this is simply not true. The church seems to understand witness as its primary political function—through its way of life, its commitment to nonviolence, and the allegiance it offers to Christ through worship. It understands itself as a political body with internal political practices. However, this does not prevent it from engaging with the political mechanisms of the world. "As a congregation, we recognize that we're part of a community," Art said. "We put a high value on working outside the walls of the church in the community where God has placed us." Its commitment to reconciliation includes the secular world, reconciling its mission with the world and including it in the work God has called it to do.

We were surprised that the two definitive missions activities of the church involved direct petition to political authorities. Pledging sole allegiance to Jesus Christ does not prevent the church from connecting with the political structures of this world on behalf of those in need, Nelson told us. Prairie Street's commitment to South Central Elkhart necessitated direct political involvement on a local level if the church was going to help its neighbors in any substantial way.

The church understood itself to have used its political power to sway the decisions of the city council. Prairie Street is not a wealthy congregation, Alan told us, but its members are well educated. The congregation has an abnormally large number of PhDs, and therefore a large degree of class power. And as Art's story of recognizing the plight of their voiceless neighbors illustrates, the church chose to wield this class power politically by educating itself on the issues, using the social resources at its disposal to engage with the local community on its behalf in both the Roosevelt School and mega shredder initiatives.

IN COMMUNITY

As the worship service came to a close, the speaker stepped down from the pulpit and walked around the pews with her microphone. One by one, congregants stood to offer a word of praise for something God had done for them this week or to request prayer from the congregation. Nearly ten people stood up to speak in this crowd of fewer than 200, and often went into great detail about their struggles. When we asked members about this practice after the service ended, they all highlighted communal sharing time as a key ingredient not only in their corporate worship, but in their communal identity.

Turning over the mic during a worship service is risky, Nelson admitted—but after leaders explained to the congregation that the time was not for announcements like "selling tickets for the high school raffle," the practice has been extremely formative for the congregation on several levels. "It's spiritually invigorating for a worshiping community to give anybody and everybody a voice," Nelson said. Worship becomes multivoiced, and includes those that do not normally have a chance to lead. This is important to mark worship as something that involves the entire community; everyone has a chance to participate and contribute. It is also another chance to see how "our stories fit into the big story" of God's reconciliation, according to Alan Kreider, whether they are stories of praise or struggle. Members become united to one another in their suffering and adoration, and begin to see themselves as part of the larger people of God. It helps move the worship of the church outside the church walls and into the world by connecting it to people and current events, and forcing the church to reckon with its place and purpose in the world. "We don't really believe in a church to which people can't bring their lives," Alan said.

Moving by Consent

The term *community* defines the social ethos at Prairie Street. Like many Anabaptist congregations, there is much attention to doing things "in community": eating, worshiping, interpreting Scripture, making decisions. The structure of the congregation enables this communitarian ethos. Mennonites are well-known for nonhierarchy and open church meetings—everyone has a voice and the congregation must move toward a consensus before a decision can be made.[11] We discovered that Prairie Street embodies these values, but in nuanced and interesting ways.

Like several of the churches we visited, Prairie Street had recently adjusted its leadership structure, and in fact, was in the midst of doing so again. Nelson explained to us that the old structure had become too complex for the size of the congregation. As membership numbers began to dwindle, the leaders decided they needed a simpler model. There were too many committees, too much bureaucracy for such a small congregation. Eleanor Kreider told us the old model was "wearing people down," and they decided to empower teams to make decisions, to cut out the "middle man" (the church council) between the pastors and congregation. Likewise, the former pastor, Andrew Kreider, felt like he had too little decision-making power since everything had to be approved by a majority of the church council.

The first move, a year after Nelson arrived, was to become more pastorally centered, to move towards "empowering the pastoral team."[12] The pastors and ministry teams then make all decisions within their own spheres of ministry—an education project, building renovations, a Hispanic ministry[13]—without requiring church council approval. In theory, this shifted decision-making power from the council to the people actually charged with that area of ministry (a prominent theme in all the churches we visited).

However, as the church has settled into this new model, Nelson explained, "It's felt to me like the pastoral team ends up becoming the nerve center of a little bit too much information and too much processing." The ministry teams defer to the pastors, which has only shifted the bureaucracy rather than eliminating it. According to Nelson, the ministry teams are too fragmented, working in silos, and the congregation is often not aware of what is going on.[14]

Now the church is in the process of tweaking the model once more, to an even more streamlined and flat structure, hoping to remove more responsibility (and power) from the pastoral teams. The ministry teams will be trusted to do whatever they want as long as it is within their team's role and budget, and the mission of the church. They will meet regularly to overcome the temptations to silo or defer to the pastoral team.

With the lay-led ministry teams fully empowered in their respective areas, church meetings, once a significant part of the decision-making structure, have now become times for information dissemination and seldom for decisions. This means the entire congregation spends much less time making decisions than it used to. In fact, there have been only two congregational meetings so far this year, they told us. The only things that now come before the congregation are large budget items, board members, elders, pastors, pastoral review, or a change in relationship to the denomination or its confession of faith—"We wouldn't want to become Catholics without at least talking about it first!" Nelson joked.

When the church is faced with a decision requiring the entire congregation's input—like its current deliberation over starting a Spanish-language worship service—it moves by *consent* rather than consensus, Eleanor explained. The meetings are a means to gauge the leanings of the congregation, not to take a definitive vote. At times a single decision may require several meetings over a period of time. The aim is ultimately to have each person give his or her "consent" to move forward, even if he or she still disagrees. Consensus allows one person the power to hold up the entire process, Alan noted; consent still gives the minority the chance to know they've been listened to, and requires the majority decision-makers to "hold that reservation in mind" as they move forward.

Creating Community

After several days in the self-proclaimed RV capital, having exhausted every local restaurant and the only brewery in town, we decided to take a trip back into Chicago for the night, to sample some Chicago-style pizza and catch a jazz show. Prairie Street had been surprising in a number of ways, and it typically helped us to take a day off to process. En route to Chicago, I (Kris) gave Sam a surprised look when we passed a sign welcoming us to Michigan. He quickly checked the (unsurprisingly faulty) GPS. "But I think you have to go through Michigan to get from Indiana to Illinois," said Sam, who did not win an eighth-grade geography bee.

When we finally arrived in Chicago, famished from our protracted tri-state excursion, we immediately located a recommended deep-dish joint. We enjoyed the hefty slices, sitting on some steps outside of Grant Park as tie-dyed, head-banded, glow-stick-bedeckd teenagers filtered out of the annual Lollapalooza rock festival. We had just missed the Mumford and Sons show we hoped to catch from the free seating in the park across the train tracks. Sam typically eats his food faster than anyone I know—I think half his plate is usually gone before we even finish the blessing. (He insists he is a very normally paced eater and that I just talk too much during meals.) But on this evening, with festivalgoers eyeing our slices like ravenous zombies (some even offering to buy them from us), we both devoured them with unprecedented speed and intensity.

Feeling a bit bloated as we walked across the Chicago River to a nearby jazz club, we managed to finally process our thoughts about the communitarian organization of Prairie Street. The church followed a trend we noticed in all five churches, toward empowering the congregation—often in the form of ministry teams—to make most of the decisions affecting the church's ministry. Trimming away bureaucracy and leveling hierarchy have become values for all of these congregations, I told Sam, though perhaps for practical rather than theological ones. Sam agreed, but replied that it still helps to move congregants from spectators to participants when they take some ownership of the church's ministry. This move has important theological implications, even if they remain unstated.

I admitted that I was somewhat surprised to see this new structure in a Mennonite church. Eliminating the requirement of consensus implied a higher value on *efficiency* than I had expected.[15] Still, this value was balanced by an underlying commitment to communalism. If a decision passes the team stage and comes before the entire congregation, then the process slows down and the church leaders seek the "consent" of all members. Decisions are not made through voting, which Nelson, like Doug at Solomon's Porch, considers an "act of violence." Votes are taken only to assess the leaning of the congregation, and all members, even those dissenting, have an opportunity to voice their reasons. Nelson will ultimately make major decisions, but not until the entire congregation has given its consent, even the minority who do not agree with the decision.[16]

The downside of this approach is that major decisions take a long time. The church is willing to sacrifice the speed of results for the integrity of the process. There is no quick referendum where a simple majority can ratify or reject any proposal. Ideally, the process pivots not on the preferences of individual members, but on spiritual discernment, a community attuned to the leadings of the Holy Spirit through a careful process (though we did not hear church leaders mention the significance of prayer in the process). Unlike the team structure, the church meeting for major decisions is not agile or nimble, and perhaps makes the church unable to respond to urgent issues that may arise in congregation. "Kind of reminds you of Entmoot in *The Lord of the Rings*, right?" Sam asked me as we approached the jazz venue, smiling and obviously proud of his (apparently) clever analogy. "You know, the council of ancient trees that take so long to make decisions?" I had no idea what he was talking about. "Sure, just like that," I replied. Nerd.

The sharing time during worship models these same communal values, I told Sam. "Quality control" is given up for the sake of granting everyone a voice during the worship time. Differences between clergy and laity are minimized and everyone has the chance to contribute to the formation of everyone else through sharing each other's burdens and celebrations (Gal 6:2; Rom 12:15). Still, ministry roles are not disrupted, Sam reminded me: the senior pastor ultimately takes responsibility for the final decision, team leaders lead, and congregants share their input. Everyone has a voice, but also a particular role corresponding to her or his gifts and calling (1 Cor 12:12–31).[17]

This practice, though slow and at times tedious, works to create a true community out of disparate individuals. Though the absence of prayer seems to leave a significant theological void, in many ways this models the image of the early church in Acts (2:42–46), and a witness to a wider world that has been co-opted by individualism. This practice creates a counterpolitics in which disagreements are worked out together, not settled by votes, where the common good is deliberated, and where dissenters are heard. The community is not always harmonious—deep disagreements occur—but it is unified in its allegiance to Christ. In this way, this practice exhibits a new political imagination, forming the consciousness of the congregation and witnessing that another form of political existence is possible.

"FROM ALL TRIBES AND PEOPLES"

During the worship service we had noticed a small crowd of Hispanic congregants sitting in a back corner of the sanctuary. None of them had spoken during the share time, but a man sitting near the front, named Angel Miranda, stood to thank them for their contribution to the life of the church. Angel was from Puerto Rico, and was married to Lora, an Elkhart native and longtime member of Prairie Street. They returned to Elkhart from Puerto Rico in 2006, and now Angel spearheads the burgeoning Hispanic ministry at Prairie Street.

Multiethnic ministry is a practical and theological issue that many churches are beginning to address—some intentionally and some, like Prairie Street, out of necessity as their commitment to the local neighborhood brings shifting demographics literally to their front doors. Churches are faced with questions about how to unite people with different language and cultural experiences into a single congregation. How do churches welcome outsiders and include them without glossing over significant cultural, and often theological, differences? The rapidly changing South Central area required this congregation of mostly older white members to contend with these questions for the first time.

I (Sam) reflected on the importance of multiethnic ministry as we drove to the retirement community in Goshen where Angel and Lora lived. Neither of us had anticipated this as a major issue at Prairie Street before we arrived, but this reinforced my sense of the rapidly changing cultural and ethnic realities for most churches in America. "It would be great if there was just some easy way to search for ethnic demographics about this local area," said Kris, who is incapable of explaining how the Internet works without using the word "magic."

A Hybrid Congregation?

We sat around a small table in the Miranda's modest apartment, drinking *café con leche* and enjoying a plate of cookies and cakes. We asked them how a fairly homogenous congregation found itself exploring multiethnic ministry. They told us that the church's Hispanic ministry is still a small program, consisting of ESL classes, a Spanish Sunday School class, and a monthly small group called *Peregrinos* (Pilgrims). It began when Hispanic folks "just started to show up at our church," starting with one family in 2010 and growing to four or five families, now comprising twelve to nineteen people most Sundays.

The next step for the church is to make a decision about launching a separate Spanish language worship service—a question that has generated some contention in congregational meetings. Angel has been the most consistent advocate for a separate service, insisting that if the group continues to grow the church should provide a worship experience that makes Spanish speakers feel at home. Worship already includes a Spanish song in every service and Scripture readings in both languages. While some of the Latino attenders are taking ESL classes, most of them cannot speak English. Angel's idea was to grow a Spanish-language Mennonite church out of the Hispanic visitors that had been attending for some time, though this was in conflict with the vision of many others in the church—including his wife. Lora and Angel explained their positions to us, occasionally talking over

119

one another, and then smiling as they offered us more coffee. The Latino attenders are divided as well, Angel said. Some would prefer their own service and others want a more integrated experience. "I don't really think that we need to be separating ourselves into different groups," Lora insisted. According to her, most members want the church to be a "hybrid congregation," not two congregations.

The church has been engaged in this discussion for a few years now, taking a slow, "Entmoot" approach again. While Angel insists that they are missing a ministry opportunity by not giving Spanish speakers a worship experience in their own language, Nelson believes they are gradually settling on this hybrid model. On the advice of an African American colleague, Nelson contends that the congregation should do something harder than splitting into two services—and therefore two congregations, he worries. It should attempt to more closely model a Revelation 7 vision: "I looked, and there was a great multitude that no one could count, from every nation, from all tribes and peoples and languages, standing before the throne and before the Lamb" (7:9). This hybrid model would create one congregation that is "neither Anglo nor Hispanic but something new."

Nelson explained that a "hybrid congregation" model would involve real-time translation of the worship service, and the church is currently constructing a sound booth for this purpose. They would use Spanish in every service somewhere, sing Spanish songs, and read the Scripture in both languages, as well as continue a Spanish Sunday School class and small group. The plan also includes hiring a Spanish-speaking staff minister charged with leading the Hispanic ministry. This is not integration, as in "you do it our way," but the creation of "something new."[18] They won't be able to serve the needs of every Spanish-language person in the neighborhood, Nelson admitted, especially those who want to stay immersed in Spanish-language culture. "Our vision is for the Anglos in our community to, as much as possible, learn from the other," he said. "We want people who are patient enough to take the time for the Scripture reading in two languages in every service." This cultivates a congregation that is serious about breaking down linguistic and racial divides.

We asked Nelson what impacts these attempts at multicultural worship were having on the congregation. Has he noticed any changes in the community or its worship with the presence of these Hispanic visitors? With tears in his eyes, Nelson told us the stories two Hispanic women in the congregation had shared last Sunday during worship. One revealed that a close relative had recently died crossing the border in the Arizona desert, and the other had a relative in Mexico who had just been kidnapped. They asked for prayers from the congregation, and the congregation will certainly grieve with them, Nelson said.

Shared stories from across cultures shape the way this community cares for one another, and change the way they worship together. The text that week was the story of John the Baptist preparing a way in the desert (Matt 3:1–12). Nelson said they discovered that what they want is for "a way to be made in the desert" for people suffering in Latin America. "We know these people now; it's not just some distant connection," he said. Because of the existence of these new relationships they do not worship the same way anymore. "It changes your perspective on what it means to be an American living in the security of all the plenty that we have," he observed, "as well as your attitude about immigration reform and the smug and self-serving things people say about immigrants." When congregation members have relationships beyond the comfort zones of class and race, it helps them see people "not as statistics or threats, but as beloved sisters and brothers." Now the church consists of people of different ethnicities relying on one another for support and praying for those they know across the globe and right next door. Made concrete in their worship practices, Revelation 7:9 has become for them a "hybrid vision" itself. It is a real possibility in the corporate worship of the community here and now, he told us, and not just something that happens in heaven.

The Challenge of Multiethnic Ministry

Like many churches wrestling with how to do multiethnic ministry, Prairie Street faces competing values. On the one hand, most members want to preserve the unity of the congregation by sticking to one worship service, and feel vaguely uneasy about "self-segregating." This desire is well-founded —the church's majority-white population is happy to have new Hispanic congregants, and wants to feel that they are embracing new cultures rather than partitioning them. After all, the eschatological kingdom of God in Revelation 7:9 includes people of every tribe and tongue worshiping together—why shouldn't the local church do the same here and now?

On the other hand, there is a minority (represented by Angel) who think the best way to reach Elkhart's growing Spanish-speaking population is to start a separate Spanish-language service. Nelson may be right in thinking that this falls outside Prairie Street's scope of ministry, but Angel raises an important point. It's a small inconvenience for a congregation of white English speakers in Indiana to hear a little Spanish in church once a week; but for a Spanish-speaking immigrant family, for whom communicating and being understood in an English-speaking world is a daily struggle, church with fellow Spanish speakers may be the only time of the week that truly feels like home. Even if Prairie Street's decision to keep the service together is the right one for them (and it may be), this decision comes at the expense of creating a truly comfortable cultural space for the Spanish speakers in the congregation. Creating a hybrid service, which requires patience and understanding from both cultural groups, is a great step, but it's not all that is necessary to create balanced cultural space. A bilingual service with equal parts English and Spanish will not be experienced the same way by both groups in a still overwhelmingly English-speaking cultural context (and Nelson seems to recognize this).

Prairie Street's situation illustrates the complexity of doing multiethnic ministry in a church with a clear majority culture. Sometimes staying true to the vision of multiethnic worship in Revelation requires creating space for a minority culture to flourish when the odds are stacked against it. This is often counterintuitive to conscientious majority-culture church leaders who just want everyone to be together, without realizing that this involves greater sacrifice from the minority culture than from the majority. The majority culture doesn't need specially designated cultural safe space because their entire environment is a safe space. But churches should recognize, affirm, and protect the value of such space for the minority cultures in their midst.

This is not to say that churches should be culturally divided—the body of Christ is multiethnic to its very core, and unity across cultures in worship is a beautiful expression of this truth. However, Scripture affirms both unity and distinction in culture (see Rev 7), and too often majority culture unintentionally glosses over the latter in pursuit of the former. Caring for minorities requires paying disproportionate attention to their cultural situation—a "preferential option" for the cultural minority.[19] This means churches should sometimes decide in favor of the minority opinion when that opinion is supported by the cultural minority. It also means that deciding in favor of the majority when opinion is split (even partially) along cultural lines requires sensitivity to the lived experience of cultural minorities, even if the majority opinion happens to be right. Understanding the church as a political body gathered from among the nations, united by an allegiance to Christ that relativizes national allegiance even as it maintains and affirms its own cultural diversity, may help the church hold these values in tension.

Worship and Allegiance

The growing Latino presence in the church taught the mostly homogenous and well-educated congregation that "church is not about speaking English and being white middle-class Anglos," Nelson asserted. "Worship is about joining a global community of those who call Jesus Lord." This is one way, he claimed, that worship takes on profound political significance for Prairie Street. In fact, this theme shapes much of Nelson's thought and teaching on worship. He has published a book, *Apocalypse and Allegiance*, on how the vision of worship in the book of Revelation impacts politics: "The way we worship . . . expresses and shapes allegiance," he writes.[20]

In fact, true to their Anabaptist heritage, church leaders at Prairie Street understand that worship forms the congregation. Against the trend of many "seeker-sensitive churches" (and opposed to Saddleback's notion of the worship service as the entry point to the Discipleship Funnel, Kris noted), Alan asserted that worship is not merely a strategy for "getting people in." A professional theologian in a church swarming with them, Alan is currently researching Christians during the Roman Empire, and explained to us that he is struck by the way the early church grew despite refusing to admit nonbaptized people into its services. While he would not suggest the contemporary church become that restrictive—it should "be attentive to the outsiders who come in"—he thinks the tendency to view worship primarily as a means of evangelism curtails the formative power of corporate worship. "It is first about God. It is praise," he said. But it is also a practice that shapes allegiance. "The aim of our worship is to glorify God and to get us involved in what God is involved in." And often that includes discussing issues that are political and intentionally shaping the way the congregation thinks about politics.

In what ways, then, does worship shape allegiance at Prairie Street? When we asked Nelson, he responded that the pastoral prayer and sharing time almost always include references to economic and political injustice throughout the world, as well as petitions for political leaders. The prayer requests of the Hispanic visitors has galvanized within the congregation a strong commitment to advocate for immigration reform on both the local and national levels.

People are encouraged to bring up issues of public policy during Sunday School. Often, songs from the Mennonite hymnal and the sermons involve issues of justice, he added. "Nelson is quite explicitly political in his sermons," Eleanor revealed. "Not party political, but political." He refuses to shy away from political issues that are relevant to the gospel, she explained, particularly issues like immigration reform or health care (though we noted that these do typically fall along party lines). And Nelson agreed. "My sermons often delve into politically engaged topics," he said, though not every sermon is political. "I don't want to bring party politics into the church," he said, meaning he never promotes a candidate or platform, "but I don't hesitate to stand up and say what I think the gospel is calling us to." He added that most people who don't like this kind of message have already left the church.

This belief that the church's call to action is necessarily political is grounded in the congregation's reading of Scripture. The Bible calls "followers of Jesus Christ to alternative allegiance and alternative identity," Nelson said.[21] Alan seconded: "The Bible is a political book; it's about the building of a people of God who will develop their own form of politics." This is the way the Bible is taught and read at Prairie Street, he said—"we are talking about our congregation's life as politics."

COMMITTING TO COMMUNITY

With our time at Prairie Street winding down, the Kreiders invited us to join them for dinner and conversation at their home. Longtime members of the church, Eleanor and Alan are both successful academic theologians who have taught locally and abroad, and even written a few books together. As we have noted, their son Andrew served for a time as pastor of Prairie Street. Though retired from teaching, they continue to reflect and write on practical theology.

The Kreiders live in a modest garden-style house just a few miles from the church. Alan met us at the front door with a warm, grandfatherly smile, and we settled around a table on their back patio overlooking a serene flower garden. Rosy and welcoming, but deeply sincere about their faith and love of their church, they talked for hours about theology, the history of the church, and their friendship with John Howard Yoder (of particular interest to Kris). Waxing nostalgically, the Kreiders insisted that Yoder's legacy, while understated, was still the underlining reason for the congregation's emphasis on community action, connection of worship to ethics, and its deep understanding of the church as a "body politic." They regaled us with stories from the past, musings about the church's future, and earnest inquiries about our perceptions of the church, and proudly showed us a collection of Mennonite daily prayers that they had just written.

For me (Sam), daily prayers called to mind a practice of High Church denominations like Catholicism and Anglicanism, yet this represents just one of the simple practices of piety emblematic of Mennonite faith. Personal devotion and daily practices of spiritual formation have long been an essential part of this community. For Mennonites, personal piety leads to a deep sense of moral urgency. Often this ethical gravity manifests itself in restrictions on behaviors like drinking or dancing (Kris noticed a disappointing lack of alcohol during any of our visits or meals—though as two white guys with little rhythm, we were thankful for no dancing). This emphasis on personal purity is also manifested in their well-known imperative against violence. In Mennonite faith, however, these restrictions are not just conduits to personal purity. They also constitute the community's public witness to Christ.

Spiritual Sectarianism

Mennonites believe the church's primary mission is to witness through an alternative lifestyle and even an alternative politics to a watching world, which often requires abstaining from the corrupt political systems of the world. Under this view, Christians are not called to control the world through coercion, public policy, or Christianizing the social order (Mark 10:42–45).[22] Because of such stances, Anabaptists are often charged with sectarianism—removing themselves from the messy political process and also, it is claimed, from the ability to create real substantive change. This is why we were so surprised to encounter overt political engagement at Prairie Street. For this church, personal devotion seemed to result in participation in worldly life and politics. Piety led to political action on behalf of the powerless. And while we were excited to find a church that challenges this sectarian stereotype, we realized that Prairie Street's political engagement does not actually absolve the church from all forms of sectarianism.

Here is what we mean. Because of their practical resistance to "reinventing the wheel" and recognition of their limited resources and aging congregation, the church encourages its congregants to join community service organizations rather than initiate its own mission programs. At the same time, church leaders admit that the congregation struggles with reaching out spiritually to the community. We agree with Alan's sense that something is lost in this approach.

When a church's mission consists only in partnership with other groups, we worry that the church may grow to see itself as just one among many other voluntary organizations in civil society, or it may allow its partners' agendas to set the terms for its own mission. In partnerships with others the church must work diligently to avoid being instrumentalized into the service of another agency, or subsumed into some other project that may ultimately be at odds with the gospel.[23] There is something important about partnering with others who share the same reason for your work, and not just the same goal—it ensures that the church operates out of its own countercultural values rather than simply reflecting those of the wider culture.

This missions approach may also fail to explicitly witness to the Lordship and redemption of Christ. The church may be forced to "remold its witness" around the terms and conditions of these outside agencies, and thereby lose important distinctive church (and political) practices like evangelism.[24] In other words, we worry there is something missing when a church acts as if there is no difference between helping someone and helping someone in Jesus' name. We do not doubt that the church's motivation for social transformation arises from its devotion to Christ as King. Yet the church's social and political activities are not done with explicit reference to this motivation. Piety inspires political activity, but does not carry over into and shape the contours of this activity in its public witness.

In this way, we worry that Prairie Street's sectarianism is not political or social, but may be spiritual—its pietistic, devotional, worshiping life still takes place largely in isolation from the world. The church offers a public, political witness, but, leaders admit, little spiritual witness. And this gives us the opportunity to make an important point about political witness. If a church is a political body, then its ambassadors must represent what the church cares about, and also why it cares about it—the theological and spiritual reasons behind its public actions. We recognize that this could be seen as a nitpicky criticism. But, for a church to align its commitments to King and kingdom and offer a faithful, holistic mission, we believe it needs to fully connect and integrate these two commitments publicly—not merely maintain them both. And while Prairie Street does embody both of these commitments, it seems to keep them separated: their mission has gone public while they allow their Christian convictions to remain privatized.

By this, we do not mean that every good deed must be immediately followed by some sort of gospel presentation! But we do think there is something significant about allowing the gospel message to not only form a church's concerns and activities, but to become explicit in the midst of those activities. In our social and political work, we are called not only to alleviate suffering and stand up against injustice, but to be ambassadors of the good news that God's world order has been inaugurated. We are called to give a reason for our hope (1 Pet 3:15), and that reason is all important if what we believe to be true about the gospel really is true.

Faithful Political Practices

While we consider this a serious point for reflection, Prairie Street offers a great example to other churches that miss the political dimensions of worship. According to church leaders, worship first transforms the congregation and then calls it to participate in God's work in the world. "Worship forms us, as forgiven people, and converts us to God's way of operating in pursuit of God's mission," Alan writes. "Such worship gets us involved as grateful collaborators with God as we learn to live in keeping with God's mission."[25] King and kingdom are linked: the church's commitment to its local community arises from its devotion to God, and worship practices like sharing time lead to concrete political activities like advocating for immigration reform.

In addition, Prairie Street's practices of communal sharing, transgressing cultural boundaries, and giving voice to everyone in church meetings affect life beyond the walls of the church. "We Christians, who discover in worship that we have something to contribute," the Kreiders suggest, "find that we also have a voice in a staff meeting at work or in a neighborhood association or in a parent-teacher meeting." Reflecting on the experiences of the last few years at Prairie Street, they say, "When the city council is meeting, we can ask for the floor, tell of our experiences, and give voice to our insights. The multivoiced *ekklesia* functions as a political reality, and we who are trained in it learn to function articulately in other assemblies as well. The culture of the church . . . influences the cultures of work and extended families, of civic organizations and political debate."[26] Worship shapes active political agents and turns worship spectators into socially engaged ministers in their everyday activities.

Body Politics

These practices are examples of the kind of new political imagination we advocate, one based on the church's allegiance to Christ as Lord. They offer a more faithful representation of how people are to live together, and live *for* others for the sake of Christ. In this way, the church is a people of God who will develop its own form of politics, according to Alan, but this does not mean that a church cannot call for the state government to enact just policies or address an issue that happens to align with some partisan issue. Issues like immigration reform and deportation, for example, are key to the proclamation of the gospel and the witness of Christians. "In fact, most issues we've been involved in would be championed by one party rather than the other—and you may not have to think very hard to guess which party that is," Nelson quipped.

And while we still worry about red and blue politics co-opting and dictating the church's mission—often without the congregation realizing what is happening—we hope the emphasis on allegiance to Christ over any earthly affiliation in Nelson's theology and preaching precludes any mixed allegiances. He insists that Prairie Street doesn't allow partisan politics to determine what issues it will address, because he believes it is the gospel that calls them to take this action. In other words, these are kingdom issues.

It is allegiance to Christ as King, not to the Democratic Party, that ultimately defines their politics, he insists. But this does not mean that Christians should not still be "wise as serpents" in their political discernment in the world (Matt 10:16). Christians will always be troubled by the way politics happens in the world. "There are some [times] that as Christians we must say, 'This is part of the world that is slipping away and will not be here when the reign of God comes in its fullest,'" Nelson said. Even so, "We are called to make use of it in the interim."[27]

On one hand, Nelson believes that many Mennonite congregations—and churches of other denominations, we might add—fall into one of two traps of passivity. Some marginalize the political dimensions of the gospel and proclaim a spiritual individualism that calls Christians to an otherworldly spirituality. Others practice a "comfortable middle-class civil religion" that makes itself too at home in the world. Both of these tendencies create a passivity in the face of economic and social injustices. He hopes that Prairie Street avoids these temptations and lives faithfully as "a corporate discernment of the body of Christ who gather around Scripture and together discern what it means to follow Jesus and the gospel, even if it is costly."

On the other hand, we also worry that churches involved in as much social action as Prairie Street risk cultivating "morality without doxology," as Alan put it—action not grounded in faith and Scripture, that does not arise out of response to God.[28] Many churches are "anorectically doxological," he warned. But a healthy church integrates faith and mission, piety and politics. We agree: love of neighbor must arise as a response to God's love for us (1 John 4:19). It is because God acted first in Christ that we are free to act, to witness to our own alternative form of politics *and* engage in earthly forms. It is first as a forgiven people that we are to engage the world in a process of reconciliation and redemption that may at times employ a city council or school board, and maybe sometimes a state or national policy, to work for God's kingdom. In other words, if a strong commitment to worship and spiritual formation is present, a radical security in its allegiance to Christ, then a church can form a people who are able to faithfully engage in the messy work of worldly politics.[29]

One of our favorite stories from Prairie Street was Nelson explaining that the mayor of Elkhart, the politician who presided over the mega shredder incident, later began attending the church. Sitting and worshiping with a community that opposed his actions and convinced him to change his mind, and this mayor became involved in worship and children's time—a witness to the way the politics of God can overcome the politics of this world. According to Alan and Eleanor, it is the simple act of worship that can shape churches into "cultures that embody the reconciling *missio dei* and equip us with practices that question and transform the cultures that surround us."[30]

Seeking the Welfare of the City

We came to identify this model of political engagement as *committing to community*. Prairie Street commits, first, to a communal ethos in its order of life together. Its decision-making process and spiritual life are oriented toward communal empowerment, discernment, and sharing. The church organizes itself to give everyone a voice. But, as in the example of the prayer request for the relative who died while crossing the border, this internal commitment also leads to a social and missional commitment to the community it finds itself in. Like the prophet Jeremiah's words to the Hebrew exiles in Babylon—"Seek the welfare of the city where I have sent you into exile, and pray to the Lord on its behalf, for in its welfare you will find your welfare" (Jer 29:7)—Prairie Street engages with its community on its behalf in a variety of ways. Committing to community sometimes necessitates direct political action when the situation calls for the church to utilize its political clout on behalf of others. But healthy political activity arises not from partisan persuasions, but from a deep devotion to Christ and the transformative power of worship.

As our evening with the Kreider's drew to a close, I (Sam) let slip that I played the piano, and they insisted I play something for them. After a couple of songs, Alan brought out their daily prayer book and invited us to join them for evening prayer, their nightly family ritual. Eleanor scolded him, saying we were surely in a hurry and would not want to join some old couple for family prayer. But of course we did. We knelt down in their small corner prayer room and read Scriptures, sang a hymn, and joined them in prayer for themselves, for their church, for Elkhart, and for us.

Our time at Prairie Street helped us identify several practices that may serve as examples for other congregations.

First, Prairie Street acts as a beacon of reconciliation in its own community. The congregation committed to staying in its neighborhood when it would have been easy to leave for a better, safer location. As communities and demographics change rapidly, churches that choose to remain in difficult neighborhoods encounter opportunities for ministry often abandoned by those who pack up and leave.

Second, the church focuses its social work on those whose voices are marginalized. It uses its "class power" as an educated, white congregation and turns it into political power—not for its own gain, but for the good of its city. Entering the political arena in this way comes with certain risks. But a church that is able to gather and organize its resources—in partnership with community members—and join with them in their own advocacy efforts expands the scope and authenticity of its witness.

Third, the leaders at Prairie Street understand and clearly articulate the interaction between worship and mission. They understand worship as a formative practice and seek to harness its power to cultivate spiritual as well as deeply political commitments to Christ as King.

Finally, Prairie Street is committed to not reinventing the missional wheel. While we have noted some dangers of this missional model, this approach allows a small church to keep its members actively engaged in socially transformative work. Too often churches reproduce programs rather than partnering and sharing resources. Engaging in such projects can open up new avenues for influence, as well as critical self-reflection when confronted with groups that do not share the same values.

* * *

We sat around Sam's kitchen table after an exhausting journey home, still stunned by the events of the past eight hours (try boarding an airplane these days when all your forms of ID have been stolen). It was late, and we were tired and hungry.

We shared some leftovers Sam warmed up from his fridge, and opened a couple of bottles of beer. We still hadn't said much since our things were taken, and as my (Kris's) mind drifted to the extra work that now lay ahead—trying to reproduce what was lost in order to write this chapter—the shock began to fade and despair settled in. Everything was gone. "There's no way we can replace this stuff," I told Sam. Without our recordings and notes, we were going to have to drop this church's story from the project.

As I sunk into my chair, eyes staring blankly into the plate in front of me, Sam spoke sternly. This didn't happen often, but he knew how to get my attention. Talking this way wouldn't do us any good, he said. The frustration was too fresh to make a decision about this tonight. We needed to rest, take some time, and make a decision about what to do in a few weeks.

My sense of guilt was too much to keep in. "Look, man, I'm so sorry. This is all my fault. You'll never get that stuff back." I was responsible. *I* had convinced Sam to do this project with me in the first place and *I* had left the car unlocked. What a stupid mistake.

I hung my head. Sam gave me a hug. "I'm not mad at you. This isn't your fault." I still couldn't look at him. He assured me that despite whatever responsibility I felt he did not blame me. "I think we can still pull this off."

And with these words, I could finally relax. I didn't know if it would turn out all right (it would). I didn't know if we would even be able to write this chapter (we would—thanks to many Skype "reinterviews"). But sometimes you have to rely on someone else's faith for a time. I took a deep breath as Sam opened up the fridge to look for more food.

Chapter 6

Living Their Story
Ebenezer Baptist Church

THE MORNING SUN SEEPING in through the skylight in the vaulted ceiling would have provided a peaceful beginning to our long day of interviews, were it not for the shrill alarm ringing throughout the empty sanctuary. I quickly glanced over at Kris, who was wandering in the foyer, apparently oblivious to the deafening tone. It was his idea to explore the new sanctuary and take a few photos, and now he had somehow tripped the security system. "I think we should probably leave," I called out to him, not one to want to get into any trouble ("I think the technical term is a 'goody-two-shoes,'" Kris wants you to know). But as we rounded the corner for the exit we ran into the security guard, shaking his head at us. Ever the stealthy researchers—"like flies on the wall," Kris says.

The previous day, this sanctuary was the setting for a lively worship service. From the fiery preaching of Dr. Raphael Warnock to the crescendoing choral anthem that brought the entire audience to its feet in response, a passion and earnestness for worship seemed to engulf the congregation. With a capacity of over 2,000 (full for two services most Sundays), the Horizon Sanctuary at Ebenezer Baptist Church in Atlanta was built in 1999 to accommodate the overflowing crowds of church members and weekly visitors to the home church of Dr. Martin Luther King Jr.—hence its moniker as "America's Freedom Church." Its airy interior, highlighted by windows at the pinnacle of the ceiling and along both sides, gave it a warm, welcoming feel, despite the imposing pulpit and large stage in the front, boasting a full choir, small orchestra, and interpretive dancers each Sunday morning.

Across Auburn Avenue, opposite this large modern cathedral, sits the old Ebenezer sanctuary, identified by a small, blue neon sign hanging from the brick exterior—one that looks more suited to a '50s diner than a church. Small and quaint, the sanctuary is lined with stained glass windows, reflecting colorful rays on the dark wooden pews and worn burgundy carpet. The simple pulpit stands on a raised altar. Though it looks rather solitary in front of the small choir loft, it boasts a tremendous history of speeches and sermons that sparked one of the most significant movements in American history. As we sat in one of the front pews in the empty worship space, the warm evening light streaming through the stained glass, we could imagine this room fifty years ago, brimming with people, heat, and energy, as Martin Luther King Jr. rose to deliver a sermon during the height of the civil rights struggle.

Like many other historically African American congregations, Ebenezer was founded during the Reconstruction era, by Rev. John Parker, a former slave. At this time many churches that had been integrated during slavery separated into black and white congregations, as white control felt threatened by the newfound freedom of former slaves. In order to maintain some degree of superiority, many church leaders dismissed their black congregants and left them to start their own churches. Ebenezer moved several times before arriving at its current location in 1922. Martin Luther King Sr. assumed the pastorate in 1931, and after nearly thirty years of service, in 1960 was joined by his son, Martin Luther King Jr. as copastor. Today Ebenezer features a socioeconomically and generationally diverse congregation—one relatively well-educated, but also with "homeless brothers in the choir," as one church leader noted.[1] Most members grew up in the Sweet Auburn neighborhood that surrounds the church, though the majority of members now commute in. Still, the congregation understands itself to be a "beacon" in the neighborhood, which results in a diverse and complex mission.

Our visit to Ebenezer would mark our final church visit of the project, and our first to a congregation composed primarily of members of another race. We expected this church to be the most politically active of those we visited, with a long and proud history of direct political engagement. While Kris could sense his views changing after encountering the work of many of these churches, he remained concerned about the formative power of

Christians aligning too closely with one political party. The stories of election night services, Barack Obama guest preaching, and voter registration in the lobby following worship services all made him uncomfortable with the direct political action he anticipated encountering here. Going into the trip, I shared some of his concerns; Kris had all but convinced me that churches working alongside political parties was bad news, and I hadn't yet seen an example of this kind of work that I could get behind.

A "STORY-FORMED" COMMUNITY

"And if 'ML' was not in the balcony when Daddy King [King Sr.] started preaching, he would send someone to get him, and wouldn't start until somebody found him."[2] One woman leaned back with laughter as she and two other longtime choir members at Ebenezer recounted stories of Martin Luther King Jr. during King Sr.'s long tenure as senior pastor. We had been guided to a small conference room in the old office building next to the former sanctuary. Sitting between giant portraits of Ebenezer's former pastors—A. D. Williams, Martin Luther King Sr., Martin Luther King Jr.—and framed newspaper clippings from the civil rights movement, we listened as three choir members (one a member since the 1930s) shared memories of the church's past. As we leaned in to hear them over the grinding sound of the window air conditioning unit, we began to gain a sense of this church's rich history.

Another choir member recalled how she joined the church after encountering Mrs. King Sr. at a fellowship dinner at the family home. "Her goal was to make sure if you joined, you were an active part of this church." Another remembered how Daddy King would give her a ride home from church every Sunday since her mother was working. "They pulled us in and nurtured us," she said. Worship pastor Tony McNeill explained that through worship, he tries to connect contemporary issues to the church's history. "It is important for those who are new, who don't know the history of this church, to experience it . . . to be connected to what's brought us this far."

At The Midnight Cry

That weekend, as we walked through the bright narthex in the new sanctuary, into the Sunday morning worship service—a few minutes late, of course—ushers clad in white gloves and black dresses and suits escorted us to our seats. Dancers, wearing white gowns and carrying white banners, surrounded the altar. The energy in the congregation grew steadily through several hymns and anthems, and by the time the musical guest had finished singing—"At the midnight cry, when Jesus comes again, we'll be going home!"—the congregation was on its feet, applauding ecstatically. Pastor Warnock delivered a sermon on letting go of your personal "baggage" and not hiding behind it like King Saul (1 Sam 10:17–24). Far from the overtly political message we had anticipated, this sermon sounded strangely similar to the personal, therapeutic themes we heard at Saddleback.

"Worship is the nerve center of the congregation," Warnock reflected to us later. "All that we do emerges from that moment when the people of God come together to bear witness to someone larger than ourselves, and to proclaim through preaching and in song the meaning of that reality, and God's claim upon our lives."[3] The church's mission emerges from its worship, he insisted. "The proclamation of the gospel itself is what calls the community of faith into being."

But this requires casting a balanced vision of ministry, Warnock said, upholding both the pastoral and prophetic dimensions of the church's life and mission. Often, he lamented, we find a natural bias in the American church towards individualism, prosperity, wellness, and upward mobility, a bias towards "an evangelical consciousness that emphasizes personal piety." But that is only half of its mission; worship is also meant to inspire prophetic social action. In fact, one sermon before the presidential election centered almost exclusively around social concerns and recollections of the community's long history of political involvement. But today's music and message emphasized the spiritual dimension, focusing on individual faith and growth.

One story highlights the way Warnock connects worship to the practical needs plaguing this local community. The Sweet Auburn and Old Fourth Ward neighborhoods that surround the church have been greatly affected by HIV over the last few decades, explained Jermaine McDonald, director of Christian Education until 2011. For years the conversation had pivoted around the sinful ways people contract HIV. Warnock committed to shifting the conversation toward combating the stigma of HIV/AIDS. To tangibly remove the stigma of the disease and frame it as a spiritual *and* social issue, Warnock began taking an HIV test from the pulpit every World AIDS Day Sunday. In addition, the church sets up HIV testing areas in the lobby, and all of the ministers commit to being tested each year. This infusion of social ministry into worship creates an environment in which "people don't bat an eye when the mood shifts from spiritual inward focus to social transformation."[4]

And while worship is the primary catalyst for social action and the primary means of connecting faith and justice, church classes offer a continuous way to develop and internalize the church's mission.[5] The church offers new-member and discipleship classes, and Wednesday night Bible study—with 300 to 500 people participating regularly. All of these deal with individual faith, says Associate Pastor Michael Wurtham. The new-member classes roll over into discipleship classes, breaking down the major tenets of faith (prayer life, Scripture reading, fellowship, stewardship, etc.). We were surprised to learn that a few years ago the congregation adopted Rick Warren's "40 Days of Purpose" program, connecting their mission to Saddleback's Purpose Driven model.[6] In fact, in 2010, Ebenezer invited Warren to speak at its annual Martin Luther King Day service, where he delivered a message on living "Purpose Driven."[7] Like Saddleback, the church is creating second- and third-level courses, and planning to launch small groups, Wurtham says. Both small groups and higher-level classes can meet the growing "need to redisciple those that have been in church for a while."

Classes help to integrate these two dimensions in the life of the congregation. A few years ago the teaching ministry decided to write their own curriculum in order to better contextualize their teaching and connect Scripture to the tangible needs of the neighborhood.[8] "Growing in your faith should push you into doing something in the community," Wurtham told us. "We tell our new-members class that it is fundamental to the Christian to serve." Discipleship requires a Christian to understand that loving God and loving neighbor go hand in hand. "Once people get here they can't help but connect [social activism] to their faith," explained Wurtham. "Dr. King wasn't able to do what he did without his faith." And while some people still struggle to make this connection, he claims, "it's our job to make sure they do."

Remembering Their Story

It was quickly apparent to us that the history of the civil rights struggle shapes the worship, culture, and mission of this church even today. Pastor A. D. Williams was instrumental in starting the first NAACP chapter and in establishing Booker T. Washington High, the first Atlanta high school for African Americans, in 1924. Martin Luther King Sr. encouraged African Americans to register to vote long before the 1960s. Martin Luther King Jr. emerged out of the "liberating culture" generated by these two men, noted Shannon Jones, pastor of community affairs. "We must always remember that this is the church he came from," he said. "We are built on the bones of King."[9]

This history is remembered weekly during the worship service and most explicitly during the annual Martin Luther King Day celebration. But in addition to forming the church's social justice activity, the living story of the civil rights movement also inspires personal faith in the congregation. The civil rights movement was a spiritual movement with social implications, not the other way around, Warnock claims.[10]

We expected Dr. King's legacy and the history of the civil rights movement to inform the practices and identity of Ebenezer—the "spiritual home of King" and "America's Freedom Church." But our conversations at Ebenezer also revealed a deep commitment to the biblical narrative that seemed more influential in the church's everyday practices and mission than any other church we visited. For Ebenezer, Scripture, like the civil rights movement, requires commitments to both devotional faith and social justice. The Bible does not separate the two—Isaiah reminds us that true fasting involves feeding the hungry and giving shelter to the homeless (Isa 58:6–7). Jesus healed the sick and fed the poor, and also proclaimed release from sin through his death and resurrection. The Bible is the vehicle for personal growth, for developing a deep faith in the salvation and presence of Jesus Christ, and for growing closer to God as Creator and Savior.

These two narratives are interlinked at Ebenezer; the stories of civil rights and Scripture work together to shape the contours and practices of the congregation. Ebenezer is a "story-formed community," to borrow a phrase from one of Kris's favorite theologians.[11] According to Warnock, these narratives form the congregation first through worship as they are recalled in Scripture readings, prayer, song, sermon, and commemorations of significant moments. Warnock as preacher serves as the storyteller of the community, the one charged with recalling and interpreting both "stories."[12] They are further developed through classes, and then manifested in pastoral and prophetic ways in the church ministries, missions activities, and political engagement.

These stories take on political significance for the church—not just by changing Jim Crow laws in the '60s, but by continuing to shape a people committed to justice and reconciliation through worship and missions. Ebenezer draws on both narratives to connect its spiritual life as a church-community to its commitment to love its neighbors.[13] This story-formed community continually reminds itself that it is bound to both King and kingdom. Piety and social transformation combine at Ebenezer to produce a clergy and a congregation committed to both, in ways we did not see at the other congregations we visited. Jermaine McDonald told us that he believes black churches may balance these better than white mainline churches because of the ways they integrate their own history with Scripture and tradition.

Most importantly, the church understands this dual commitment to be modeled on Jesus' life. McDonald explained that Jesus would go out and heal and preach and then retreat for his own inner, spiritual renewal "in order to do the work he was called to do." The pattern at Ebenezer is this: "Let's go empty ourselves and then get recharged, and then go empty ourselves again."

WE SHALL OVERCOME

"We thought about grandmother and granddad that night," Rev. Shannon Jones recalled as he described the election day Watch Night service held in 2008. "We thought about 'strange fruit,'[14] about folks hanging from trees. We thought about the invisible institution of slavery and we voted our conscience."[15] I (Kris) was living in Atlanta at the time, and I remembered walking toward the sanctuary that November night, when I began to hear singing, sounding faintly like the civil rights anthem "We Shall Overcome." When I turned the corner, I saw the flickering lights of candles held by a crowd of more than a thousand lining the walkway to the church doors. Excited conversations were drowned out by those singing along with the gospel choir inside, where two giant screens were set up displaying CNN's election coverage. Television cameras and lights overshadowed the candles everyone was holding. Soon, Rev. Al Sharpton and Pastor Warnock moved through the crowd and into the overcrowded sanctuary to begin the service.

Election Night

Rev. Shanan Jones walked hurriedly into the small conference room in the old office complex, a few minutes late for our scheduled interview. He apologized, explaining that he had been called out of the office to help a couple of church members who had been evicted from their apartment. "At Ebenezer," he said, "you can be in a planning meeting for an Obama event one minute and driving to an apartment the next minute pleading with them not to throw someone out!" As he recalled that election night service in 2008 and anticipated another one in just a few weeks as the 2012 election drew near—complete with a panel on black support of Obama's presidency—he told us that "Watch Nights" have been an ingredient in black religion since the days of slavery. The clandestine "hush harbor" worship gatherings of enslaved Africans continue today in the established churches of black communities.[16]

The black church formed out of necessity, Jones said. "It grew to show the world that there is a God who understood our oppression; the same God that fed the hungry." While blacks were not respected in society, they "could come into the black church, put on a suit, and be somebody. It was not *an* institution, it was the *only* institution we had." During segregation, while blacks were excluded from many social organizations and political activities, the church had to serve multiple roles—it was a forum not only for spirituality, but also fellowship, education, and politics.[17] It was the hub, the "lifeblood" of the community.[18] Its role as an institution expanded further than that of white churches out of necessity—there was no other place to go or organize. If African Americans were to accomplish anything, especially in the political arena, they had to turn to the only institution truly and completely theirs: the local church.[19] This developed the church into a community that took responsibility for its local neighborhood or city—both in terms of pastoral care and more systemic, even political, involvement. Community missions and political action are intertwined in the life and mission of the church, Jones said. "We are not just feeding—we are engaging."[20]

Community Outreach

"Ebenezer is about doing something, not just talking. You draw people into the church when they see that you're not just giving lipservice," worship director Tony McNeill told us. Ebenezer views itself as the pastor and care-taker of the Sweet Auburn community, engaging with the neighborhood through what it calls "community outreach." Most church leaders empha-sized that despite serving "multiple roles," Ebenezer is a *church* first, a com-munity of care and worship; political action is simply an extension of this primary identity. One of Dr. Warnock's first new programs when he arrived was not a political program, but a Bible study for local community youth.[21] In a community plagued by oppression, discrimination, poverty, drugs, and violence, most members need compassion before they need political action, Jones added.

Ebenezer hosts a Crisis Closet on Saturdays, providing free cloth-ing and public transportation vouchers, and offers free haircuts for local homeless men in a program it calls "Cutting through Crisis." The line often wraps around the block as the deacons fry fish for the guests. "We don't just hire barbers," said Jones, "we hire the absolute best barbers around and cut about 500 heads of hair each week." The idea is not to offer Band-Aid solutions, but to build relationships with their neighbors, to "begin to dig in and demonstrate that love."[22]

Each church organization—Sunday School classes, the choir, church musicians—has a person dedicated to organizing some sort of mission proj-ect in the community. Wurtham was making plans to lead the youth group in a sex trafficking symposium. They will partner with existing organiza-tions, "as opposed to reinventing the wheel." In a program called "Ishmael's Promise," deacons mentor first-time legal offenders for minor violations and help them secure jobs. The county court system agreed to include the program as part of an initiative to find alternative methods of dismissing charges against these youth. The youth must complete a financial literacy course, résumé writing program, and volunteer hours. A judge later ruled that this was an infringement of the separation of church and state, even though it was nonproselytizing, and no longer allows this to be an option for alternative service.[23]

According to church leaders, the congregation gets behind these ef-forts quickly. Ebenezer, a church of almost 4,000 members, operates with just three full-time ministers, four part-time associates, and a few semi-narian interns. The senior pastor and Board of Trustees make most major decisions; other pastors' ideas are always filtered through Warnock and he ultimately makes the final decision. The ministerial staff should always be listening to and in conversation with the congregation. The church is "leadership driven and membership inspired," claims McDonald.

Wurtham admits that the pastoral team couldn't lead a church of this size without congregational participation and, especially, an active deacon ministry. The church relies on a team of 40 to 50 deacons, men and women who serve lifelong tenures after being appointed. After participating in a year-long "catechism" process, deacons are spread out among all the ministries of the church and are responsible for providing "pastoral care" for every person in the church—every member is assigned a deacon. Every pastor we spoke to highlighted congregational participation. The key to making this participation effective, McDonald told us, is to be sure that people are working where they are best gifted: to have a local teacher consult on the teaching training, or a social worker help with the social services ministry. With so many gifted professionals in the church, he says the goal is "connecting what you do with your faith life."

"The Gospel Is Political"

While the pastoral role is primary, the missions activities of the church do not stop at pastoral care or "community outreach." They often lead to direct political activity. "It's in the DNA of the church," Wurtham told us. "We can't be Ebenezer and not fight for justice. We can't be Ebenezer and not try to transform the world." It is in the history and nature of this church to be actively engaged on both local and national levels.[24] "Ebenezer has a history of recognizing that the gospel is political. Making real changes in the real world is part of God's saving work," says Jason Myers, director of discipleship. "So the work of the church is always going to be political in addition to spiritual."

I (Kris) recalled that the Sunday morning before the 2008 election, for example, Warnock preached from Numbers 13:25–31, where the Hebrew spies come back from their venture into Canaan with dire news that the inhabitants are simply too large to fight. He likened this narrative to the story of African American struggles, claiming that when no other spy trusted God or thought victory was possible, Caleb exclaimed "Yes we can!"—an overt reference to Barack Obama's campaign slogan.[25] Now, four years later, and a few Sundays before Obama's reelection, a guest preacher made reference to Mitt Romney's "47 percent" gaffe.

The church is able to do some things that seem political, McDonald explained, "because we don't endorse." For example, Senator Barack Obama came to preach at Ebenezer the Sunday before Martin Luther King Day, in the heat of the presidential primaries in 2008. Warnock introduced the senator by saying, "This is Ebenezer. Giants have stood here, so we don't take this pulpit lightly. . . . All of you be proud that this brother can run, because of Dr. Martin Luther King." At the conclusion of the service, the entire congregation, Obama included, linked arms to sing "We Shall Overcome."[26] "We had to fight, bleed and die just to be able to vote," Warnock told the crowd. "Now we can select presidents. And now with credibility and intelligence and power, we can run for president."[27]

A few years later, Warnock preached an entire sermon on the universal health care bill prior to the congressional vote on Obamacare. "He took a biblical perspective on why we should support universal healthcare," McDonald told us. But he also addressed what you can do as an individual even without healthcare. McDonald concedes that this may have been too political for many in the congregation, though "this is a congregation in which many people could benefit from universal health care." McDonald noted a difference between defending policies and endorsing candidates. Warnock will often mention policies that he thinks align with the church's theological perspective—and this is not partisan, he contends.

Hearing about a presidential candidate in the pulpit made us uncomfortable, but church leaders insisted there was no conflict here, because they did not endorse him. When the church holds a political forum, they always invite representatives of both parties. Often only Democrats show up, but they always leave an empty chair to represent the missing party.[28] Repeatedly, church leaders told us that they "walk a fine line." It may not be a good idea to have a rally in the sanctuary to "turn Georgia blue," Shanan Jones joked with us, but they feel the freedom to talk from the pulpit about "voting your conscience." Still, church leaders believe the unity of the congregation is most important: "We recognize that we can step into political conversations, without being so overtly political that we turn people off or make people feel unwelcome." And they allow this to temper any partisan fervor, "because our ultimate goal is advancing the name of Christ."[29]

Political activity expands beyond the pulpit. As we left the church after worship, a few weeks before the election, we saw tables set up to register voters. When we asked church leaders about this, they said that the church does this every election cycle, setting up voter registration booths in the lobby for several weeks leading up to the election, and organizing a "Souls to the Polls" transportation program to enable people to vote. Jones also recalled the "Freedom Caravan," a bus caravan designed to carry displaced New Orleans residents back home to vote after Katrina. "We operated like a campaign. We created a war room to find people's precincts. . . . [It] took over a month to plan." Jones noted that many in the congregation became engaged in the process, with several church members taking time off of work to help out and make the trip. After a grand jury in Ferguson, Missouri chose not to indict a white officer who killed an unarmed black teenager, Attorney General Eric Holder chose Ebenezer as his first stop on a national tour on race and public safety in December 2014. The church hosted a town hall meeting led by Holder as well as an interfaith service.[30]

"The Empire Strikes Back"

The church understands its community outreach activities and its more directly political efforts to be integrated. They are both forms of community engagement, and are all in some sense "political," on a continuum. The church leaders want to focus on the neighborhood first, but sometimes an issue calls for deeper involvement to create systemic change, and at those times, "we are unapologetic about being involved."[31] They are equally willing to give out haircuts to the homeless, partner with nonprofits, *and* "march on the capital steps and work behind closed doors under the gold dome. All of those avenues are open to us."[32]

As the pastor for community affairs and public relations, Shanan Jones is on the leading edge of the church's political activity. He explained to us that sometimes the church can't help but seek political measures in order to fulfill its mission to its neighbors. "Our work is not just handing out a sandwich, but working to get the person who needs the sandwich a job," he said, "and working to fix the structural issues that put that person in that position in the first place. And that requires political action." He thinks it is a serious mistake when the church goes silent in the political arena, when it decides to "just to fix sandwiches and go under bridges." Leaning forward in his seat, he insisted, "When the city wants to make begging for a dollar a crime, it is our job to say, 'That is an unjust law,' but also to ask, 'Why are so many people homeless in the first place?'" In cases like this, he sees no problem with the church having a "lobby day," as long as it also works to investigate the underlying causes of injustice. If the church is to care for its neighbors, to work on behalf of the "least of these," then it is called to engage in the methods and processes that can bring about real change for those people. "What happens under the state dome affects the lives of people right outside our doors."

But there is an even deeper motivation at work here. "Jesus gave us the mandate," he said. With this, he recited the Luke 4 passage that we heard numerous times during our visit at Ebenezer—a de facto scriptural mission statement for the church: "The Spirit of the Lord is upon me, because he has anointed me to bring good news to the poor. He has sent me to proclaim release to the captives and recovery of sight to the blind, to let the oppressed go free, to proclaim the year of the Lord's favor'" (4:16–19). Here Jesus was talking about economics, society, and even politics, Jones says.

"But why exactly does this mandate call you to become involved in political activity, rather than simply seeking your own solutions to the problems of hunger and poverty (a la Saddleback)?" we asked him. He responded that Jesus himself was deeply political, so the church is called to be political as well. We often forget, he explained, that "our Lord was executed not in the temple, but by the state. There was something in his mouth that was deeply upsetting to Caesar, the self-proclaimed son of God. 'Wait a minute, a kingdom? What kingdom?' Something about him put him against the kingdoms of this world, something that was deeply political." We often act "as though Jesus just danced his way to the cross," Jones laughed. But no, "He was killed by the state. . . . It was 'the empire strikes back'; this notion that the reign of God is over against the empires of this world." When you look at the gospel in this way, to see that it speaks truth to power and calls the church to do the same, you begin to see that the church is inescapably political. "So at some point you might see a Senator Obama running for president standing in our pulpit. And then the next day you may see a letter for Obama asking, 'Where is the conversation about the poor?'" For Ebenezer, with a healthy and critical distance, politics is no more dangerous for the church than any other method of eliciting change, leaders insist.

"The gospel is inescapably political," Pastor Warnock added. "I think it requires you to take sides, where issues of justice and human dignity are concerned."[33] The problem is that in the American church issues of justice and peace have become marginal. "There's a theological problem at the root of our silence on so many issues," he said, "a truncated view of the gospel at the heart of American Protestantism." This idea that body and soul are separate, and that the church is called to care only for souls, is part of the agenda of the American slaveocracy, he told us, an ideological system that "puts the church on the side of the powers." It is his job every Sunday to preach a gospel that "pushes against that grain." That is why it is so important to integrate body and soul, spiritual and physical, personal and public, and in this, "the black church traditionally has been a corrective." To attend to the physical needs of the neighbor, he said, the church *must* employ political measures. "To the degree that churches are silent on the public policy issue, I think we actually advance the systems of inequality and injustice."

That is why Warnock decided to advocate for healthcare reform in a Sunday service, and even to flag that day as "Health Care Sunday." That is also why he came out against the death penalty, and lobbied diligently to save Troy Davis from wrongful execution, "as his pastor."[34]

It is important for the church to take stands, Warnock told us, because despite fashionable opinion, churches still have influence. "Churches can make a difference; we've seen it," he told us. "We do still live in a world where religion is influential." Especially for African Americans, the church is still the most influential institution and can offer a strong collective voice. And like Shanan Jones, Warnock thinks it is important to hold community outreach and social transformation in tension—they are tethered to one another, though still distinct.

Social transformation requires direct political action because, he insisted, there's a limit to what a church can achieve without using channels of public policy and government. The church's charity work with the poor can even become part of the problem, especially if churches only work through nongovernmental channels, because it allows churchgoers to feel good about their work without addressing systemic problems. Warnock observed, "To limit ourselves to charity . . . is to get just a piece of what we're called to do." He added with a serious tone, "It's to banish the church to small enclaves of activity rather than seeing the ways in which our public voice has to be heard on issues of public policy."

The Paradox of Politics

This trip afforded me an opportunity to introduce Sam to good Southern food—fried chicken, collard greens, sweet tea. He mercilessly ridicules the South for such cultural paragons as NASCAR, Carhartt pants, and (particularly hurtful) "Podunk" accents. I thought that my last chance to redeem the South in his mind would be through its food. During our stay in Atlanta we tried out a plethora of fried chicken joints, country "meat and potatoes" diners, and barbeque shacks. While I thought such exposure to southern delicacies might finally convert him—or at least expose him to the gospel of Southern charm—the only food he kept returning to were the free chocolate chip cookies in the hotel lobby, which he seized every time we went in or out.

During a culinary excursion to Mary Mac's, a famous Southern diner that serves dishes like hoppin' John and potlicker, we attempted to make sense of Ebenezer's political activity, and what we thought about it all.

Throughout our research visits, Sam always provided helpful counter-points, gently prodding me to consider other perspectives (and not always about theology): "Kris, you know it's dangerous to drive with flip-flops, right? Are you sure you want to wear a *t-shirt* to this interview? Do you know you hold your fork like an eight-year old?" You would think such kind-hearted corrections would get annoying. But usually, Sam's careful, reasoned thoughts temper my tendency toward rash judgments. This was especially true when it came to discussing church involvement in direct political activity.

I had never encountered a church as prominently political as Ebenezer. Their explicit political activism challenged me, and initially, made me uneasy. The church was unashamed about its political involvement. "I own the fact that what we do is political—I just think the gospel is," Warnock told us.

Reaching for another piece of cornbread before Sam could take them all, I told him that I worried about this on several levels. I understood Jesus to have inaugurated a new form of politics in the church, one that stood against the politics of this world. To me, this meant that churches should abstain from utilizing the political channels of the world to fulfill their mission. I worried about the potential of corruption, of churches allowing their allegiance to Christ to become superseded by commitment to nation or party, and their missions and ministries to be determined by partisan agendas. Electoral politics operates out of a separate set of values and com-mitments than does Christian faith, and their intermingling has produced disastrous results in the past. While many single out the religious right as *the* example of religion cuddling too closely with electoral politics, this is a risk for both conservative and liberal congregations. Becoming too aligned with earthly politics risks diluting the witness and mission of the church. "What it really comes down to," I told him, pausing dramatically for a sip of sweet tea, "is an issue of faithfulness." I argued that a church would struggle to remain faithful to its calling if involved too closely in electoral politics.

As Sam listened patiently to a speech he had suffered through many times before, he identified the issue that we both knew lay under the surface of our analysis. We had to recognize our own whiteness and attempt to understand how it affected (and limited) our research and our theology.

This church emerged from a time in which few social options were available to African Americans. The local church became more than a place of worship—it was the center of political life, out of necessity. Sam suggested that as two white people from churches laden with political privilege—and therefore the luxury of keeping a great distance between church and politics—we have a hard time understanding this context. Some of the concerns we have about politics in church—though certainly not all of them—may not be as relevant to black congregations. A church of a people enslaved or segregated until just fifty years ago would seem to face less temptation to develop an idolatrous patriotism for the state that oppressed them for so long. Perhaps my worry was not wrong, Sam told me, only misplaced.

But this still doesn't mean that anything goes in church life. There must be some limits on how far into electoral politics churches can venture without forfeiting elements of their particular vocation. Churches must seriously reflect on what criteria they will use to prudently discern faithful political activity from what is not (and I don't mean evaluating how far we can go without giving up tax-exempt status; concerns of legality should always be subordinated to concerns of faithfulness). Inviting a presidential candidate to the pulpit, for example, seems to go too far, in any context. It risks putting the church in the service of national politics or viewing the state as the only means to bring about social change, and therefore, losing a sense that God's politics is ultimate. But perhaps other direct political activities at Ebenezer like voter registration could be faithful representations of Christian witness during our "sojourn in this earthly city."

COLLABORATION AND COMPLEXITY

Atlanta is renowned for having the worst traffic of any southern city. The metropolitan area sprawls for miles, covering thirty-nine counties, with more than sixty streets named "Peachtree." With a less-than-optimal public transportation system (a justice issue occasionally taken up by Ebenezer, with some progress having been made), it can take hours to go a few miles.

This gave us ample time sitting in the car. Sam, who does not love '90s pop music, likes to maintain control of the playlist. Even though every now and then he says I may choose a song, the opportunity rarely seems to arrive—I have one job, driving, and it should take my full concentration, he reminds me. Despite his obsession with the band U2, and my impressive rendition of the Proclaimer's "I Would Walk 500 Miles," I've yet to get Sam to admit that 1990–1995 is the greatest period in music history (and he never will, he wants you to know).

Finally conquering the morning traffic rush into the city, we arrived for our visit to the new Martin Luther King, Sr. Community Resources Complex, completed in late fall of 2012 and home to the MLK Sr. Collaborative, a consortium of nonprofits partnering with Ebenezer to provide community resources. This building, adjacent to the Horizon Sanctuary, houses the new church offices, a cyber café, and the numerous partner organizations that make up Ebenezer's new collaborative.

The complex was inspired by its namesake, who took over leadership of Ebenezer in 1931 during the heart of the Great Depression. He was known for bringing people together to work with one another during this difficult time—and church leaders see the need for similar action in the surrounding neighborhood today.[35] Daddy King was more than a minister, one member told us—he was a pastor and shepherd: "If something is going on in your life, he is going to do what he can to makes sure it gets better."[36] From making phone calls to secure teaching jobs for church members to bailing members out of jail, Daddy King left a legacy of care and compassion for his church and neighborhood. Andrew Young, former mayor of Atlanta, civil right activist, and national leader, said King "ran a one-man service center" out of his office. "Now it takes this kind of collaboration just to keep up with his vision." According to Warnock, this collaborative is an extension of his legacy.

One-Stop Service

We walked through the front doors of the complex into the bright foyer. A rugged Bible and blue plaid suit and cane, possessions of Daddy King, were on display by the entrance. Dawn Brown, a lawyer by trade hired in 2012 to be the Collaborative's director and oversee the work in the Community Resources Complex, met us in the lobby. She said that this lobby would be used as a "triage" stage, where needs were assessed and clients were directed to the appropriate agency on the upper floors. A glass memorial under the staircase displayed the names of all the church members who helped fund the multimillion-dollar building.

Dawn took us upstairs and introduced us to Walter Jackson, the director of Operation Hope, one of the Collaborative Partners. The principal partners—one Catholic and the others secular—all offer different social services to the complex's clients, from foster care agencies to Operation Hope's work in financial education.[37] Each agency is part of what Ebenezer calls an "integrated service delivery" model for community engagement. In this model, the partners work in tandem to provide all the services a client family needs. Each of these families must meet certain criteria to qualify: they must be below the poverty line and have children, as well as be unempoyed or underemployed for six months. In addition to these families, the different partners will also have single-service clients who may need only job training, or disability benefits. The idea is "to be a one-stop," Dawn said.

Each partner service addresses community needs the church is already involved in. The integrated service delivery approach is innovative, according to Warnock, and he thinks this is a model that can and should be replicated by other churches. The model empowers families to make their own decisions about the care they receive. The idea is for families to come and say, "This is what we want. These are services we think we need, and we want you to help us get to that point." Dawn and her team will talk with each family about its goals in order to help them move toward self-sufficiency, home ownership, and constant employment with insurance, and will also discuss potential obstacles. "We want our services to reflect what the community is asking for."

Community Engagement

Listening to the neighborhood and allowing its voices to determine the services provided by the Collaborative is an integral part of this model. The first step was to determine whether there was a need for a collaborative resource center, or whether the church could meet community needs on its own by providing a referral service. Beginning ten years ago, Ebenezer conducted a study commissioned by the state to assess community services and needs. They discovered that many people in the neighborhood were forced into affordable and government housing—500 into one housing complex near the church.[38] Ebenezer used this information to initiate a series of meetings and surveys over three years, talking with the people in need of services, as well as community "stakeholders" like city councilors and employers. They hosted town hall meetings, attended neighborhood association meetings, and listened to those already doing work in the neighborhood. The primary needs that emerged from this process were job opportunities, financial services, entrepreneurship, and foster care services.[39]

As Dawn and Walter relayed the history of the Complex, they were happy to note that they "did not dictate to the community what it needed." Warnock determined that the neighborhood's needs were too large and complex for the church to handle on its own; they needed other organizations to locate in the neighborhood permanently. Ebenezer knew that it needed partners, and Warnock wanted to find outside organizations "who could see themselves in this vision," both to help fund the building and to contribute a greater scope of services.[40]

Dawn led us past some empty offices, soon to be filled by Catholic Charities. As we walked back toward the sanctuary, we stopped at the cyber café, complete with Macs and PCs. Central to the integrated services approach is a commitment to giving people the tools they need to take responsibility for themselves.[41] In fact, some community members have already started businesses after taking workshops at the Collaborative. According to Jackson, the most important role of the Collaborative is to offer hope to a community that had grown hopeless in its poverty. Being poor is not just about lacking financial resources, he said. As another has said, it is "a disabling frame of mind, a depressing of your spirit. When people get a taste of this Collaborative they will never be without hope and will never be poor again."[42]

While each Collaborative Partner has staff to run its own services, church members are integral to the functioning of the complex. The church sees this as an outgrowth of its community involvement. From monetary investments to a huge pool of volunteers—especially educators and administrators—many church members are involved in the work of the center. We asked church leaders about the almost exclusively local focus of their missions work. For Michael Wurtham, the Collaborative is a way the church attends to Jesus' command in Acts 1 to "take care of what is right around us," he said—to begin in Jerusalem and "*then* go to Judea, Samaria, and the ends of the earth."

We wound our way up to Dawn's office on the top floor. As we sat down around her desk sipping coffee, we asked her if the goal of the community center was to eventually influence public policy. She told us the idea is to focus on services first. Still, she thinks ultimately the Collaborative can do both: provide on-the-ground services and work to impact public policy through the solutions they find. "A lot of policy has been reactive rather than proactive," she explained, and the Collaborative could be a way to discover needs and come up with policy solutions faster. But they need to wait for data to come in before going to policy makers to document and measure the effectiveness of the services it delivers. They will not go to policy makers with problems, she said, but with workable solutions to these challenges. Material has to be presented empirically, tied to demonstrable results. "Then policy makers are more likely to listen." You can't translate the hopelessness of people into policy—their inability to envision their children going to college, or fear of lack of social security. But if you can give these families hope and show policy makers tangible results of services that actually work, "that's a much more dynamic argument for change and I think that will drive the policy."

Warnock echoed Dawn's vision for the complex. Much of what will happen here falls under the umbrella of outreach, he said, but it "bends towards social transformation." Citing Latin American liberation theologians who work alongside the poor, he lamented the fact that churches are comfortable running soup kitchens, but often uncomfortable asking the deeper question, "Why are people poor in the first place?" They often avoid confronting systemic inequality and raising issues of public policy. "That's where politics comes in," he said. "We do it all. If we can move the average credit score in this neighborhood by 100 points, that will achieve something a march will never achieve. It's got to be both-and, all of the above."

Strength in Partnership

After a long day of interviews, we decided to unwind at the Brick Store. This bar in downtown Decatur is reminiscent of a old British pub, with gothic chandeliers, a heavy wooden door like something out of *The Hobbit,* and of course, an abundance of brick. Kris, who is overly prone to dramatic superlatives—his favorite beer, top five Kevin Bacon movie roles, best song of the 1990s that is not "I Would Walk 500 Miles"—claims this as his favorite bar "in all of America." As we sat down at the horseshoe-shaped bar, Kris remembered that this was the first place he ran across Doug and Tony from Solomon's Porch, many years ago after a youth ministry conference (they were the token radical voices).

One of our questions after visiting the MLK Sr. Center was about churches partnering with secular organizations. Do these kinds of partnerships allow churches to remain faithful to the specificity of their calling and the integrity of their witness? This question emerged for us at several of the churches we visited, but featured most prominently at Ebenezer. Outside partnerships were more engrained into the political theology and even identity of the congregation and what it understood to be its mission in the community. All of the church's ministers told us there was no reluctance at Ebenezer to working with government groups or officials, and most often cited pragmatic reasons for partnering. "We recognize that we can't do it all by ourselves so we partner with these other groups that are doing it at a much larger level than we can," Shanan Jones told us. The church was using $70,000 out of its operating funds every year to meet people's emergency needs. This was simply unsustainable, and the needs in the neighborhood were not diminishing. This community center provided a way to meet needs beyond what they could do alone. Partnering allows them to have a greater impact; "two cords are stronger than one," Warnock quoted. The partners benefit from the legacy of the church and its existing networks, and the church benefits from the expertise the partners provide.

Most of all, the neighborhood benefits. "The Collaborative gives us an opportunity to increase our capacity to be a servant church in ways that we would not be able to if we were depending solely on our own resources," Warnock explained. This denotes an intentional blurring of any division between sacred and secular. Warnock's message to his congregation is always one of living missionally and collaborating with anyone with similar goals, even if they are not Christian. The only thing lost in partnering, he says, is the ability to proselytize. But this would not be the primary focus even if the church was doing these things all on its own, he said: "We seek to bear witness through service."

This seemed a bigger loss to us, however, than church leaders suggested. Aside from missing out on opportunities for direct evangelism, community mission efforts look differently when done with an evangelical end versus through purely secular means. As we have noted in previous chapters, the transformative impact of social justice efforts suffers when the name of Christ is left out. And while Ebenezer's leaders acknowledged this loss, Kris, especially, remained skeptical. The motivation for this work—for the sake of the kingdom—needs to be made explicit. It should emanate from and shape the work that is done. If ministry is to be a witness for the kingdom, then ministers should be able to give the reason for the hope they have. He also worried about government co-opting the church for its own ends—and the church opening itself up to this through partnerships. Churches must work diligently to avoid being used in the service of a secular agenda. This danger exists to varying degrees with organizations, and while most of the Collaborative Partners seem to be grounded in similar aims and methods, the church should remain judicious.

I thought Kris was still seduced by the lofty rhetoric at Saddleback, and envisioned a network of churches taking the lead in curing social ills, rather than the corrupting "powers and principalities" of the world. And while that had also appealed to me during my visit there, I was beginning to question whether that was really a feasible position for most congregations.

In the end, I reminded Kris, church leaders at Ebenezer offered a helpful counter to the more church-centric rhetoric we heard at Saddleback. They explained, rightly, that context matters. Some churches have the means to engage in socially transformative activities on their own, and can envision themselves changing the world without having to rely on non-church groups. "Based on our social location," McDonald explained, "we see that churches do not have the resources or funds to engage in the types of projects that Saddleback insists churches can do. We recognize that our role is to hold government and other agencies more accountable, so that people in our pews and neighborhood can get the care they need."[43] This vision of collaboration and partnership sees the Saddleback model as too idealistic. "We are a bit more realistic in knowing that the problem is too big for churches to handle alone," Jones had told us.[44] But that is not the only reason for the Collaborative. Warnock also cites a deeper theological reason. "We believe the church itself is a citizen in the community, and should find ways to cooperate [with others]." For Ebenezer, the Collaborative is a way for the community to engage as one citizen cooperating with other citizens, businesses, and government and nonprofit agencies.

LIVING THEIR STORY

After another long day of talking with church leaders, we met Rev. Warnock at the door to his spacious office. Young, vibrant, and bald, he wore jeans and wingtip shoes, along with square, clear-framed spectacles. He gave us both a swift, firm handshake, flashed a wide smile, and welcomed us to the new office building. The church offices are connected to the

Martin Luther King, Sr. Complex, and opened in the fall of 2012. He led us past the conference table and wrap-around desk to the lounge area with couches, a flat screen TV, mini-kitchen, and chessboard, next to an expansive window overlooking the sanctuary.

Warnock was called to pastor Ebenezer in 2005 at age 35, making him the youngest senior pastor in the church's history. A graduate of Morehouse College in Atlanta, one of the most prestigious historically black colleges and the alma mater of Martin Luther King Jr., Warnock earned his PhD in systematic theology at Union Seminary under the watch of James Cone, scholar, activist, and father of "black theology." He began his pastoral ministry serving in several prominent black congregations, including Abyssinian Baptist Church in New York City, where his hero Dietrich Bonhoeffer attended during his brief tenure in America. Warnock immediately displayed a sharp wit and sense of humor, blended with a scholarly astuteness.

Spiritual Formation and Social Transformation

Rev. Warnock had recently published his dissertation, *The Divided Mind of the Black Church*, and we began by asking how this project connected with his experience as a pastor. The premise of the book, he told us, is that "the black church needs . . . a deeper understanding of the relationship between the ministry of social activism, embodied in the civil rights movement, and the reality of a liberationist faith rooted not only in the black church's history but in Scripture.[45] Both are in the DNA of this place," he told us, but the church must still be intentional in cultivating a deep affinity between them. He said that he works to maintain a productive tension between activism and faith in the congregation.

This is reinforced in several ways, most obviously by reciting the church's mission statement at every worship service: "Ebenezer Baptist Church is an urban-based, global ministry dedicated to *individual growth and social transformation* through living in the message and carrying out the mission of Jesus Christ."[46] Both elements of the church's mission—the spiritual and social—are embedded in this vision, and this statement, he told us, informs all the ministries of the church. They are also both reflected in his preaching, by the Scriptures he chooses and messages he plans. "Ebenezer tries desperately to hold those two things together," McDonald had told us. "We are not talking about universal health care every Sunday. Some Sundays we are talking about getting yourself right with the Lord."

For Warnock, social justice proceeds from worship, but never leaves it behind. "Worship becomes the platform and rallying place where you frame and articulate, in light of the demands of the gospel, why we should show up and do this in the first place," he told us. Warnock's staff believes he is successful in integrating the social and personal: "He finds a way to preach from the newspaper and the Bible," Rev. Jones said. "He finds a way to take the ancient gospel and make it contemporary for the work of this church—economic issues, political issues, our role in society, our role in the community, our role in our families."

In some ways, Warnock explained, he would be unable to minister in any other way. Both elements are a part of his story: he grew up evangelical Baptist and then was exposed to liberationist theology at Union Seminary under Cone.

We asked how he thought the congregation was doing in linking both of these elements of its mission. He responded that he wants the congregation to be more intentional about discerning how to engage people in this "postmodern moment," how to engage in spiritual formation that takes people's intellect seriously and generates a mature faith. They need a piety that moves beyond spiritual platitudes and pushes against consumerist and narcissistic forces in our culture. He worries that the American church has adopted the "consumeristic orthodoxy" of American culture, and thinks that a strong connection between faith and social action is the only antidote.

"Then how do you keep these things connected in the life of the congregation?" we asked. Sitting back in his seat and cracking a wry smile, he replied, "Believe it or not, I find the Bible pretty helpful!" In Scripture you don't sense a disconnect between the spiritual and social ministry of Jesus, he reminded us; Jesus is talking about heaven one moment, healing a social outcast the next, and challenging the ruling authorities the next. They are all integrated into one vision. This is also engrained in the history of the black church, he said: "You cannot understand why King does what he does without understanding the depth of his faith and prayer life." Here Warnock, like others we interviewed, recalled the story of King's kitchen conversion moment. When faced with a moment of crisis during one of the darkest nights in the civil rights movement, sitting alone at his kitchen table, he felt God's comforting presence and promise never to leave him. This was a classic evangelical conversion moment, when "the individual soul reckons with the question of salvation," and when King's leadership in the civil rights movement received its most potent spiritual calling.[47]

155

The black church began with two sensibilities, Warnock said: protest *and* revivalistic piety.[48] This means, on the one hand, that politics emerges from piety, and churches "cannot afford to marginalize the importance of personal piety." Too often the church has done this, Warnock believes, "and to that extent it disconnects itself from the internal freedom evinced in black evangelical piety and celebrated in worship."[49] But on the other hand, he observes that the church, the most "prominent instrument of liberation within the African American community," has recently become a "conservative custodian of an uncritical evangelical piety that undermines the aims of liberation."[50] Most evangelical black churches focus on piety at the expense of social justice, leaving the call to prophetic social action to the scholars and activists of "black theology."[51] Churches are "burning up with piety and emotionalism" while those attending to social change operate outside the church structure. "The black church . . . embraced a bifurcated understanding of salvation that privileges individual souls, not seeing the redemption of black bodies and the transformation of the whole of society as central to its vocation as an instrument of God's salvation."[52] While the church had become merely a "dispenser of spiritual aspirins" to a community still marginalized and downtrodden by institutional racism and systemic poverty,[53] the legacy of King calls the church back to both the personal and social dimensions of salvation—to bring the reality of the church's social mission to the forefront and challenge the accommodationist view of many black churches.

The black church must be challenged to "more fully integrate its pietistic and protest dimensions into a more holistic understanding of what it means to truly be a prophetic church and a liberationist community," Warnock argues—one that sees authentic piety and social liberation as inextricably linked.[54] "It is not as if piety is one thing and social justice is another," he observed. "One proceeds from the other." He has heard from some of the congregation, especially young members, that they appreciate finding a place that connects with their everyday personal struggles but also refuses to ignore "issues that are screaming for a gospel response." In a solemn moment, he recalled the Trayvon Martin verdict coming in late on a Saturday night. He knew it meant he had to change his sermon for the next day. He could not preach the sermon he had already written; he had to address "the pain and angst around the implications of that verdict."

All of this means that churches are in need of a "politically engaged piety,"[55] one that does not uncouple the spiritual from the social, the personal from the public. The mission of liberation that emanates from the black church's history, Warnock insisted, must derive its motive, power, and validation from the church's piety.[56] For Warnock, the mission of the black church—or any politically minded congregation for that matter—cannot be reduced to the quest for political liberation. It must always remember that liberation starts with evangelistic piety, and "both are grounded in the 'living reality' of Jesus."[57]

Liberation and spiritual renewal must be tied together through the history of the black church's struggle for political liberation and testimony to the faithfulness of God along their journey. While Warnock specifically addresses the black church in his book, we saw the same sort of division in all kinds of churches across the country. As we looked back on our visits to all five congregations and our own personal experiences in many different churches, we recognized a tendency in most to identify with one dimension over the other. Most focus their attention either on saving souls and growing members in individual faith or on seeking to change the social order in a myriad of ways. Few churches achieve a balance of both, it seems, because few are able to theologically (and then practically) integrate these aspects of its mission.

Protest and Partnership

While the black church has a particular history and struggle that is not the story of more privileged congregations, we believe (and Warnock insists) that the mission of developing personal faith and transforming the world is the mission of all churches—of *the* church. And we believe that Ebenezer's example can apply to churches of every kind.

This integration happens best, we believe, when the church understands itself to be an inherently political community, as Ebenezer does. It is political through and through, from its ordinary worship practices—practices of piety—to its efforts to impact public policy. Only by considering a wide range of its practices to be political is it able to draw the formative connections between devotion to the King and work for the kingdom—and therefore to fully engage in both. Spiritual formation and social justice are mutually impactful because they are both politically formative. A community's worship forms it into a congregation prepared to go into the world and find creative ways to transform it. For example, recalling God's promise to call us "home" with a "midnight cry" forms people to trust in a hope beyond what this world can imagine. There is a sovereign power that deserves and requires our ultimate devotion because of God's faithfulness. And God's faithfulness demands a response from us here and now, in the time before the midnight cry, a response to bring this message of hope to those around us. And this is a message that requires a tangible, concrete hope. For Ebenezer, concrete hope necessitates political action.

These political practices operate on two levels, Warnock said, levels that resonate with the types of political practices we have outlined in this book. He distinguishes between a "reactionary, political over-againstness" in which a church reacts to a political stimulus through protesting or lobbying, and an "ontological over-againstness," which manifests itself in the preaching, singing, ordinary programs, and ministry of the church. This second category points to something deeper, and essential, in the soul of the faith community.

Yet, we also noticed an inherent tension in the way church leaders talked about engaging in the first type of politics. On one hand, they seemed to approach the issue like Kris did: the kingdom of God is set against the kingdoms of this world—it has an inherent "over-againstness," to use Warnock's term. Like Kris claims, the post-Constantinian Christian church has often slept too comfortably beside the ruling political powers. But we must remember the kingdoms of this world executed the Son of God and continue to oppress people all over the globe. Christians, therefore, need to embody a "principled restlessness, a conscientious malcontent" (to borrow phrasing from Dr. King). But on the other hand, Ebenezer also wants churches to work alongside the governments of this world, and partner in addressing and rectifying the social evils of our day. For Ebenezer, such partnerships are necessary to meet the needs of its neighborhood.

When we asked the church ministers about this tension—opposing *and* working with government—none gave us clear answers. The closest they came to reconciling this was by connecting the urgency of their work for justice—which, they claim, sometimes necessitates government involvement—with their allegiance to Christ. The rule of Christ the King is threatened by pervasive injustice, and the church should engage in *all means necessary* to stop it. "Oppression insults the sovereignty of God," Warnock said. "It's important for the church to speak out because every time we do so, we affirm that God and God alone is sovereign." This theological commitment permits the church to engage in earthly politics, to participate in the electoral process, because God is sovereign over both church and state. The church stands over against earthly governments, but can also participate in and with them because God's sovereignty rules over both the church and earthly governments.

With this tension in mind, one of our lingering questions about Ebenezer is whether it occasionally ventures too far in its political activity, overemphasizing the "reactionary, political over-againstness," and too closely aligning with individual candidates, parties, or specific policies. As one influential theologian has noted, all of electoral politics is "morally ambiguous."[58] Engaging in activities like inviting a candidate to preach or calling for a congregation to support a particular, and assuredly complex, legislative bill always risks undercutting the prophetic stance of "over-againstness" that Warnock envisions for the church. Still, despite these questions, we are always reminded of our own cultural position and recognize that Ebenezer frames these activities as part of a holistic, scripturally grounded ministry.

Striking this balance is not easy work. Any direct political action must be grounded in and accountable to the church's worship and faithfulness to Scripture. And while we worry about things like presidential candidates preaching and an overemphasis on voting as a Christian duty, we know that Warnock fully recognizes this difficulty: "It's a dance. And the danger is when you don't recognize the inherent tension." Dr. King challenged the state and challenged the laws, but was also willing to partner with elected officials to draft a bill. He fought for policy change one minute but talked about the importance of faith in the love of Christ the next. And the church today can do the same.

But this is only faithfully possible when the church operates with a deep sense of its own politics, a radical security in its ultimate allegiance. For Ebenezer, the church is political when it enters into the political realm through voting, lobbying, or appealing to public figures, but it is also political (and provides just as powerful a political witness) when it praises God as King and offers free haircuts to the homeless.

In practices like operating the Community Resource Center, in partnering with outside agencies to bring tangible changes that it could not accomplish on its own, the church offers a practice of politics that transcends the typical narrow vision of politics and draws others into the mission of God in the world. This means that a church must understand everything it does as politically formative—from reading Scripture to negotiating a partnership with the Department of Children and Family Services.

Warnock closes his book by arguing for the political engagement of the black church in a surprising place—with the story of his congregation's children's ministry. "The mission of the true church is to save bodies *and* souls," he writes. "The efforts to educate black children by church women such as Arenia Mallory, no less than the civil disobedience of Martin Luther King Jr., constitute a revolutionary act, bearing witness to 'the beloved community' and the coming reign of God."[59] Ebenezer considers its children's ministry to be political. The ordinary is political. Few opportunities arise for many neighborhood children to escape the poverty they see around them. Many paths seem to end up only in deeper oppression or even prison. In these circumstances, a literacy program in a neighborhood with a high dropout rate is a political act. Any way of empowering these little ones by giving them a voice in a world that seems set against them from the beginning is a political act. "Giving these kids self-esteem and sense of achievement, and opening their imaginations to vistas beyond their neighborhood," Warnock said, "that's political in that it has the potential to shake up the order of things." Like the early church shaking the social structure simply by meeting together and refusing to eat meat sacrificed to idols or joining the emperor's army, the church today, through practices as simple as children's ministry, can still "turn the world upside down" (Acts 17:6).

"And Called Its Name Ebenezer"

We identify Ebenezer's model of political engagement as *living their story*. By recalling in its liturgy, its decision-making meetings, and its local missions efforts the church's history of liberation and embeddedness in the political ministry of Jesus, Ebenezer allows these stories to form its way of being in the world. It is attuned to the deep dimensions of faith and spiritual growth, and it allows this faith and the worship it inspires to shape its concern for those on the margins.

In all this Ebenezer remains true to its name: "Ebenezer" was the name Israel gave to the stone of help they raised as a monument to God's faithfulness. Every time they passed by, Ebenezer called them to remembrance of God's faithfulness (1 Sam 7:12). Ebenezer marked Israel as a story-formed community, one shaped and guided by the remembrance of its past and its faith in God's work in the world.[60] As a congregation, Ebenezer Baptist Church does the same. Through its political practices it remembers its past—the deep struggle of the civil rights movement and the faithfulness of God expressed in the story of Scripture. It remembers its calling to follow Jesus' example in bringing good news to the poor and freedom to the oppressed. It integrates a commitment to growing in faith with its work to transform the social order, and allows both dimensions of its vocation to influence the other. Because it roots its mission efforts and political practices in its commitment to Scripture and discipleship, Ebenezer offers a faithful example for churches on the Left and the Right of when (and how) it is appropriate to engage in direct political activity.

While we have emphasized how Ebenezer draws from its own unique history to become this story-formed community, we do not believe that this approach to political engagement is confined to black or minority-culture churches. While some congregations may be unable to appeal to their own particular past, all Christian congregations can appeal to an ecumenical history of liberation, beginning with Scripture.

We believe several aspects of Ebenezer's political engagement can serve as examples for other congregations.

First, Ebenezer has a unique history that informs its current identity, worship, and missions. While not every congregation will have a history as distinguished as this church, we think that most congregations would benefit from recalling their own stories and allowing that to shape them and their practice. Sometimes this will mean acknowledging and confessing shortcomings or evils in your history—like racism—and using that reminder to chart a new path forward. Sometimes this will mean celebrating saints of days past or moments of profound grace. Practices of remembrance can help remind a congregation of who it is and, most importantly, whose it is.

Second, when Ebenezer began planning for community missions, it did not offer a predetermined solution, but listened to the local neighborhood inform it of its needs. Many churches would benefit from following this example of performing diligent research to discover what needs a community has and then fashioning missions and outreach programs around these needs. Practices of listening, like town hall meetings, can help churches be more faithful in their call to love their neighbor.

Third, while Ebenezer remains committed to strong political activism, this activism is thoroughly grounded in the call of Scripture. Ebenezer thinks through issues theologically before entering the political arena in advocacy of or opposition to policy issues, and continually checks to ensure that its activism remains within the political vision of Scripture.

Finally, Ebenezer recognizes the limits of its resources and finds partnerships to help it achieve its missional goals, while still retaining ownership of missions. This serves as a helpful example of the way a church can balance its own missions—with its particular Christian reasons and methods—while still incorporating others into God's kingdom work. Not every church has the resources to meet the needs around it, and Ebenezer offers a vision of faithful partnership with other Christian and non-Christian groups.

* * *

When we squeezed into the pew at the beginning of worship, the older gentleman next to me (Sam) introduced himself. Alexander—tall and balding and moving cautiously in his age—greeted us warmly. He pointed out his wife in the choir loft, and explained with a coy smile that they used to attend Rev. Warnock's church in Baltimore, and were overjoyed that Ebenezer had called him to Atlanta. He occasionally leaned over to talk to me during the service, grinning mischievously.

When the service was over, he asked where we were from and how long we were staying. It was clear we were visitors. The congregation that day included a few white families and young adults—including an all-white university group on a civil rights tour—but for the first time during any of our visits, we stuck out, and felt it. Wishing us well on our travels, he asked me if I had any friends in Atlanta. When I told him I had a few friends at Georgia Tech, he said, "Be sure to tell them about us. Invite them to come." He reached out to shake my hand. "We're not a black church—we're a church."

As I looked around at this historic congregation, "America's Freedom Church," I remembered Rev. Warnock's insistence that his church's mission of balancing spiritual growth and social transformation was the mission of all churches. When we first approached Ebenezer we had some reservations about their level of political activism. But as we joined the congregation spilling out from the sanctuary and into the world, a congregation that knew itself to be deeply political because the gospel is political, I looked over to see Kris nodding thoughtfully. We had both come a long way. What if the thing we had been worried about was actually the answer all along? What if a new way of doing politics was possible?

Conclusion
Kingdom Politics

THE WORST PART OF taking a class on St. Augustine's magnum opus, *The City of God*, was having to lug that 1300-page book back and forth from class. As Kris and I packed up our things to leave, I asked him what he thought about Augustine's concept of politics—our class topic that day. We were compiling thoughts for our budding research project, and the fourth-century church father who lived during both the Christianization and the decline of the Roman Empire seemed an obvious place to start.

Early in *The City of God*, Augustine outlines a Christian vision of politics that has influenced political philosophy ever since. Augustine broke from leading philosophers of antiquity by claiming that politics is not simply a common sense of justice or order. Politics cuts much closer to the core of humanity: humans are created with a desire to worship, and politics is a way of ordering that desire. For Augustine, a political community is not defined by its laws, but by what it worships. As we walked back from class, we began recalling moments in our lives that caused us to ponder the relationship between church and politics, and to suspect that some churches were worshiping the wrong thing! These were the questions that drove us to this project in the first place.

I (Sam) remembered sitting in church as a kid around July 4 while the band played the armed forces anthems. At the time it didn't strike me as something that might not belong in church. This was what church was supposed to be, right? I laughed as Kris recalled his teenaged self, dressed as a wounded soldier carrying the American flag to the altar during a youth group production at his small-town Baptist church, limping down the aisle in all his patriotic glory. It was not much different, he confessed, from his first Sunday as pastor of a rural North Carolina congregation—also around

July 4—when the worship leader played a video of religious quotes from former US Presidents scrolling to the tune of the national anthem in front of a waving American flag.

We now see in these stories the idolatrous linking of Christianity and patriotism, the baptism of American political interests into the Christian mission, and the muddling of American and Christian identities. Some churches go even farther, venturing boldly into the world of electoral politics. I recalled one sermon I heard at a nondenominational church during an election year, in which the pastor attempted to educate his congregants on the ballot issues and offer an "objective" approach to faithful political engagement (so far, so good). However, the sermons leaned heavily on moral issues typically associated with the religious right, and failed to mention reasons why Christians might have a stake in social programs and immigration reform.

Kris recalled his involvement with a progressive Christian religious freedom organization that worried over the Bush-era religious alliances (so far, so good). But rather than framing its concern theologically, the group grounded its mission—and even its name—in the US Constitution. While at the time I did not quite understand his reservation with this, I came to appreciate the dangers in churches grounding their political mission in the state or national politics rather than the gospel. Many scholars claim that Christians increasingly tend to articulate their positions on social issues in political rather than theological terms.[1] Any time Christians look to a secular political document as the basis for their work, it should raise questions of misdirected allegiance.

* * *

These initial thoughts and conversations, over two years before we began writing this conclusion, led us to identify politics as the problem. Like the voices behind the statistics we cited in chapter 1, we thought the church in America had become too political! But as we visited and got to know the five churches discussed in this book, our perspective began to change, and we realized that, like many churches, we were throwing the proverbial baby out with the bathwater. To make politics the problem only contributed to the divide between prophetic and pastoral congregations—those focused outwardly on changing the social order and those focused inwardly on personal faith and piety. We began to see that the problem is not politics itself, but the way churches understand what politics means.

An understanding of politics limited to action directed toward the state or political party—voting, lobbying, campaigning, preaching about political issues from the pulpit—leads churches to either retreat from this dangerous world into their own ethereal realm or march directly into it to the beat of a partisan drum. But another vision of politics is possible.

Understanding the inherently political character of the church integrates the prophetic and the pastoral within the church's God-given mission. Both worship and mission (faith and practice, pastoral care and social justice, personal and public, etc.) are political, so there is no inherent division between them. The rift in so many churches between social justice and "personal faith" was not caused by politics, but perhaps it could be bridged by a deeper understanding of the church's own political character—a politics oriented around allegiance to Christ as King and citizenship in his kingdom. In that sense, while politics is not the problem, it can be part of the solution.

We have made this claim often in this book, and have attempted to describe the political character of the churches we visited. Now, let's step back 2,000 years and think theologically about why the church is inherently political.

Why the Church is Political

Hungry and weary from forty days of fasting, Jesus stood on the pinnacle of a mountain (Luke 4:5–8; Matt 4:8–10). The devil showed him all the kingdoms of the earth below: "I will give you authority over all of these," the tempter promised, "if you will only worship me." Jesus, who began his ministry by announcing the inauguration of a new kingdom—God's kingdom—quickly refused the offer. Earthly kingdoms and authority and glory turned out to be no great temptation for Christ. But it is important to understand that here Jesus did not reject politics, but redefined it. He refused to accept politics on the devil's terms: the kind of politics that merely seeks to wield power over a nation, proclaimed by the Zealots in Jesus' day and accepted by most scholars, pundits, and even church leaders in ours.[2]

The Jewish Messiah, the one about whom the prophets foretold "the government will rest on his shoulders" (Isaiah 9:6, NASB) proclaimed a new form of politics. This government would not be a rival government to the rulers of this world; it would not take the same form or follow the same patterns. The politics of Jesus was not politics as usual. You see, Jesus was already King. He already had authority in his kingdom, over and against all the kingdoms of the world.

Jesus brought a new vision of politics. And the next three years of Jesus' ministry would begin to show just what this newly inaugurated kingdom, this new political imagination, would look like.[3]

At the end of his ministry, Jesus would be faced with another political question: "Are you King of the Jews?" The Roman governor Pilate attempted to uncover just what type of political threat this carpenter from Nazareth posed to the religious authorities and to the empire. Bound and beaten, Jesus responded the same way he had three years earlier, redefining politics: "My kingdom is not of this world" (John 18:33–37). Jesus' politics is not like the politics that perverts justice or limits itself to coercive action, that nails dissidents to a tree. His authority and his means of making change are not like the world's: "If my kingdom were of this world my servants would be fighting." The kingdom of God looks different from earthly kingdoms, but Jesus is still King: "It is for this purpose that I have come into the world."

From beginning to end, Jesus' ministry was about inaugurating a new kingdom, an alternative form of politics in the world. As N. T. Wright puts it, "Jesus' launch of the kingdom—God's worldwide sovereignty on earth as it is in heaven—is the central aim of his mission, the thing for which he lived and died and rose again."[4] This was a different sort of King, one who rules because he humbled himself unto death (Phil 2:5–11); who sits on his throne in the form of a Lamb that was sacrificed (Rev 5:6–7); who is proclaimed King while dying for the sake of the world (Mark 15:26). And this is a different sort of kingdom, one that belongs to the little children, to prostitutes, and tax collectors (Mark 10:14; Matt 18:3; Matt 21:31; Luke 18:16); it is not run by the rich and powerful (Matt 19:23; Mark 10:23; Luke 18:24–25), but belongs to the poor (Luke 6:20); it requires sacrifice and commitment, but also the posture of a servant: "the rulers in this world lord it over them . . . but not so with you" (Matt 20:25–26). This is a different form of politics.

And at its foundation, the church's political nature is rooted in the person of Jesus Christ. The church is a group of people who are ruled by another king (Acts 17:7). Jesus did not say to the Herods and Pilates and Caesars in power, "you can have your politics and I'll do something else more important."[5] Rather, he demonstrated that the way we do politics down here on earth was really screwed up (to use a theological phrase). As Reverends Warnock and Jones from Ebenezer contend, it was because Jesus' message and action were political that he was executed by the state. In fact, Jesus was such a formidable political figure that Pilate chose to release the Zealot insurrectionist Barabbas over him.[6] "Jesus is Lord" is therefore the ultimate political claim; it constitutes a challenge to present political powers and represents a new way of doing politics in the world.

In the same way, the church's beginning at Pentecost was politically charged (Acts 2:1–13). By speaking the language of people of other nationalities, ethnicities, and political identities at its very first gathering, the church became a body that crossed political lines.[7] The church's very foundation required political reconciliation between Jew and Gentile (Eph 2:14). From the beginning, the church has existed as a political reality. It began by "[upsetting] the particular ideological arrangements of nations, peoples, and corporations" at Pentecost, and is called to continue this political work.[8]

The political character of the church is proclaimed throughout the New Testament. In fact, the New Testament word for the gathered church is *ekklesia*, the same word used for the "assembly" of citizens in a city. The origin of the word we translate as *church* therefore implies citizenship, the cultivation of a common identity.[9] When this community of the "citizens of heaven" gathers in worship, it witnesses to a different form of political body, one that pledges allegiance to a heavenly King over all earthly rulers (Phil 3:20). Creating a new citizenship apart from (and within) worldly citizenship, reorienting our allegiance, and concluding with the creation of a new city (polis) when God's future finally recreates the world (Rev 21:1–5). The early Christian writers tell us over and over again that the church is a political body, a witness to a new kingdom. When the King arrived, the kingdom came with him.

We chose the terms *King* and *kingdom* to describe the divided dimensions of the church's mission because both terms communicate the political nature of the church. Personal devotion to Jesus as King is a fundamentally political response. Faith, spiritual growth, evangelism, personal devotion— all of these are political acts that witness to the new political reality we have been describing, and direct our allegiance away from earthly powers to the one "ruler of the kingdoms of the earth" (Rev 1:5).

Faith is always personal, but never private. And because faith is always public, worship is always public, and thus, *both* are political. King and kingdom, spiritual and social, pastoral and prophetic—these should never be separated in the life of the church. Understanding them as equal and unified elements of the deep political mission of the church is essential in keeping the church's attention directed at its King, while deeply involved in the earthly work of his kingdom.

How Churches are Political

As our focus shifted, we began to see the ways the congregations we visited were embodying this new form of politics. One church (Saddleback) attempted to avoid overt politics; another (Solomon's Porch) insisted on partisan neutrality; and still another (Ebenezer) wore its politics on its sleeve. Yet each congregation expressed an important, and unique, aspect of the political mission of the church that we highlight in this book. A quick review of a few of the core practices of each congregation (both negative and positive) will help illustrate. First, the negative.

The rhetoric we heard at Saddleback belies a narrow understanding of politics. In its worship services, Saddleback embodies a passive strand of church politics—it attempts to avoid anything political to protect its higher priority of evangelism, and introduces controversial issues only further down the Discipleship Funnel. The church distinguishes between worship and missions, understanding worship as having to do only with spiritual growth and evangelism, and limiting politics to the realm of its missions—a method also influenced, to some degree, by a partisan (libertarian) view of the role of government. At its surface this appears to be the partitioning of spiritual and social that we think is symptomatic of the typical American view of politics. First & Franklin also appeals to this narrow concept of politics, but adopts a more activist stance, despite their hesitancy to use the term *politics*. The repeated assertions of "deeds over words" by the congregants betrayed a stark separation—and hierarchy—of faith and public missions (despite the pastors' efforts, it seems). Its overt (and partisan) political activism appeared to be unmoored from a strong scriptural and theological foundation—activism for activism's sake. For both congregations, King and kingdom seemed to be divided.

Solomon's Porch, with an inward-focused, community-oriented approach to church, provides a unique case. Its theologically savvy church leaders perceive two strands of politics—the narrow sense of electoral action *and* a deeper sense of community formation that comes closer to the vision we advocate. However, its overarching commitment to unintentionality in its life together—along with Doug's (Lutheran) separation of church and politics into two divergent realms—seems to obstruct any effective cooperation between spiritual and social. Its hands-off approach to spiritual formation, coupled with its refusal to offer substantive theological or political guidance, undercuts true communal formation and severs the church from its historic and ecumenical tradition. By avoiding most controversial political issues, presenting both angles of political arguments, and understanding church and government as two polities that should not infiltrate or interfere with the other, the church transcends partisanship but falls short of its responsibility to shape the way its members think socially, morally, and politically. The church's commitment to King and kingdom seems to be hindered by a limited public witness and an overly detached approach to the community's faith development.

Prairie Street does recognize the deeply political character of the church. Its worship informs its commitment to its local community, and its leaders articulate its worship practices in political language. Worship practices deepen the faith of the congregation and lead to political action. But this church also helped us realize that understanding the political nature of worship and missions is not enough. For Prairie Street, faith and devotion inform missions but do not always accompany it out into public. Its public expression of faith relies heavily on indirect community engagement through nonchurch social service groups. The church risks falling into a type of spiritual sectarianism that fails to publicly articulate the reasons behind its actions, and thereby hinders its public witness. In that sense, the church remains committed to King and kingdom, but these two do not seem to infiltrate and shape the character of its public witness.

The good news is that the story does not end here. Each church also provides an important example of a new political imagination (sometimes despite itself), one that transcends a narrow vision of politics based on parties and policies, and points to the church as an inherently political body founded on the politics of the kingdom of God. In this way they offer examples of ways for churches to connect King and kingdom. They embody a vision of politics not marked by anxious avoidance or blind acceptance, but by ultimate allegiance to a common King and kingdom that unifies the church in pursuit of a common love and mission. Each church offers important political practices that point to this new political vision.

Saddleback's grand vision for global missions demonstrates a deep sense of the church's political vocation, even if they rarely talk about it this way. For this congregation, the church itself is a distinct political body— sometimes set against the state government and sometimes willing to partner with it, but always on the church's own theological terms. The church universal is God's instrument to change the world, to bring the kingdom to earth in its fullest, and this is nothing if not a deeply political understanding of its vocation. Saddleback is fully committed to King and kingdom, and offers a helpful counter to churches that tilt to one extreme or the other. Their commitment to the radical political mission of the church is the starting point for the vision of church that we suggest here. The church is God's "superpower," sent to bring God's healing and redemption to the world.

Solomon's Porch recognizes the deeply partisan culture of American society and works to transcend partisanship in its community. Whereas Saddleback fails to acknowledge the political dimensions of its practices, Solomon's Porch adds another layer to our developing vision of the church as a political body by infusing its church practices with political meaning— from the way communion is served to the dialogical sermon to the physical arrangement of its Gathering Room. As "church reimagined" it seeks to bring God's healing to those hurt by previous church experiences. Its flattened leadership structure and elimination of sacred/secular distinctions imbue the congregation with a democratic ethos that church leaders hope will impact the way their congregants interact with the world. The unique political fabric of the congregation offers an important witness to churches stuck in old patterns of hierarchy and unhealthy distance between leaders and members.

First & Franklin and Prairie Street both emphasize the works of the kingdom, and both understand that worship animates this work. At First & Franklin, practices like the passing of the peace and memorializing war victims are deeply political (even if church leaders don't like to talk about them that way). They suggest that there are ways apart from electoral politics to work for social transformation, within a church's ordinary practices. These two practices serve as examples of just the sort of ordinary activities that constitute Kingdom Politics. Prairie Street adds another layer to this working vision of the church political by demonstrating how worship practices can inspire faithful ventures into electoral politics. The congregation's practice of open-mic sharing time during worship, for example, generated a shared political mission to work for immigration reform. This practice both reorders the church's internal priorities—how does it best embrace its immigrant visitors?—and refocuses its missional efforts to advocate for immigration reform at a local and national level. It is important to note that this effort to change public policy only comes from first theologically wrestling with a social issue that emerged from the community's own worship. Prairie Street's activism emanates from its worship and witness to the church's political allegiance to Christ as its primary motivation for entering electoral politics.

Ebenezer offers what we consider to be the best example of a congregation witnessing to an alternative political imagination. It fuses its commitments to King and kingdom and allows both dimensions to inform its identity, mission, and political work. Many observers have noted the American church's difficulty in theologically articulating the reasons for the work that it does. But Ebenezer bucks this trend by grounding all of its public work in scriptural mandates and in the congregation's own missional history. Its commitment to spiritual formation undergirds its mission efforts and its involvement in electoral politics. It discerns the needs of its neighbors and responds in ways that are framed by a deep commitment to faith—even if this means partnering with nonchurch groups to accomplish its mission. This church demonstrates a way that congregations can faithfully act as political bodies, internally and externally, shaping the deepest commitments of its community and the ways it behaves publicly as an agent of change in the world.

Implications of the Church as Political

Our interactions with these churches helped us to identify three practical implications of the view of church and politics we have proposed. The first two deal with *when* the church can faithfully engage in the narrow political activity of entering electoral politics and partnering with non-Christian, even governmental, groups. The third is a more general implication about church practices.

1) Entering the Political Arena

Only when a church understands itself as deeply political (that even its ordinary practices of worship, education, decision-making, missions, and ministry are all politically formative) is it able to faithfully engage in the politics of the state. If political efforts are separated from its devotional practices, it risks doing social activism (on the Left or Right) for its own sake, and is not truly functioning as a church.

Bonhoeffer suggests that the church is "necessarily political," but in two senses. The "first political word" of the church is beyond party politics. Only once a church understands this "first word" can it ask if there ought to be a "second word." "It would always be necessary to ask," he writes, "whether it is really worthwhile risking the highly political substance of a church, which in its first word is beyond party politics, by entering in the second word into party politics." The church must examine its motives carefully when it enters party politics, he warns, because its very character is at risk; still, "the second word with all its consequences cannot be excluded as an ultimate possibility for the church."[10]

This sense of the church as political can help reform the way churches understand their mission. When a church begins to allow this vision of church as political to inform its practice, the primary question isn't, "is your church using partisan political channels?" The primary question becomes, "where does your allegiance lie? Is it with a particular cause, party, or nation—or with God and his kingdom?" If a church practice is motivated by allegiance to Christ and aligned with the objectives of the kingdom, the question of whether the church is using partisan political channels becomes secondary.

This point has two further implications:

First, for churches (on the Left and the Right) that are prone to align themselves too closely with a particular party or overemphasize a particular social or moral issue, recognizing the scope of the church's political mission might keep the church from a disordered allegiance to party or issue, and free them to engage more broadly. There is nothing inherently wrong, theologically, with church engagement in electoral political action as long as it is vested within a deep sense of the church as its own political body. If the church's God-given agenda lines up with the agenda of a worldly political body on a particular issue, then it may be appropriate to work together, though we doubt a major American political party platform would ever line up closely enough with the church's agenda to warrant unilateral support for that party.

And second, for churches that avoid talking about important social or moral issues for fear of being "too political," recognizing the deeply political character of *all* of the church's activity might help recast the act of taking a stand on controversial issues, not primarily as an act of allegiance to a party, but as an act of allegiance to the King. This means that the church's job is not to avoid issues that are controversial in the partisan political realm just because they are "political." The church's job is to align itself politically with the gospel and the kingdom of God. Some kingdom objectives will line up with objectives of politicians in the realm of partisan politics. When they do, churches may work alongside government, always keeping in mind that this is a horizontal partnership based on a common goal, not a vertical relationship of allegiance. When kingdom and partisan objectives do not align, the church must still act as a political body through the witness of its life together (like the countercultural witness of Solomon's Porch's governance structure or First & Franklin's passing of the peace).

This point signals a departure from our theological position entering into this project. We were initially concerned that entering into any electoral or narrow political activity—even one as minor as voter registration in the church—was too risky and could lead to mixed allegiance. But the faithful practices of these churches changed our minds—especially the ways that Prairie Street and Ebenezer grounded their political action in careful theological and scriptural reflection (and even then proceeded with due caution). This is still a dangerous business. We cannot reduce Christianity to political action and separate activism from the nourishing center of faith in Christ. The church cannot become a political action committee. Political action must always remain grounded in worship and Scripture. This keeps us "uprooted from our own experience," continually taking us back to the story and mission of God, and allowing that story to continually shape our mission.[11]

We must diligently remember that the meaning of faith is not found in its instrumental value for society. The church's job is not to try to fix all the world's problems through the channels of partisan political activity. The church must remember that its first task is to "call upon God," as Augustine reminds us.[12] But, a church that is radically secure in its identity as a political body with allegiance only to the King is free to engage controversial issues all over the political spectrum without being crippled by the fear of being pigeonholed as merely "conservative" or "liberal."

2) Partnering with outside Organizations

The church's witness requires not just acting from our spiritual center, but also *demonstrating* that we are doing so. Faith and devotion must not only *inform* missions, but also *accompany* them. Therefore, it is important to primarily work with people who share the reason for our work and not just the end goal. This does not exclude partnering with all "secular" groups, but it does mean we must carefully research the motives of these groups and ensure that such partnerships do not hinder the full expression of the church's mission. It may mean altering the method of that witness—from direct proselytizing to a more embodied form of witness—but it should never mean the elimination of that witness to the King.

Therefore churches, in order to fulfill their mission, should be careful about when, how, and with whom they enter into partnerships. Churches must work diligently to avoid being instrumentalized in the service of another agenda, or subsumed into some other project at odds with the gospel. We must avoid partnerships and alliances with groups or activities that could draw us away from the Kingship of Christ. We certainly would not want to rule out all cooperation, but only suggest that a church should be cautious and discriminating about its alliances, so that the allegiance of its members will not be compromised and it can remain faithful to its God-given mission in the world.

3) The Politics of Church Practices

In all this we must remember that all church practices are political. All practices—from the seating arrangement in worship to the youth group's mission trips—form our allegiance, and therefore churches need to be careful and intentional about everything they do. When the church fails to do this, it squanders the formative potential of its practices, and may even unintentionally form its members in harmful ways. Failure to think about all practices as political often causes the church to sever its worship practices (spiritual) from its work of social transformation (social/political). Understanding the inherently political character of the church, however, integrates worship and mission (faith and practice, pastoral care and social justice, personal and public, etc.) and proclaims them both as political. There is no inherent division between them.

A more careful intentionality about formative worship practices like confession, communion, baptism, singing, and sermon will help congregations to understand that even personal devotion to Jesus as King is a fundamentally political response. Piety is political. Faith is always personal, but never private. Spiritual growth, evangelism, personal devotion—all of these are political acts that witness to the new political reality we have been describing, and direct our allegiance away from earthly powers to the one "ruler of the kingdoms of the earth" (Rev 1:5). King and kingdom, spiritual and social, pastoral and prophetic—these should never be separated in the life of the church. Understanding them as equal and unified elements of the deep political mission of the church is essential in keeping the church's attention directed at its King, while deeply involved in the earthly work of his kingdom.

Thus, when the church understands itself to be political, it is better able to be faithful to the fullness of its God-given mission. The church's political task is to introduce the world, call the world, and witness before the world to the rule of Christ. It is not to bring about a new Christendom—to Christianize the social order or "take back America for Christ." It is to witness before the world that a new order is already here, and demonstrate the graceful character of this new world order.

Why "Kingdom Politics"?

We have chosen to frame our understanding of the political vocation of the church as "Kingdom Politics." *Kingdom* is the word Jesus used to describe the political character of God's new creation, and it tells us how the church is called to understand politics. First, "kingdom" implies a King, an absolute and unchallenged personal authority to which we owe all our allegiance. The kingdom is ruled not by just any king, but by the King of kings—Jesus, Lord over heaven and earth for all eternity, over every earthly power and physical reality, in every time and place. There is no parallel authority on earth with which he must share his subjects' allegiance; he is King over all. The global and historical church is united in its allegiance to this all-encompassing cosmic authority, who is worthy not only of obedience, but also of worship. The King is the object of both fear and love; and, as Augustine suggests, this love is what binds his subjects together as a political community that is not of this world (John 18:36). The character of a king affects the nature of his kingdom. The politics of this kingdom are oriented toward *shalom*—not simply because there *is* a king, but because of who the King is.

Second, a kingdom is a human political reality, earthly and physical. Its very existence affects the lives of its subjects in real, tangible ways. A kingdom is not merely an impersonal political structure; it is a community of people under a common political authority. It doesn't end at the boundary of the throne room; it shapes its subjects' experience of life in their homes and workplaces. Likewise, the kingdom is a physical reality in which God's will is done *on earth* as it is in heaven, not just in the church but in every corner of its territory. The church, which will one day "reign on the earth" with Jesus (Rev 5:10), is called to seek the welfare of the cities it finds itself in (Jer 29:7) until the day when the King finally makes all things new (Rev 21:5). Thus, Kingdom Politics is concerned both with ultimate allegiance to a heavenly King who is due worship and obedience, and also with the concrete reality of life in the kingdom on earth, the community of people who live under the authority of the King.

* * *

Epilogue

It was the coldest morning Atlanta had experienced in decades: digits were in the teens as we parked the car and began walking through the biting chill toward Ebenezer Baptist Church. For the first time in two years of church visits and interviews, we had actually shown up early! The Ebenezer staff, however, had decided to open late to avoid the cold, giving us a few hours to spare.

To pass the time and escape the polar vortex, we walked across the courtyard to the Martin Luther King National Historic Site. The church actually sits on government-owned property in the middle of the historic site—a strange territorial meshing of church and state. The Visitor Center houses an interactive exhibit chronicling the life of Dr. King, through his many famous speeches and numerous arrests. Several large photos depict King behind a pulpit, rallying a congregation to put its faith into action. Recently scholars have brought to light the Christian roots of the civil rights movement. What has often been construed as a secular political movement that utilized churches' influence for its legal ends was in fact a distinctly spiritual movement, founded on the deep faith of southern black churches. Christian faith gave rise to the movement and sustained its progress along the way.[13]

Dr. King often described the situation during segregation and the civil rights struggle as "darker than a thousand midnights." The exhibit featured images of marchers pushed back by fire hoses, attacked by dogs, singing the anthems and spirituals of the movement, beaten but resilient in the face of the dark midnight of Jim Crow. The task King and his followers faced required both a dedicated personal faith and a strong commitment to social change. His goal of a free and equal society was rooted in a concrete vision of the kingdom of God—and of the gospel. "The gospel of Jesus Christ," King once wrote, "is a two-way road. On the one side, it seeks to change the souls of men and thereby unite them with God; on the other, it seeks to change the environmental conditions of men so that the soul will have a chance after it is changed."[14] The gospel aims for both "justice and brother-hood," he said, "which is the Kingdom of God."[15]

The civil rights movement is one of the best examples of the church integrating its spiritual vocation with its calling to help bring the kingdom of God to earth—of committing to King and kingdom. Its political struggle is well documented, but it is important to remember that it also arose from a deep sense of politics within churches.

Professing ultimate allegiance to Christ as King over any earthly political allegiance frees us to be used as God's instruments of reconciliation, healing, and hope. This deep sense of politics, manifested by Dr. King and other civil rights leaders, emanates from many churches today: First & Franklin altering their worship practices to welcome the outcast; Solomon's Porch breaking down barriers between church and world; Prairie Street allowing worship practices to inspire acts of justice; Saddleback acting boldly as God's instrument of world change; and Ebenezer, humbly partnering with other organizations to bring hope to the poor. These churches demonstrate how our love for God compels us to take responsibility for our neighbor. As Bonhoeffer reminds us, the church is the church only when it exists for the sake of others.[16]

These models of political engagement represent a politics of hope in a world that often lacks it. They demonstrate the power of the church to change the world, one step at a time. They also point to a deep—and deeply political—devotion to the King of kings and Lord of lords (1 Tim 6:15, Rev 19:16). They require trust that everything has already been made subject to

Christ the King, though at present we do not yet see this reality (Heb 2:8)—injustice, poverty, and spiritual hunger are all around us, and the political solutions available to us are so often morally ambiguous. Still, Scripture calls us to remember that despite it all, "we do see Jesus, crowned with glory and honor" (Heb 2:9). The King is on his throne, calling us to help make his kingdom a reality on earth. "The most inspiring word that the church may speak," Dr. King preached, "is that no midnight long remains. The weary traveler by midnight who asks for bread is really seeking the dawn. Our eternal message of hope is that dawn will come."[17]

Acknowledgments

AFTER VERY NEARLY FAILING to get off the ground, this project was rescued by a generous grant from the Project on Lived Theology—and then several more as it expanded from a single article into a book manuscript. Charles Marsh's faith in and generosity toward us has been remarkable, and these few lines will never be enough to thank him. We feel honored that an organization as innovative and respected as the PLT would sponsor two students to travel the country to talk with people about the infamous "conversation stoppers" of religion and politics. Charles, we are beyond grateful.

This project was completely dependent on churches generously allowing us to intrude their space, occupy their time, and then reveal our observations and contingent judgments in print. We are deeply grateful to each of these five congregations and the outstanding folks who minister in them—both for their hospitality, and for everything they taught us along the way. Our theologies have been more formed by the experience of engaging with what churches are doing on the ground than by any of our purely academic research—which speaks to the genius of the lived theology method. And so our biggest thanks goes to the folks at Saddleback, Solomon's Porch, First & Franklin, Prairie Street, and Ebenezer for welcoming us, for hosting and feeding us, for taking the time to talk with us, and most of all, for teaching us what it means to be the church.

Of course, we are also indebted to the great people at Cascade, especially our editor Rodney Clapp. Cascade took a chance on an odd little book proposal from two nobodies, and Rodney and his team worked diligently to make our dream a reality. We are grateful for their dedication and hard work. Also, this book would have never been possible without the keen eyes and sharp minds of Guy Speers and Ashleigh Elser, who read and commented on every single page of the manuscript. We cannot imagine how many hours they spent on this project for us—they are certainly the best pro bono editors we could ever ask for. We owe each of them a debt that not even a bottle of Quarter Cask or a sketchy salmon dinner could repay (sorry, Ash).

This was a thoroughly collaborative project—not only because it was cowritten, but also because of the many conversations we had with friends and colleagues during the writing and editing process. We are so grateful to everyone who read chapters and gave feedback, or were part of the many conversations that shaped our thoughts and words, including Chuck Mathewes, Paul Jones, Luke Bretherton, John Shelton, Paul Gleason, Nathan Walton, Charlene Brown, Mike McCurry, Ron Speers, Tim Hartman, Sabrina Slater, Amy Canosa, Christina McRorie, and Joe Lenow. The feedback we received at presentations of portions of this material was also extremely helpful, especially those at the Project on Lived Theology presentation in 2013, the TEC Dissertation Group at UVA, AAR/SBL 2014, and the 2014 NCSS Seminar at Wesley Theological Seminary.

So many logistical matters contributed to the success of this project. We are especially grateful to Guy and Susan Speers for great conversations over home-cooked meals and early-morning rides to the airport. I (Kris) am so thankful for Sam, who never once drove on our trips but provided all kinds of helpful driving advice. We also want to thank DoubleTree Hotels for their free chocolate chip cookies, and Laphroaig for providing the motivation to finish the manuscript by our deadline.

Finally, neither of us knew each other very well before we began this project. But through long drives, theological reflections, debates, arguments, revelations, cones of ice cream, and pints of beer, we forged both a research partnership and a friendship. And in hindsight, this project was as much a training in friendship as an adventure in theology. As Stanley Hauerwas says, "We literally cannot do good without our friends, not simply because we need friends to do good for, but because the self-knowledge necessary to be good comes from seeing ourselves through our friendships."

I (Sam) am thankful to Kris for being a wise counselor, a patient sounding board, a diligent colaborer, an adventurous traveling partner, a formidable opponent, a sharpening iron, and a loyal friend. His sharp insights and deep convictions about the church and the Christian life have been formative, challenging, and enriching, and I mean it when I say that I never could have done this project without him.

Over the last four years, Sam has taught me (Kris) a great deal about what it means to be a friend. And while his contributions to this project are manifold—expert precision in writing and reflective thought, help in correcting my tendencies toward wordiness (and series of threes), and his diligence until the end despite the many deadlines that accompany finishing college—I am most thankful to him for that.

P. S. If the person who stole our laptops, phones, and DVD of *Almost Famous* ever happens to read this, we'd still like our stuff back.

Notes

CHAPTER 1: FOR KING AND KINGDOM

1. Evangelical theologian Scot McKnight diagnoses a similar problem in his book *Kingdom Conspiracy: Returning to the Radical Mission of the Local Church* (Grand Rapids: Brazos, 2014). He humorously identifies this tension generationally in terms of two senses of the kingdom of God: the social justice agenda of the "Skinny Jeans Kingdom" and emphasis on personal salvation of the "Pleated Pants Kingdom." Like us, he suggests true kingdom work both integrates and transcends both of these visions. Many scholars, practitioners, and theologians have observed similar tendencies in churches, such as N. T. Wright, as we discuss in a note below. Raphael Warnock identifies a similar divided mission in African American congregations between personal piety and social transformation in his book *The Divided Mind of the Black Church: Theology, Piety, and Public Witness* (New York: New York University Press, 2013). We will address Warnock's assessment more directly in chapter 6. Beyond such clear diagnoses, both theologians offer intriguing proposals for ways that the church should correct for this mistake. Our book moves in a slightly different direction by investigating the political roots and implications of this problem and takes a more ground-level constructive approach by analyzing what churches are actually doing to integrate the social and personal elements of the gospel (see the section "Our Approach").

2. One of the clearest articulations of this ecclesial division is offered by N. T. Wright in *How God Became King: The Forgotten Story of the Gospels* (New York: HarperOne, 2012). He labels these two types of churches/Christians as "kingdom Christians" and "cross Christians," one group with a social gospel agenda, the other with a saving-souls-for-heaven agenda (159). Framing this as a New Testament scholar, he writes that most Christians tend to highlight one element or the other: "whether the kingdom, to validate a contemporary social agenda (and to leave a question mark as to why the cross mattered at all), or the cross, to emphasize the mechanism by which God rescues sinners from this world and enables them to go to 'heaven' (leaving a question mark as to why either Jesus or the evangelists would think it mattered that much to do all those healings, to walk on water, or to give such a remarkable teaching)" (176).

3. Robert Putnam and David Campbell, *American Grace: How Religion Divides and Unites Us* (New York: Simon & Schuster, 2012), 442.

4. David Kinnaman and Gabe Lyons, *UnChristian: What a New Generation Really*

Thinks About Christianity . . . And Why It Matters (Grand Rapids: Baker, 2007), 155.

5. Paul A. Djupe and Brian R. Calfano, "The Deliberative Pulpit? The Democratic Norms and Practices of the PCUSA," *Journal for the Scientific Study of Religion* 51:1 (2012) 97.

6. See Robert Putnam and David Campbell, *American Grace,* 121, and Peter Beinart, "The End of American Exceptionalism," *National Journal,* February 1, 2014, 19.

7. Putnam and Campbell, *American Grace,* 121.

8. Ibid., 419.

9. James D. Hunter, *To Change the World: The Irony, Tragedy, and Possibility of Christianity in the Late Modern World* (Oxford: Oxford University Press, 2010), 103.

10. Ibid.,12.

11. The lingering effects of this limited notion of politics truncate the theopolitical imaginations of church leaders, and they tend to either align their political practices with the political Left or Right or withdraw into their own ethereal realm. However, "In the church's view," argue Stanley Hauerwas and Will Willimon, "the political left is not noticeably more interesting than the political right; both sides tend toward solutions that act as if the world has not ended and begun in Jesus. These 'solutions' are only mirror images of the status quo" (*Resident Aliens: Life in the Christian Colony* [Nashville: Abingdon, 1989], 28).

12. In addressing why believers do not engage politically, Charles Mathewes writes, "The only models for faithful engagement they see are much too tightly tied to immanent political agendas, and so they hesitate to engage their faith in civic life" (*A Theology of Public Life* [Cambridge: Cambridge University Press, 2008], 5–6).

13. Hunter, *To Change the World,* 185, 186.

14. James K. A. Smith, *Desiring the Kingdom: Worship, Worldview, and Cultural Formation* (Grand Rapids: Baker, 2009).

15. N. T. Wright, *After You Believe: Why Christian Character Matters* (New York: HarperOne, 2012), 259.

16. Michael Gerson and Peter Wehner, *City of Man: Religion and Politics in a New Era* (Chicago: Moody, 2010), 72.

17. If it is not apparent by now, we agree with Mennonite theologian John Howard Yoder, who claims, "The Christian community, like any community held together by commitment to important values, is a political reality"; he explains, "The church has the character of a *polis* (the Greek word from which we get the adjective political), namely, a structured social body" (*Body Politics* [Scottsdale, PA: Herald, 2001], viii).

18. This conception of politics is formulated from a combination of the political concepts of anthropologist Saba Mahmood and theologian John Howard Yoder. Mahmood outlines two ways communities can be political in a deep sense. One, these communities engage in practices that form their communal identity, direct their behavior and goals, shape their communal decisions, and demonstrate their distinctive way of life. As such, their witness affects cultural and social transformation from the ground up. Two, these communities are political in that they constitute an alternative to the nation-state by

submitting to an alternative law or ruler (*The Politics of Piety* [Princeton, NJ: Princeton University Press, 2011], 47–48). Likewise, Yoder claims that politics involves visible markers, including: 1) a distinctive way of making decisions, 2) a procedure for defining and circumscribing its membership, and 3) a mission to carry out common tasks in the world. For Yoder, this "makes the Christian community a political entity in the simplest meaning of the term" (*Body Politics*, viii). While this may seem like a nuanced or even esoteric understanding of politics, in many ways this is nothing more than the ancient and basic definition of politics offered by Aristotle—that of free "men" deliberating about how to order their life together.

19. For a good anthropological account of this in the Muslim context, see Mahmood, *The Politics of Piety.*

20. The limits are evident within the plethora of sociological and political theory accounts of church and politics. One of the most recent, and representative, members of this corpus is Putnam and Campbell's *American Grace.* While they begin by acknowledging the growing interchange between religion and politics in America, the gradual chipping away at the infamous "wall of separation," their way of framing the issue—"Religiosity has partisan overtones now that it did not have in the past" (369)—betrays the limits of their study. The notion that the key indicator of religion's role in politics is the degree of partisan overtones it now carries demonstrates a view of politics based on party affiliation and activity. This sets the tone for the rest of the study. Claims about the connection between religion and politics are limited to religion's interaction with America's two major political parties, leading to the conclusion that "there is simply not much overt politics at church" (442). Though they concede that many ecclesial teachings "resonate politically" (419), by this the authors mean only that they have a measurable impact on a churchgoer's partisan identification. By following their predecessors and focusing primarily on "overt politicking over America's pulpits" (ibid.), the authors overlook other potential politically formative practices of the church such as group meetings, mission trips, shared meals, baptism, evangelism, confession, counseling, communal worship, and Bible study. They concede, "this hardly means that nothing of political import happens at church" (442), yet cite only subtly political sermons and self-reinforcing religious social networks as sources of this politically relevant activity.

To cite another example, Mark Chaves, in his influential *Congregations in America,* concludes that "Politics remains, for most congregations, a peripheral activity" (95). He is able to make this conclusion by limiting politics to empirical activity measurable in polls: a church 1) informed those in a worship service about opportunities for political activity, 2) distributed a voter guide, 3) distributed a Christian right voter guide, 4) organized voter registration, 5) held a meeting or event to discuss politics, 6) held a meeting or event to participate in a political demonstration, 7) held a meeting or event to lobby elected officials, 8) invited an elected government official as a guest speaker, 9) invited a political candidate as a guest speaker. His research indicated that 58 percent of congregations did not participate in any of these nine activities (*Congregations in America* [Cambridge, MA: Harvard University Press, 2004], 108).

Even a scholar as attuned to the dynamics of church and politics as James Hunter conforms to this tendency. In his critique of the politicization of Christianity, he claims that the politicization of Christianity has delimited the imagination and practice of the church, confining it largely to seeking political solutions for society's ills and rendering political action as its primary means of world engagement (*To Change the World*, 185–86). And while this critique aligns closely with our assessment, his solution subscribes to the same limited notion of the political as his sociological colleagues. He calls for the church to "decouple the public from the political" (186), taking political in the more narrowly circumscribed terms described above.

In the end, it seems that all of these scholars follow the lead of Max Weber, the architect of sociology, who considered politics "the leadership, or exercise of influence on the leadership, of a political organization, hence today, of a state" ("Politics as Vocation," in *The Vocation Lectures*, David Owen and Tracy B. Strong, eds. [Indianapolis: Hackett, 2004], 32–33). Confining politics to issues having to do directly with public policy and the state, he concludes, "Hence, 'politics' for us means striving to share power or striving to influence the distribution of power, either among states or among groups within a state" (78). Politics is inherently coercive or competitive activity having to do with power and domination. It is oriented only toward state power and the ability to influence the distribution of this power—public and legislative policy.

21. We believe that research into and reflection on the relationship of churches and politics of a theological nature (as opposed to empirically based research methods) can illuminate a deeper conception of politics hopefully at work in many congregations, and highlight important practices to serve as examples for other local churches. We believe this is especially true when folks pay attention to the actual practices and self-understanding of actual local churches. Paraphrasing Don Browning, Christian theology opens up a world where grace and transformation are possible. Because of this higher purpose, it may be better suited to detect both the pitfalls and the transformative potential of church practices (Don S. Browning, "Congregational Studies as Practical Theology," in *American Congregations* vol. 2, edited by James P. Wind and James W. Lewis [Chicago: University of Chicago Press, 1994], 206).

22. Friedrich Schleiermacher claims that in order to exert any deliberative theological influence, one must appraise the actual condition of the church at that time: "The tasks of any person who is to exert influence of a genuinely deliberative character arise out of the way in which one appraises the actual condition of the church at the present time, according to one's conception of the nature of both Christianity and of one's own particular church community" (Schleiermacher, *Brief Outline of Theology as a Field of Study*, 3rd ed. [Louisville: Westminster John Knox Press, 2011], 97–98).

23. Quote taken from a draft of Marsh's "Introduction" to a new volume on lived theology methodology, Sarah Azransky et al., eds., *Lived Theology: New Perspectives on Method, Style and Pedagogy in Theological and Religious Studies* (forthcoming). Marsh describes the three primary concerns of the lived theological method as: 1), keeping narrative space open to the actions of God in experience; 2) understanding the dynamism of theological convictions, the play of doctrinal and confessional commitments—views on Christology, the Trinity, the church, etc.—in lived experience; and 3) clarifying the social consequences of theological ideas in ways that help Christians (and for somewhat different reasons, all people of faith) more truthfully communicate and embody the good news of the risen and saving Christ.

24. In "Coming to Judgment: Methodological Reflections on the Relationship Between Ecclesiology, Ethnography and Political Theory," Luke Bretherton encourages theologians "to generate theological and political conceptualisations fully alive to the

dialectical relation between them and their epistemological inter-dependence" (*Modern Theology* 28:2, April 2012, 173). In order to do this effectively, he claims that empirical, ethnographic-type research must make a normative turn and "offer not simply interpretation, but judgments leading to better action" (169).

25. Schleiermacher, *Brief Outline*, 41.

26. For much of what follows in this section, we draw heavily on James K. A. Smith, *Desiring the Kingdom: Worship, Worldview and Cultural Formation* (Grand Rapids: Baker, 2009), 46–63.

27. "Attention to practices is helpful because it makes a way of life, which is a very big thing, more visible and more open to engagement, criticism, and transformation. Noticing, understanding, and living specific practices require us to see and do things that are of immense importance to the way of life in and for the world to which people of faith are called" (Dorothy C. Bass and Susan R. Briehl, eds., *On Our Way: Christian Practices for Living a Whole Life* [Nashville: Upper Room, 2010], 10).

28. The preeminent conception of practices belongs to Alasdair MacIntyre, from *After Virtue: A Study in Moral Theory*, 2nd ed. (Notre Dame, IN: University of Notre Dame Press, 1984), 175: "By practice I . . . mean any coherent and complex form of socially established cooperative human activity through which goods internal to that form of activity are realised in the course of trying to achieve those standards of excellence which are appropriate to, and partially definitive of, that form of activity, with the results that human powers to achieve excellence, and human conceptions of the ends and goods involved, are systematically extended." Smith points to another definition of "practice" that allows for the goods of a practice to be external to the practice itself, rather than only internal like MacIntyre (*Desiring the Kingdom*, 80–83). This is more promising for our argument about how these practices are politically formative, both within the church community and in its relationships with those outside. Theologically, we have to believe that the goods of these practices may be felt beyond the practice itself—and perhaps beyond the Christian community itself—in ways unforeseen.

Offering a definition more specifically oriented toward Christian practices, theologians Dorothy Bass and Miroslav Volf suggest: "Christian practices are patterns of cooperative human activity in and through which life together takes shape over time in response to and in God as known in Jesus Christ" (*Practicing Theology: Beliefs and Practices in Christian Life* [Grand Rapids: Eerdmans, 2011], 3). These practices form a way of life that orients believers toward a distinctive end or love, or in John Howard Yoder's words, they form "believers who for Jesus' sake do ordinary social things differently" (*Body Politics*, 75).

29. This entails a different anthropology that understands the human not as an unsituated, autonomous subject who maneuvers through life by her own free and rational choices. Rather, a human acts on a deeper level through her desires, which are conditioned and formed by regular practices within a particular social location and relationships.

30. "The Christian community carries on its life through certain 'practices' that are constitutive of the shape of its life together in the world. When a community is participating in the practices of Christianity, 'an environment is created in which people come to know the presence of God and experience new being in the world. . . . By active

participation in practices that are central to the historical life of the community of faith, we place ourselves in the kind of situation in which God accomplishes the work of grace" (Dorothy C. Bass, "Congregations and the Bearing of Traditions," in *American Congregations* vol. 2, edited by James P. Wind and James W. Lewis [Chicago: University of Chicago Press, 1994], 178).

31. For an analytical history of this shift toward attending to practices as formative and constitutive of identity, see Manuel A. Vasquez, *More Than Belief: A Materialist Theory of Religion* (Oxford: Oxford University Press, 2010), 211–60.

32. Arguing against the established concept of a "people" as a community bound by only justice, Augustine claims that "a 'people' is an assembled multitude of rational creatures bound together by a common agreement as to the objects of their loves. In this case, if we are to discover the character of any people, we have only to examine what it loves" (*City of God,* edited by R. W. Dyson [Cambridge: Cambridge University Press, 1998], 19.24) . We thank Chuck Mathewes for framing Augustine's thought in this way for us.

33. livedtheology.org.

CHAPTER 2: SADDLEBACK

1. Rick Warren, *The Purpose Driven Church* (Grand Rapids: Zondervan, 1995), 194.

2. Jason Byassee, "What is the Church For?," *The Christian Century,* March 9, 2004, 28.

3. Warren, *The Purpose Driven Church,* 45.

4. Justin Crowe, Susan McWilliams, and Sean Beienburg, "A Pilgrimage to the Disneyland of Faith," *PS: Political Science and Politics* 43:2 (April 2010) 360.

5. "The PEACE Plan," brochure.

6. Warren illustrates this target demographic in the form of a model—"Saddleback Sam"—complete with a drawing in *The Purpose Driven Church* (170). He claims that a church will attract and retain people most similar to those who already attend, who tend to image the church leadership. Targeting is simply good evangelism, he says—"Jesus did it" (158).

7. Worship Arts interview, May 28, 2013; Warren, *Purpose Driven Church,* 230. Saddleback previously held a midweek service for believers for the purposes of edification and discipleship, leaving the weekend services to target the unchurched, but this "Believers' Service" was dropped more than ten years ago.

8. Dave Holden interview, August 4, 2012, Lake Forest, California. All subsequent references to Holden are from this interview.

9. Crowe et. al., "A Pilgrimage," 361.

10. For example, see Mara Einstein, *Brands of Faith: Marketing Religion in a Commercial Age* (New York: Routledge, 2008), 102.

11. Dave Holden interview.

12. Class 101, "Membership," is a characteristically alliterative introduction to the

church: salvation, symbols, structure, style, and statements. Class 201, "Maturity," explains the basic personal practices of the mature Christian life: the four essential spiritual habits of daily time in the Bible, prayer, tithing, and fellowship. Class 301, "Ministry," uses the acronym of SHAPE (Spiritual Gifts, Heart, Abilities, Personality, and Experiences) to help people discover how they were "created to serve." This class serves as the catalyst for Saddleback's foundational conviction that "every member is a minister." Finally, Class 401, "Mission," offers a brief history of the church's mission, teaches people how to articulate their own testimony, and introduces them to the PEACE plan, Saddleback's model for global mission. Orienting members to local and global mission work, it promises to help them "discover their life mission and how to reach the world with God's love." Each class meets once for four hours, and members progress at their own pace, typically completing all four in about two and a half years (Saddleback brochure).

13. Justin Wilford, *Sacred Subdivisions: The Postsuburban Transformation of American Evangelicalism* (New York: New York University Press, 2012), 142.

14. Ibid., 153–54.

15. According to sociologist Nina Eliasoph, this parallels a wider trend in American society. In her study *Avoiding Politics: How Americans Produce Apathy in Everyday Life* (Cambridge: Cambridge University Press, 1998), she concludes that Americans in general avoid talking about politics in public contexts. The public sphere exhibits a surprising evaporation of political discourse, creating what she calls "a culture of avoidance." She suggests that while most people want to create a sense of community through various public settings, they do not want to talk politics, but relegate political talk to their private contexts. She concludes, "Civic etiquette made imaginative, open-minded, thoughtful conversation rare in public, front-stage settings," creating a sense of political apathy among American citizens (230).

16. Warren, *The Purpose Driven Church*, 252.

17. Mara Einstein argues that this is aversion to politics is typical among most megachurches like Saddleback. She writes, "Megachurches, which began to develop in the 1970s as well, are now seen as part of a trend toward a 'kinder, gentler' Christian conservative. These churches are all-accepting, with language that allows for inclusiveness. Instead of blaming women for abortions, crisis pregnancy centers are used; instead of gay bashing, they pray for the sinner to become heterosexual and promote conversion therapy and the ex-gay movement. All of it is a repackaging of conservatism, a revision in the marketing strategy, and it has helped megachurches gain more and more congregants, increasing their influence in the political sphere because of their numbers, while at the same time more liberal churches decline" (Einstein, *Brands of Faith*, 179).

18. Robert Putnam, *Better Together: Restoring the American Community* (New York: Simon & Schuster, 2003), 140.

19. Robert Putnam even suggests that it is "consumer" friendly: "The Saddleback experience, from parking facilities and child-care arrangements to the music, messages, and ease of coming and going anonymously . . . weekend services are as carefully shaped to 'consumer' preferences as any commercial product" (ibid., 125).

20. For a discussion of "cheap grace," see Dietrich Bonhoeffer, *Discipleship: Dietrich Bonhoeffer Works vol. 4* (Minneapolis: Fortress, 2003) (previous versions entitled *The Cost of Discipleship*). Bonhoeffer describes cheap grace as follows: "Cheap grace means

grace as bargain-basement goods, cut-rate forgiveness, cut-rate comfort. . . . It is grace without a price, without costs" (43). And then in more detail, "Cheap grace is preaching forgiveness without repentance; it is baptism without the discipline of community; it is the Lord's Supper without confession of sin; it is absolution without personal confession. Cheap grace is grace without discipleship, grace without the cross, grace without the living incarnate Jesus Christ" (44).

21. As James K. A. Smith puts it, "Worship marks us out as and trains us to be a peculiar people who are citizens of another city and subjects of a coming King" (*Desiring the Kingdom: Worship, Worldview, and Cultural Formation* [Grand Rapids: Baker, 2009], 154). He comments further, "I think it is important to own up to the fact that perhaps some of our worship habits are a missed opportunity. . . . While we might be inclined to think of this as a way to update worship and make it contemporary, my concern is that in the process we lose key aspects of formation and discipleship" (153).

22. Warren, *The Purpose Driven Church*, 56, 79, 244.

23. Ibid., 135.

24. This understanding of politics supports Putnam and Campbell's conclusion that "there is little politics in church." Several Saddleback pastors are friends with Robert Putnam.

25. "Rule out the political questions," Oliver O'Donovan writes, "and you cut short the proclamation of God's saving power" (*Desire Of the Nations*, [Cambridge: Cambridge University Press, 1996], 3).

26. Crowe et al., "A Pilgrimage," 361.

27. See Warren, *The Purpose Driven Church*, 377.

28. Mike Constanz interview, August 4, 2012, Lake Forest, California. All subsequent references to Constanz are from this interview.

29. Madison Park, "Rick Warren and church tackle obesity," cnn.com, January 24, 2012.

30. David Chrzan interview August 8, 2012, in Lake Forest, California.

31. Warren, *The Purpose Driven Church*, 355

32. Byassee, "What Is the Church For?," 28.

33. Brandon Lyons interview, May 29, 2013, Lake Forest, California.

34. During a trip to South Africa in 2003, Rick Warren became acutely aware of the magnitude of global need. The body of Christ had become primarily a mouth, he observed. It is a body that is now in need of reattaching its hands and feet. "I found those 2,000 verses on the poor," he recalls, recounting his experience one night during his trip. "How did I miss God's compassion for the poor? I was not seeing all the purposes of God." After meeting local pastors in South Africa, he prayed, "God, what are the other problems that you want to tackle? What are the problems so big that no one can solve them?" (Timothy C. Morgan, "Purpose Driven in Rwanda," *The Christian Century*, September 2005, 34).

35. "The PEACE Plan," brochure.

36. Brandon Lyons interview.

37. David Chrzan interview, May 30, 2013, in Lake Forest, California.

38. Morgan, "Purpose Driven in Rwanda," 35.

39. Mike Constanz interview.

40. On the global level, 8,000 congregants have participated in Global PEACE Team trips. By 2010 a Global PEACE Team had visited every single nation-state. The church now has plans to send teams to the remaining 3,800 "unreached people groups." To accomplish this, in 2012 they began the Twelve City Initiative, a plan to plant Saddleback "outpost" churches in twelve strategically chosen cities to help mobilize other churches to reach these groups (Dave Holden interview).

41. "The PEACE Plan," brochure, and Bill Mugford interview, May 30, 2013.

42. David Chrzan interview.

43. Randy Craft interview, May 29, 2013, Lake Forest, California.

44. Mike Constanz interview.

45. Jon Meachem, "The End of Christian America," *Newsweek*, April 13, 2009, 36.

46. In many ways, this vision is surprisingly similar to those of contemporary theologians like Stanley Hauerwas. For them, the church is a community aligned with the seismic shift in the world that occurred in the life, death, and resurrection of Jesus Christ—all of creation becoming new (2 Cor 5:17). Building on the work of Dietrich Bonhoeffer, who claims that the church literally *is* the present body of Christ in the world (1 Cor 12)—Christ existing today as the church community (*Christ the Center* and *Discipleship*)—theologians like Hauerwas highlight the church as God's primary instrument of healing presence and saving action in the world. For both these theologians and Saddleback, the church is *the* community that has been commissioned to do these things. It is the people, the *polis* that God uses to bring about change in the world, to witness to the kingdom of God by calling for repentance, proclaiming the saving faith of Christ, and embodying the radical practices of kingdom life in its example to others. It is a society ruled by another King, pledging allegiance to another leader above the rulers and officials of this world, and constituted by another mission (Acts 17:7).

47. Warren, *The Purpose Driven Church,* 358.

48. Dallas Willard, *The Divine Conspiracy: Rediscovering Our Hidden Life in God* (New York: HarperCollins, 1997), 36–37.

49. O'Donovan, *Desire Of the Nations,* 3.

50. See Hunter, *To Change the World,* 124.

51. Theologian J. B. Metz articulates this vision of church and world well: "The Church [as] the historically tangible sign and the institution of this grace within the world is not the opponent but the guarantor of the world. The Church exists for the sake of the world. . . . The Church itself is in the service of the universal will of God for the world. The Church, then, bears witness to, and makes present, the power of that will made flesh in which God finally makes the world over to himself" (*Theology of the World* [London: Burns & Oates, 1969], 50).

52. "God's Great Mission for My Life," brochure, Saddleback Church.

53. Warren, *The Purpose Driven Church*, 354.

CHAPTER 3: SOLOMON'S PORCH

1. Tony Jones describes the Emergent Church with the following points: it practices a "generous orthodoxy" that finds little importance in the differences between various "flavors" of Christianity; it believes friendship and reconciliation must mark all debates about doctrine and dogma; it believes in the ever present newness and power of the gospel; it is a global movement; it sees God's activity in all aspects of culture; it rejects a division between what is considered sacred and what is secular; and it rejects the politics of Left versus Right (Jones, *The New Christians: Dispatched from the Emergent Frontier* [San Francisco: Jossey-Bass, 2010]).

2. The term "Emergent" and the general movement of these disenfranchised church leaders has come under a significant racial critique recently. This is offered profoundly by Soong-Chan Rah in his book *The Next Evangelicalism: Freeing the Church from Western Cultural Captivity* (Downers Grove, IL: InterVarsity, 2009): "I personally find the use of the term 'emerging church' to be offensive. I believe that the real emerging church is the church in Africa, Asia, and Latin America that continues to grow by leaps and bounds. I believe that the real emerging church is the hip-hop church, the English-speaking Latino congregation, the second-generation Asian American church, the Haitian immigrant church, the Spanish-speaking store-front church and so forth. For a small group of white Americans to usurp the term 'emerging' reflects a significant arrogance" (124). He notes that most of the leaders and pastors in this movement are only emerging out of a disgruntlement with baby boomer evangelicalism. Rah laments the fact that when these emerging white evangelicals chose to leave the baby boomer churches, they did not consider joining the real "emerging" immigrant or African American churches, but chose instead to cluster homogeneously with those who looked and acted like them, and thus retained their own positions of ecclesial power. This only perpetuates the church's "captivity to white, Western culture" (125). Nearly every person we met at Solomon's Porch, except for Ben Younen, who is on church staff, was white—as were, admittedly, the two researchers asking them questions and making judgments.

3. Tony Jones interview, May 19, 2012, Edina, Minnesota. All subsequent references to Jones are from this interview

4. Doug Pagitt, *Community in the Inventive Age* (Minneapolis: Sparkhouse, 2011), 57.

5. Tony says that the embodied character of this worship setting cultivates a *habitus* of openness and inclusivity in the congregation, citing the term made popular by sociologist Pierre Bourdieu. Theologian Mary McClintock Fulkerson, also applying this concept to ecclesial formation, offers the following definition of *habitus*: "a bodily knowledge, not caused by principles but done in a way that responds appropriately to a situation; it draws from the past but in an improvisational way" (*Places of Redemption: Theology for a Worldly Church* [Oxford: Oxford University Press, 2007], 151). That is, in the case of Solomon's Porch, congregants develop an ethos of openness because of the ways their bodies are situated every Sunday. This does not occur because of some predetermined

principles, but happens improvisationally, in response both to positive elements of the historic tradition retained by Solomon's Porch (such as communion, lay participation in worship, etc.) and in response to the current circumstances of a church that they perceive has become too rigid and hierarchical.

6. Doug Pagitt, *Church Reimagined* (Grand Rapids: Zondervan, 2003), 77.

7. Interview with Ben Johnson, May 20, 2012, Minneapolis, Minnesota. All subsequent references to Johnson are from this interview.

8. Pagitt, *Community*, 61.

9. Pagitt, *Church*, 65, 72.

10. Ibid., 65.

11. Pagitt, *Community*, 139.

12. Ibid.

13. Ibid.

14. Ibid., 164.

15. Tony Jones interview.

16. James Davison Hunter, in his book *To Change the World*, labels this an "identity of negation." Charging this to the Neo-Anabaptists of the Yoder and Hauerwas ilk, he describes this as an identity that is defined and shaped by what the community or group opposes (164). The project of the community is dependent on the existence of this opposing community to serve the role of enemy and grant them their collective identity, one rooted in *ressentiment* (175).

17. Even the primary consideration for the Porch's local missions efforts is to be a place of healing for those who have been hurt by other churches. When we asked about their missions efforts to their relatively affluent local neighborhood, Cecka Parks, facilitator for the Faith, Health, and Wellness Center at Solomon's Porch, answered, "These people are not outwardly struggling to pay rent, but I wouldn't be surprised if a lot of people here grew up in conservative church homes and are jaded by the church." Solomon's Porch can be a new form of outreach and ministry to those who have been hurt by a church. The church's unofficial (of course) motto is: "To be with Christ is to be a benefit and blessing to the world," not to try and "save" people, she added. Visitors will "find this tight-knit community that maybe they could belong to. Because really that's what most people need is a place to belong." In some ways, perhaps, the church must structure its identity around the object it wants to heal people from in order to be an effective source of that healing. (Parks interview May 25, 2012, Minneapolis, Minnesota. All subsequent references to Parks are from this interview.).

18. Philosopher Alasdair MacIntyre would claim that Solomon's Porch's tendency to eschew traditional elements is predicated on a deficient conception of "tradition." More specifically, their legitimate concerns about coercive power orient them toward a hostile view of tradition (also legitimate in light of the way tradition has been wielded as a weapon by churches), and thus undercut a broader, more flexible understanding of tradition. But for MacIntyre, and others following him, tradition is shaped by a community's continual deliberation about what they ought to be, "constituted by a continuous argument" (*After Virtue*, 206). To be a part of a tradition is to be in dialogue with one's inherited modes of

being and vision of community—its crucial beliefs and practices—and to pass these on to future generations. But it is also to continually elaborate, revise, amend, and even reject parts of this inheritance (*Whose Justice? Which Rationality?* [South Bend, IN: University of Notre Dame Press, 1989], 101). Solomon's Porch seems to understand tradition in this first sense, but ignores the flexible, continually transforming dimension of tradition. This broader understanding of tradition in communities, notes MacIntyre commentator Romand Coles, "develops a distinct order that is more than an arbitrary imposition of power and exists with a combination of determinacy and openness" (*Beyond Gated Politics: Reflections for the Possibility of Democracy* [Minneapolis: University of Minnesota Press, 2005], 91). In this vein understanding themselves as part of the church tradition, even if on the borderlands of that tradition, rather than an outlier, will not necessarily inflame their concerns about coercive power.

19. The image of Christ and the church as vine and branches, while affirming the interconnectivity of all congregations into one organism with Christ as their foundation, also suggests both organic growth and the need for occasional pruning (trimming from the inherited tradition). Solomon's Porch has certainly emphasized these important themes in their community, though we worry that an overemphasis may undercut any sense of connectivity to other churches or the tradition in general.

20. Interviews with Doug Pagitt, May 21 and 22, 2013, Minneapolis, Minnesota. All subsequent references to Pagitt, excluding his books, are from these interviews.

21. Sociologist James Hunter observes that "the dominant public witness of the Christian churches in America since the early 1980s has been a political witness"—by which he means a partisan witness—and that this is true of Christians on both sides of the political aisle (*To Change the World,* 12). Hunter laments the "politicization of everything"—that institutions and issues are now defined in relation to state politics—which has "delimited the imaginative horizon through which the church and Christian believers think about engaging the world" (103; see also 185–86).

22. Doug's clean delineation between the church realm and civic realm points back to Luther's famous "two kingdoms" theology. Luther distinguishes between these two "governments," claiming that one is tasked with producing inner righteousness, the other to bring about external order and prevent evil deeds (*Temporal Authority: To What Extent It Should Be Obeyed*). His claims that a Christian should therefore be the first to sign up if there is a lack in hangmen notwithstanding, the most disturbing aspect of this ethic is the way the two kingdoms actually manifest themselves within each solitary Christian in the schizophrenic categories of the "inner" and "outer" man or the office and the person: "here we have two different persons in one man" (*The Sermon on the Mount,* 596). He goes on to say, "Thus when a Christian goes to war or when he sits on a judge's bench, punishing his neighbor, or when he registers an official complaint, he is not doing this as a Christian, but a soldier or judge or lawyer. At the same time he keeps a Christian heart. . . . It grieves him that his neighbor must suffer grief. So he lives simultaneously as a Christian toward everyone . . . and as a secular person" (*The Sermon on the Mount,* 600). This seems to be one theological framework at work in Doug's easy partition of his personal Christian self and his electoral, partisan self. He does not have to worry that one will interfere with the other because they are separate realms and distinct elements within his one person. He can, in Luther's words, "employ [his] secular person" in running for public office (602). (All references from Oliver O'Donovan and Joan Lockwood

O'Donovan, eds., *From Irenaeus to Grotius: A Sourcebook in Christian Political Thought* [Grand Rapids: Eerdmans, 1999].

23. See Martin Luther, *The Freedom of a Christian* and *Sermon on the Mount,* in ibid.

24. Doug identifies his style as progressional, implicatory preaching. "Implicatory" is contrasted with "application," meaning that Doug seeks to implicate listeners in the story of God, not apply life lessons. "Progressional" refers to the way the sermon is formed and conducted, a dialogue where "the content of the presentation is established in the context of a healthy relationship between the presenter and the listeners, and the substantive changes in the content are then created as a result of this relationship" (*Preaching Re-Imagined* [Grand Rapids: Zondervan, 2005], 23). Rather than one preacher developing a sermon in the isolation of a private study filled with exegetical accessories, the sermon preparation meeting allows those present to contribute substantively to the sermon, he says.

25. Pagitt, *Church,* 77.

26. See Paul A. Djupe and Brian R. Calfano, "The Deliberative Pulpit?," 90–109. A recent study shows that 40 percent of church leaders think churches should foster egalitarian debate and help congregants to seek their own views rather than persuading them from the pulpit to take a particular theological line of belief (98). Churches should simply supply members with information that assists them in applying their own values in concrete contemporary situations (93). Over one half of clergy say that they provide multiple viewpoints on a public or political issue when they address it from the pulpit (98). Counterintuitively, this is truer with more conservative churches—those more concerned with outreach—who want to integrate diverse perspectives without alienating any potential seekers (102). In fact, politically liberal clergy are less likely to provide multiple viewpoints on an issue (104).

27. This odd claim, repeated in several of Doug's books and to us in person during interviews, seems to invoke Stanley Hauerwas's concern about severing the Bible from the context of the interpretive community and placing it into individual hands. "The Bible becomes the possession not of the Church but now of the citizen, who has every right to determine its meaning" (*Unleashing the Scripture: Freeing the Bible from Captivity to America* [Nashville: Abingdon, 1993], 32). By freeing the Bible from church authority and placing it in the possession of each individual as his or her own interpreter, we risk making it captive to other ideologies that have already overtaken the individual's world view, be they nationalistic, consumeristic, or other. Hauerwas claims this happens when the distinctive role of the clergy becomes secondary (31).

28. Interviews with Janelle Vick, May 24, 2012 and May 22, 2013, Minneapolis, Minnesota. All subsequent references to Vick come from these interviews.

29. Doug Pagitt interview and *Community,* 23, 48.

30. It is important that the facilitator represents the staff to Central Casting while also representing the staff to the community. If the staff member was not doing his or her job, the facilitator would be the one to address that to the staff member and to Central Casting (Cecka Parks interview).

31. Though Janelle recalls a congregational vote only two or three times during their twelve-year history, she says they did ultimately vote on purchasing the new building. (In

the meeting Doug asked, "I guess we should vote now?") Another, more typical example of Solomon's Porch decision-making process was their decision to open the Faith, Health, and Wellness Center. When questions arose in 2011 about how to use the building in a more sustainable fashion, along with the growing need to generate revenue streams for the church and also justify the purchase of the building to some members, the leadership decided to convert the entire second floor into a wellness center. When the idea generated with Alan Bachman, Doug suggested they talk to Central Casting ("We probably should talk to Central Casting, right?," Janelle remembers) and get their feedback. Then Doug held a meeting for all covenant participants (read, members) in order to see if there were any objections.

32. Interview with Alan Bachman, director of the Faith, Health, and Wellness Center at Solomon's Porch, May 22, 2013, Minneapolis, Minnesota.

33. Pagitt, *Community*, 36.

34. Ibid., 40.

35. Ibid., 51.

36. Pagitt, *Church*, 130.

37. The sermon is always a political act, whatever its form. The power to interpret Scripture for the community, Hauerwas claims, is always a political exercise (*Unleashing the Scripture*, 21). In this way, the sermon is one of the most potent political acts at Solomon's Porch because it expands the scope of interpretation of most churches and embodies the shared goods of the community: those of equality, diversity, and abjuring authority. Every person listening to the sermon is equally empowered to interpret the sermon and the biblical text for themselves, under no hermeneutical authority other than themselves. Because the sermon is intrinsically political, Hauerwas insists that the church community is the proper polity for reading and interpreting Scriptures (27). This seems true at Solomon's Porch, as the entire community engages in the action of interpretation, though without any communally derived application it can seem as if each autonomous individual is his or her own polity.

38. Here we follow Mennonite theologian John Howard Yoder, who notes the exemplary, democratic governance of the church as a potential model for other polities. He perceives an "egalitarian thrust" within the Christian community that may prove instructive to the larger society (*Christian Witness to the State* [Scottsdale, PA: Herald, 2002], 18). That is, one could easily extrapolate these communal practices into a secular or pluralistic setting, and that they can be commended to most any society as a "healthy way to organize" and "prototypes for what others can do in the wider world" (*Body Politics*, 44, 46). For Yoder, this exemplary nature of the church and its democratic practice emanates from his conviction that the church is the true, paradigmatic polis (not the state), and even provides the justification for the legitimation of secular government (*Body Politics*, xi; *Christian Witness to the State*, 16).

39. In "The Deliberative Pulpit?,"Paul A. Djupe and Brian R. Calfano conclude that religious organizations do model democratic practices, especially democratic deliberation (that is, debate over public issues using common terms). In some ways this is similar to Yoder's notion of the church as a political model for democratic practice. In fact, 75 percent of Djupe and Calfano's respondents claim that promoting democracy is essential to God's plan ("The Deliberative Pulpit?," 93).

40. For a resonant vision of "radical democracy" on a more general level that incorporates some of these same constitutive elements, see political theorist Romand Coles (*Beyond Gated Politics*) and Stanley Hauerwas and Romand Coles, *Christianity, Democracy, and the Radical Ordinary: Conversations Between a Radical Democrat and a Christian* (Eugene, OR: Cascade, 2008).

41. Drifting too far from the contours of tradition can enervate constructive dialogue and progressive movement just as easily as remaining constrained within the rigid limits of tradition. Romand Coles notes, riffing on MacIntyre, "A too-radical contingency—a too-radically heterogeneous relationship to heterogeneity—can kill enquiry just as surely as a closed structure" (*Beyond Gated Politics*, 90–91). In other words, operating with a hermeneutical and deliberative structure that is too radically open and contingent—an "anything goes" ethos—is equally as disastrous for any type of constructive formation, be it spiritual, theological, moral, or political. Without any positive center or ordered structure, there can be no constructive formation. In fact, Coles suggests that the contours of one's inherited tradition or identity provide a helpful space in which to provoke meaningful questions and arguments by granting a fundamental level of meaning and relatively stable (yet open) horizon of inquiry. Without this structure, "the contingency and partiality of our concepts and relations" often become so radical as to become unintelligible to one another and irresolvable. Intelligible and intelligent moral, spiritual, theological, and political life becomes impossible (90).

42. Doug Pagitt interview. Appropriately, this unintentional ethos is grounded in Emergence theory, a paradigm that provides no direction or intended outcomes, but only a loosely held structure, one that is generative and created as the community proceeds—one that is ad hoc, in other words.

43. This procedural vision of democracy—on the level of national governance—is critiqued by political philosopher Michael Sandel (*Democracy's Discontent: America in Search of a Public Philosophy* [Cambridge, MA: Belknap Press, 1998]) among many others. For other helpful critiques of liberal/procedural versions of democracy see Jeffrey Stout, *Democracy and Tradition* (Princeton, NJ: Princeton University Press, 2004), and Christopher Eberle, *Religious Conviction in Liberal Politics* (Cambridge: Cambridge University Press, 2002). Sandel describes this vision as a form of government that refuses to affirm any vision of the good life, but provides a "framework of rights that respects persons as free and independent selves, capable of choosing their own values and ends" (4). It is founded on a liberal, voluntarist conception of freedom—the "freedom to choose"— that prioritizes individual rights over a common conception of the good.

44. While Solomon's Porch provides an important example of democratic church structure, it is a democracy that is purely *procedural* rather than *substantive*, a form that does not easily cultivate a cohesive community. Political theorists such as Cornel West suggest, alternatively, that community building is just the sort of work democracy is meant to accomplish. A deeper form of democracy "is not just a system of governance" but cultivates "a cultural way of being," he claims (*Democracy Matters: Winning the Fight Against Imperialism* [New York: Penguin, 2005], 68). It is not only about the inner workings of a political system but about sustaining a genuine community (69). For Solomon's Porch, however, their form of democratic organization does not galvanize people around shared goods in common, a set of goals to achieve, or a commitment to an authority beyond the procedural goals of giving everyone a voice and allowing everyone the autonomy to be

their own authority. Our concerns are akin to those made by Alexis de Tocqueville many years ago and more recently by sociologist Robert Bellah, that democracy—especially a procedural version—actually engenders an individualism because of its focus on equality and freedom (Alexis de Tocqueville, *Democracy in America* [New York: Penguin, 2003], 501, 587–89; Robert Bellah et al., *Habits of the Heart: Individualism and Commitment in American Life,* 2nd ed. [Berkeley: University of California Press, 2007], 22–23). This model of church politics, in contrast to Saddleback (come on, everybody else is making the comparison!), prioritizes *procedure* over *purpose.*

45. At least Doug does this.

46. Mark Chaves observes that most congregations do more to encourage individual political activity than they try to engage politically as a congregation (*Congregations in America*, 111).

47. This is not meant to be an endorsement of the Purpose Driven model (see chapter 2 for more information on that). Rather, it is to note that by virtue of being the body of Christ and the community living in anticipation of the coming kingdom of God, the local church should be gathered around a common purpose guided by these two identity markers. The particular purpose may look different in each local church, but it should be oriented toward witnessing to Christ's redemptive and world-changing mission, now given to Christians as the body of Christ.

CHAPTER 4: FIRST & FRANKLIN

1. Jeff Watson interview, June 16, 2012, Baltimore, Maryland.

2. Jim Schroll interview, June 17, 2012, Baltimore, Maryland.

3. The PCUSA has experienced the second sharpest decline in the most recent figures of all denominations, dropping another 3.5 percent in just one year, from 2009 to 2010, according to the National Council of Churches' *2012 Annual Yearbook* (National Council of Churches, "Church giving drops $1.2 billion reports 2012 Yearbook of Churches," *Yearbook of American & Canadian Churches 2012,* March 20, 2012, http://www.ncccusa.org/news/120209yearbook2012.html).

4. Barna Research Group, December 7, 2009, https://www.barna.org/barna-update/article/17-leadership/323-report-examines-the-state-of-mainline-protestant-churches#.UlTXYiSxOLo.

5. Phil Adams interview, June 16, 2012, Baltimore, Maryland.

6. Alison represents a slow increase in female pastors in mainline congregations. The number of female pastors has jumped from 15 percent of all mainline pastors to over 20 percent over the past ten years (Barna Research Group, December 7, 2009, https://www.barna.org/barna-update/article/17-leadership/323-report-examines-the-state-of-mainline-protestant-churches#.UlTXYiSxOLo).

7. Pam White interview, June 17, 2012, Baltimore, Maryland.

8. Ibid.

9. Alison Halsey interview, June 17, 2012, Baltimore, Maryland.

10. Phil Adams interview.

11. Jason Kissel interview, November 4, 2012, Baltimore, Maryland.

12. Phil Adams interview.

13. Alison Halsey interview.

14. It may be that Diana Butler Bass's idea of a "practicing congregation" was influential in directing the Sankofa process. Bass describes these types of congregations as "Communities that choose to rework denominational tradition in light of local experience to create a web of practices that transmit identity, nurture community, cultivate mature spirituality, and advance mission" (*The Practicing Congregation: Imagining a New Old Church* [Herndon, VA: Alban Institute, 2004], 14). She says that many congregations struggling with the fragmentary nature of culture and the disestablishment of Protestantism's position of cultural influence have turned to nondenomination and posttraditional paradigms. Practicing congregations, on the other hand, are attempting to rejuvenate their own tradition in a process she calls "retraditioning." This describes a process in which a congregation responds to cultural changes by recreating itself into a sacred space for the formation of identity and meaning. Echoing the language church members used regarding Sankofa, retraditioning implies "reaching back to the past, identifying practices that were an important part of that past, and bringing them to the present where they can reshape contemporary life" (50). This requires reflexivity (a willingness to challenge and change its old ways of doing things), reflection, and risk taking, all activities employed in the Sankofa process (14). While it seems that Bass has in mind incorporating ancient spiritual practices like *lectio divina* into the life of the church, First & Franklin has attempted to do this by reaching back into their own past and revitalizing practices of music, outreach, and social ministry.

15. Dietrich Bonhoeffer claims that a church seeking only its "self-preservation, as though that were an end in itself, is incapable of taking the word of reconciliation and redemption to mankind and the world" (*Letters and Papers from Prison*, edited by Eberhard Bethge [New York: Collier, 1972], 300).

16. This is not to say that every struggling church needs to fight to keep its doors open. In his book *The Next Evangelicalism* (76–77), Soong-Chan Rah insightfully suggests that some struggling white American congregations need to give up spending their resources to maintain their own leadership and submit to the leadership of one of the many growing minority churches in their local area. Minority churches can often benefit from the resources of waning white churches, and white churchgoers can benefit from the vibrant and growing faith communities in their neighborhoods, if they are willing to submit to new leadership.

17. Maria Holt interview, November 3, 2012, Baltimore, Maryland.

18. Jim Schroll interview.

19. Betty Schroll interview, June 17, 2012, Baltimore, Maryland.

20. Holt interview.

21. James Cone puts it nicely: "The mission of the Church is defined by its proclamation, and the proclamation is authenticated by the mission" (*God of the Oppressed*, rev. ed. [Maryknoll, NY: Orbis, 1997], 34).

22. The original Greek meaning of liturgy—*leitourgia* in Greek—is inherently socially formative: "an action by which a group of people become something corporately which they have not been as a mere collection of individuals—a whole greater than the sun of its parts," according to Alexander Schmeman. He goes on to more explicitly connect the concept of liturgy and mission, writing, "It means also a function or 'ministry' of the man or of a group on behalf of and in the interest of the whole community" (*For the Life of the World*, 2nd rev. ed. [Crestwood, NY: St. Vladimir's Seminary Press, 1973], 25). The liturgy of ancient Israel, he says, was the communal work of preparing the way for the coming of the Messiah, and in this act of preparation, Israel became who it was called to be—the people of God. In the same way, the church is a liturgy, a ministry to prepare the way for the coming of the kingdom of God.

23. The social and political significance of corporate worship has become a popular theme in the writings of Neo-Anabaptist, postliberal, and radical orthodox theologians (see John Howard Yoder, *Body Politics*; Stanley Hauerwas and Sam Wells, eds., *The Blackwell Companion to Christian Ethics* [Malden, MA: Blackwell, 2006]; William Cavanaugh, *Torture and Eucharist: Theology Politics and the Body of Christ* [Malden, MA: Blackwell, 1998]; and Catherine Pickstock, *After Writing: On the Liturgical Consummation of Philosophy* [Malden, MA: Blackwell, 1997], just to name a few prominent recent examples). While such contemporary sentiments can often be parodied (i.e., taking Eucharist will simply solve everything), we think that it is important to see that the connection between worship and ethics has an important theological history. Friedrich Schleiermacher connected common worship and the development of morality as the two interrelated functions of the church: "Both morality and worship, however, are also so closely conjoined in their ongoing cultivation that when they diverge too much from each other, in either movement or repose, then either common worship comes to look as though it has degenerated into empty ceremonies and superstitions while the Christian life is clearly demonstrated in morality, or, vice versa, Christian piety is maintained through common worship while prevailing morality appears merely to convey the consequences of motives foreign to Christianity" (*Brief Outline*, 170). And Schleiermacher seems to be revitalizing a theme that was central to the early church. The *Didache*, a catechesis and liturgy guide of the late-first-century church, grounded the Christian way of life, Christian "training" as it puts it, in the liturgical practices of baptism, communion, and corporate prayer.

24. Emmanuel Katongole observes this implicit and persistent Docetism in our churches—not just evangelical churches but liberal ones as well. As he says, this "haunts the way in which Christians in the West deal with race, culture, and the problem of racism" ("Greeting: Beyond Racial Reconciliation," *Blackwell Companion to Christian Ethics*, 79), and we would add, haunts the way we deal with illness and those pushed to the margins of society because of illness .

25. This is the way the *Didache* begins its explanation of Christian worship—"the training is this . . ."—as a training for initiation into the Christian assembly. The order provided in the *Didache*, a recording of the oral tradition of the first-century house churches, compiled around the time of many of the New Testament writings, details the step-by-step transformation by which Gentiles were included into the worshiping community. See Aaron Milavec, "Introduction," *The Didache: Text, Translation, Analysis, and Commentary* (Collegeville, MN: Liturgical, 2003).

26. We agree with Hauerwas and Wells that worship offers "a series of ordered

practices that shape the character and assumptions of Christians, and suggest habits and models that inform every aspect of corporate life—meeting people, acknowledging fault and failure, celebrating, thanking, reading, speaking with authority, reflecting on wisdom, naming truth, registering need, bringing about reconciliation, sharing food, renewing purpose. . . . It is the most significant way in which Christianity takes flesh, evolving from a set of ideas and convictions to a set of practices and way of life" ("Christian Ethics as Informed Prayer," *Blackwell Companion to Christian Ethics*, 7).

27. Sociologist Robert Wuthnow argues from his research that most churches offer few theological reasons for their difference from other community organizations. They provide no special insight or corner on the concept of social justice and do not identify reasons why they should be involved in social justice. He worries that when churches cannot articulate what they can offer that is distinctive from other groups, they lose an ability to speak to conditions of everyday life and end up reinforcing the cultures in which they exist. See *The Crisis in the Churches: Spiritual Malaise, Fiscal Woe* (Oxford: Oxford University Press, 1997), 99, 217.

28. At the time this ceremony would have transgressed PCUSA policy. During the denomination's General Assembly in 2014, however, the PCUSA voted to allow clergy to perform same-sex marriages in states in which it is legal. Same-sex marriage was legalized in Maryland by the 2012 referendum vote.

29. Figures on party affiliation show First & Franklin to be somewhat of an anomaly here as well, even among mainline churches. Among all white mainline Protestants, 52 percent are registered (or lean) Republican while only 40 percent are Democratic; almost 40 percent claim to be conservative and 40 percent moderate, with only 20 percent claiming to be liberal in their politics (Pew Research Center for the People & the Press, January-July 2012, Pewresearch.org).

30. Considering this, First & Franklin appears again as somewhat of an anomaly among other mainline congregations. "White moderate to liberal" congregations, according to church researcher Mark Chaves, are the most likely Christian religious group to organize political discussion groups or offer opportunities for political action (as First & Franklin does), but the least likely to attempt to directly influence the electoral process or public policy (*Congregations in America*, 119). This is certainly not the case with this church, although according to Chaves's research, no Christian church group is *likely* to engage in that level of politics, with black Protestants reporting the highest percentage.

31. Church researcher Mark Chaves concludes that because mainline congregations are more wary of appearing like they are taking sides in a partisan conflict than many other church types, they are one of the least likely groups to engage directly in politics— or at least claim that they do (*Congregations in America*, 121)!

32. Jeff Watson interview.

33. Dorothy Jantzen interview, November 3, 2012, Baltimore, Maryland.

34. Bill Bridges interview, June 16, 2012, Baltimore, Maryland.

35. Paul A. Djupe and Christopher P. Gilbert note significant barriers between the intentions of clergy and the reception of congregational members, resulting in situations like this in most churches (*The Political Influence of Churches* [Cambridge: Cambridge University Press, 2005], 18).

36. David Kinnaman and Gabe Lyons, in *UnChristian*, revealed the results of a 2007 Barna Group survey. Among non-Christians ages sixteen to twenty-nine, 91 percent said Christianity has an antigay image and 87 percent said it is judgmental. The results among Christian youth were only slightly better: 80 percent agreed that it was antigay and 52 percent said it was judgmental.

37. "Words of admonition and reproach must be risked when a lapse from God's Word in doctrine or life endangers a community that lives together, and with it the whole community of faith. Nothing can be more cruel than leniency which abandons others to their sin. Nothing can be more compassionate that that severe reprimand which calls another Christian in one's community back from the path of sin. . . . Then it is not we who are judging; God alone judges and God's judgment is helpful and healing" (Bonhoeffer, *Life Together* [Minneapolis: Fortress, 2004], 105).

38. According to Karl Barth, it is Christ's holiness that stirs the church to action, that summons the church into the world (*Church Dogmatics,* IV/1, edited by G. W. Bromiley and T. F. Torrance [Peabody, MA: Hendrickson, 2010], 701). The church's mission in the world is first and foremost a response to what Christ has done for the world. The church must act out of the right that Christ gives it to act. This means that without a strong sense of faith in Christ and realization of the gifts of Christ living and working in the community, its most holy work is only profane, its practices become religious rites, and its mission becomes propaganda (694).

39. Martin Luther King Jr., "Letter from a Birmingham Jail," in A *Testament of Hope: The Essential Writings and Speeches of Martin Luther King, Jr.,* edited by James M. Washington (New York: Harper Collins, 2003), 299.

40. Wise words from King again: "It may be true that the law cannot make a man love me, but it can keep him from lynching me, and I think that's pretty important" ("Address at Western Michigan University," December 18, 1962, www.wmich.edu/sites/default/files/attachments/u34/2013/MLK.pdf).

CHAPTER 5: PRAIRIE STREET

1. Along with several personal items, we did lose hours of interviews with church leaders at Prairie Street and observation notes. We were able to finally write this chapter after reproducing several of those interviews via Skype, phone, and email (dates cited reflect original interviews). Still, our research material on this church was reduced by over two-thirds, accounting for the limited number of voices in this chapter. We thank the people of Prairie Street for their hospitality of time in granting us make-up interviews.

2. Alan Kreider interview, August 7, 2013, Elkhart, Indiana.

3. It was during our time in Elkhart that the story of the scope of Yoder's sexual infidelity and assaults on women broke. In fact, as we were interviewing one church member on faculty at the seminary, he showed us a statement the seminary had just released that day about Yoder's actions and allegations that it helped to cover them up. It was interesting to us that Yoder was only brought up by church members when we mentioned his name. For a full account of Yoder's actions see David Cramer, Jenny Howell, Paul Martens, and Jonathan Tran, "The Yoder File," *The Christian Century,* vol. 131, no.

17, August 20, 2014, 20–23, and David Cramer, Jenny Howell, Jonathan Tran, and Paul Martens, "Scandalizing John Howard Yoder," *The Other Journal*, July 17, 2014, http://theotherjournal.com/2014/07/07/scandalizing-john-howard-yoder/.

3. Alan Kreider interview; South Central Improvement Commission, "South Central Elkhart Quality of Life Plan."

5. South Central Improvement Commission, "South Central Elkhart Quality of Life Plan."

6. Alan Kreider interview.

7. Alan Kreider interview.

8. Katie Jantzen interview, August 4, 2013, Elkhart, Indiana.

9. According to the Mennonite theologian John Howard Yoder, the church must be freed "from the urge to *manage the world*" (*The Politics of Jesus*, 2nd ed. [Grand Rapids: Eerdmans, 1974], 240, emphasis added). Therefore, the Christian should not "identify the gospel of the Kingdom of God with a plan for social betterment independent of the changing of men's minds and hearts" (*The Christian Witness to the State* [Scottdale, PA: Herald, 2002], 23).

10. For a careful critique of Anabaptists, see James Hunter, *To Change the World* (150–66), especially how their political witness reinforces an ecclesial identity of negation in which they discern nothing good in the world but yet need the power of the state to make sense of their ecclesiology: "To literally demonize such powers as the State and the market as they do means that they draw much of their identity and purpose in the here and now through their cosmic struggle with them" (164). See also Kathryn Tanner, *Theories of Culture: A New Agenda for Theology* (Minneapolis: Fortress, 1997), especially 93–119.

11. The goal of ecclesial deliberation, as Yoder describes it, is consensus: "until the consensus becomes clear . . . no decision has been reached" (*Body Politics*, 68). This process is heavily Spirit-led: "the gathered community expects Spirit-given newness to suggest answers previously not perceived" (*The Priestly Kingdom: Social Ethics as Gospel* [Notre Dame, IN: University of Notre Dame Press, 1984], 35).

12. Art Stoltzfus interview, August 5, 2013, Elkhart, Indiana.

13. We recognize that the term "Hispanic" is controversial and carries much (and often negative) political weight. However, we thought it important to retain the terminology that this immigrant community at Prairie Street uses to identify itself.

14. Alan Kreider interview.

15. As one of the most prominent Mennonite theologians, Yoder's work continually notes how the criteria of faithfulness and anticipation of the already/not yet triumph of Christ over the powers of this world supersede the criterion of effectiveness or efficiency. "The key to the ultimate relevance and to the triumph of the good is not any calculation at all, paradoxical or otherwise, of efficacy, but rather simple obedience" (*The Politics of Jesus*, 237–38). Yoder's most prominent example of this is nonviolent action, engaged "not because it works, but because it anticipates the triumph of the Lamb that was slain" (*The Royal Priesthood: Essays Ecclesiastical and Ecumenical* [Scottdale, PA: Herald, 1998], 151), though this pertains to communal life and decision-making as well. Later in the

same essay he talks about abandoning the desire "to be effective immediately" since this desire is a loyalty counter to Christian obedience (158).

16. Again, this corresponds to Yoder's notion of the church "open meeting" (*Body Politics*, 61). Yoder cites the primary elements of that practice to be freedom of speech and orderliness of dialogue, noncoercive deliberation, as well as special attention to minority opinions and the "voiceless"—those who are perpetually underprivileged (66).

17. See Yoder, *The Priestly Kingdom*, 29. The church is ordered by the gifts of the Spirit given to the people, denoting different ecclesial functions. For Yoder, however, the diversity of gifts entails no hierarchy, in importance of each gift or in the decision-making rank of the church.

18. Eleanor Kreider interview, August 7, 2013, Elkhart, Indiana.

19. This is akin to the "preferential option for the poor" that Gustavo Gutierrez reads in the Bible and has made prominent in the writings of liberation theology. This preferential option conveys God's special concern for the poor (Luke 6:20 among many others), and the church's special responsibility toward the poor: "Christian poverty, and expression of love, is solidarity with the poor and is a protest against poverty" (*A Theology of Liberation: History, Politics, and Salvation*, 15th anniversary ed. [Maryknoll, NY: Orbis, 1988], 172).

20. J. Nelson Kraybill, *Apocalypse and Allegiance: Worship, Politics, and Devotion in the Book of Revelation* (Grand Rapids: Brazos, 2010), 15.

21. Ibid., 21.

22. To "rule the world" in a Christian sense, for Yoder, is neither to assume relationships of power nor to attempt to control those in power, but to practice discipleship in light of Christ's nonviolent rule (*The Royal Priesthood*, 135). Yoder continually touts the Christian calling to powerlessness in the affairs of the world: "The kind of faithfulness that is willing to accept evident defeat rather than complicity with evil is, by virtue of its conformity with what happens to God when he works among us, aligned with the ultimate triumph of the Lamb" (*The Politics of Jesus*, 238).

23. Some degree of "instrumentalization" is inevitable in any relationship, and is not always sinister. Theologian Charles Mathewes is optimistic that the church can accept some instrumentalization by the government for particular civic ends; this may even mediate its pretensions of spiritual self-righteousness (*The Republic of Grace: Augustinian Thoughts for Dark Times* [Grand Rapids: Eerdmans, 2010], 52).

24. Writing about the dangers of partnering with outside groups, especially state-sponsored organizations, Luke Bretherton claims, "In accepting the current terms and conditions of cooperation as structured by the state, the church distorts its ministry and mission and remolds its witness around the instrumental requirements of the state" (*Christianity and Contemporary Politics: The Conditions and Possibilities of Faithful Witness* [Malden, MA: Blackwell, 2009], 45). He identifies this danger as "institutional isomorphism," defining this as the tendency of religious groups to reshape themselves in order to fit government policy or processes for the sake of collaborating more effectively. In doing this, however, they risk losing their distinctive characteristics, for example, abstaining from their practice of proselytizing. He frames this as the religious group "recast in the image of the state" (Bretherton, 43, drawing on Paul J. DiMaggio and Walter W.

Powell, "The Iron Cage Revisited: Institutional Isomorphism and Collective Rationality in Organizational Fields," *American Sociological Review* 48.2 (1983) 147–60.

25. Alan and Eleanor Kreider, *Worship and Mission After Christendom* (Scottdale, PA: Herald, 2011), 141–42.

26. Ibid., 176.

27. Just as God makes use of earthly government for God's own ends (Rom 13:1–7), so too should the church use politics. For more, see Augustine, *City of God*, book 19.17: Christians are to "make use of earthly and temporal things like pilgrims: they are not captivated by them, nor are they deflected by them from their progress towards God." While both Christians and pagans make common use of earthly things like civil politics, they do so for different ends. "But the Heavenly City—or rather that part of it which is a pilgrim in thus condition of mortality, and which lives by faith—must of necessity make use of this [earthly] peace [i.e., order] also, until this mortal state, for which such peace is necessary, shall have passed away. . . . And so even the Heavenly City makes use of earthly peace during her pilgrimage."

28. Kreiders, *Worship and Mission,* 152.

29. Karl Barth, *Community, State, and Church* (Eugene, OR: Wipf & Stock, 2004), 144, 167, 171.

30. Kreiders, *Worship and Mission,* 142.

CHAPTER 6: EBENEZER

1. Michael Wurtham interview, October 12, 2012, Atlanta, Georgia.

2. Interview with choir members and Tony McNeill, October 11, 2012, Atlanta, Georgia.

3. Raphael Warnock interview, January 7, 2014, Atlanta, Georgia.

4. Jermaine McDonald interview, November 24, 2013, Baltimore, Maryland.

5. Djupe and Gilbert note the importance of small groups in cultivating political "civic skills" and "political norms (*The Political Influence of Churches*, 19). In small groups church attenders meet discussion partners, nurture civic skills, pass along theological and political norms, and recruit into political activities (245).

6. Michael Wurtham interview.

7. Kris was in attendance.

8. Jermaine McDonald interview.

9. Shanan Jones interview, October 12, 2012, Atlanta, Georgia.

10. This claim is echoed by several scholars, including theologian Charles Marsh. "Particular ways of thinking about God, Jesus Christ, and the Church framed the basic purposes and goals of the movement. . . . The spiritual energies of the movement were born of particular forms of theological expression" ("The Civil Rights Movement as Theological Drama—Interpretation and Application," *Modern Theology* 18:2, April 2002,

233).

11. Stanley Hauerwas, "A Story-Formed Community: Reflections on *Watership Down*," in *A Community of Character* (Notre Dame, IN: University of Notre Dame Press, 1981).

12. James Cone notes, "In black churches, the one who preaches the Word is primarily a storyteller. . . . The story was both the medium through which truth was communicated and also a constituent of truth itself. In the telling of a truthful story, the reality of liberation to which the story pointed was also revealed in the actual telling of the story itself. That was why an equal, and often greater, emphasis was placed on the storyteller" (*God of the Oppressed*, 52).

13. Anthony B. Pinn frames it well: "Black Christianity as expressed through these black churches is in no sense limited to political and social activities. These churches recognize a divine motivation for their activities in that the word of God requires spiritual and material freedom" (*The Black Church in the Post-Civil Rights Era* [Maryknoll, NY: Orbis, 2002], xiv).

14. He alluded to the 1939 Billie Holiday song "Strange Fruit," based on the poem by Abel Meeropol, which famously protested lynching.

15. This interview with Shanan Jones comes from November 25, 2008 at Ebenezer Baptist Church in Atlanta, GA, with Kristopher Norris.

16. From 2008 and 2012 interviews with Jones.

17. This comprehensive nature of the black church entails political dimensions that seem completely natural to the congregation and leadership. The historical and social context of the black community forms the church into its own public communal space. "Negro churches are the only natural communities universal enough to command the loyalty and respect of the majority of Negro masses. They alone are so extensive as to form unity in political power" (Joseph Washington, *The Politics of God: The Future of Black Churches* [Beacon, 1969], 201).

18. Pinn, *The Black Church in the Post-Civil Rights Era*, xii.

19. Evelyn Brooks Higginbotham quotes E. Franklin Frazier's notion of the black church as a "nation within a nation," saying that since blacks were denied access to public space "the black church . . . came to signify a public space, the one true accessible space for the black community" (Higginbotham, *Righteous Discontent: The Women's Movement in the Black Baptist Church, 1880–1920* [Cambridge: Harvard University Press, 1993], 7). Open to both religious and nonreligious groups, she proposes that the black church historically served as a "multiple site," caring for all the needs of a community under oppression—a "church with the soul of a nation" (10). Higginbotham suggests that the lack of institutions open to blacks until recently necessitated the black church becoming "the most logical institution for the pursuit of racial self-help . . . an agency of social control, forum of discussion and debate, promoter of education and economic cooperation, and an arena for the development of leadership" (5).

20. Tony McNeill interview, October 11, 2012, Atlanta, Georgia.

21. Allison Samuels, "For Those Who've Fallen, Salvation Amid the Suds," *Newsweek*, March 31, 2008, 28–29.

22. Shanan Jones interview, October 12, 2012, Atlanta, Georgia.

23. Dawn Brown interview, January 4, 2014, Atlanta, Georgia.

24. Michael Wurtham interview, January 5, 2014, Atlanta, Georgia.

25. Worship service, Sunday, November 2, 2008.

26. Tahman Bradley, "Obama Takes Ebenezer Church Pulpit," *ABC News*, January 20, 2008, http://abcnews.go.com/blogs/politics/2008/01/obama-takes-ebe/.

27. Carrie Budoff Brown, "Obama Speaks at Ebenezer Baptist Church," *Politico*, January 20, 2008, http://www.politico.com/news/stories/0108/7998.html.

28. Shanan Jones interview.

29. Jermaine McDonald interview.

30. Katie Leslie, "Attorney General Holder: Ferguson protests present opportunity," *Atlanta Journal-Constitution*, December 1, 2014, http://www.ajc.com/news/news/attorney-general-holder-to-address-local-leaders-o/njJsF/.

31. Michael Wurtham interview.

32. Ibid.

33. Raphael Warnock interview, October 12, 2012, Atlanta, Georgia. Here again, Warnock echoes his mentor James Cone, suggesting that theology cannot help but take sides in politics, and it should always take the side that aligns with the poor and oppressed because that is the side God has already taken (Cone, *God of the Oppressed*, 65).

34. Davis was a man from Savannah who was sentenced to execution for the murder of a police officer, despite a lack of witness or weapon. He was ultimately executed in 2011.

35. William C. Bell, president, Casey Family Services, in Martin Luther King Sr. Community Resources Collaborative video "Building a Community of Hope."

36. Interview with choir members and Tony McNeill, October 11, 2012, Atlanta, Georgia.

37. The Collaborative Partners consist of Operation Hope, Catholic Charities of Atlanta, the Center for Working Families, and Casey Family Programs. A few other groups also partner with the Collaborative, including the nsoro Educational Foundation, a group that helps children who have aged out of foster care to get jobs or get into college, and the State Department of Family and Children's Services, a government agency that works with children on self-sufficiency and soft skills, as well as securing education opportunities.

38. Walter Jackson interview, January 4, 2014, Atlanta, Georgia.

39. Martin Luther King Sr. Community Resources Collaborative video "Building a Community of Hope."

40. Walter Jackson interview.

41. Bell, Collaborative video.

42. John Hope Bryant, founder of Operation Hope, Collaborative video.

43. The church can use all the help it can get. "We do not have the answers to every social problem. . . . Our job is to struggle along with everybody else and collaborate with them in the difficult, frustrating task of seeking a solution to common problems" (Charles Marsh, *The Beloved Community: How Faith Shapes Social Justice, From the Civil Rights Movement to Today* [New York: Basic Books, 2004], 210). Churches "should listen to them and should learn lessons as they catch a glimpse of a better future under a different banner than Christ. Indeed Christians should receive the discovery with humility and with gratitude for the opportunity to participate in a common human struggle for a just world" (209).

44. Shanan Jones interview.

45. Raphael Warnock, *The Divided Mind of the Black Church: Theology, Piety, and Public Witness* (New York: New York University Press, 2013), 177.

46. Italics added.

47. Marsh, *The Beloved Community*, 33. For a recounting of the experience in King's own words, see Martin Luther King Jr., *The Autobiography of Martin Luther King, Jr.*, edited by Clayborne Carson (New York: IPM/Warner, 1998), 76–78.

48. Robert Franklin suggests "The best of the black church tradition focuses on both personal and social transformation" (*Another Day's Journey* [Minneapolis: Fortress, 1997], 33–34).

49. Warnock, *The Divided Mind*, 176.

50. Ibid., 29.

51. Ibid., 13.

52. Ibid., 177.

53. Quote from J. Deotis Roberts, "Black Ecclesiology of Involvement," *Black Religion, Black Theology: The Collected Essays of J. Deotis Roberts*, edited by David Emmanuel Goatley (Harrisonburg, PA: Trinity, 2003), cited in Warnock, 73.

54. Warnock, *The Divided Mind*, 188–89.

55. Ibid., 184.

56. Ibid., 37.

57. Ibid., 102.

58. Reinhold Niebuhr, "Christian Faith and Political Controversy" in *Love and Justice: Selections from the Shorter Writings of Reinhold Niebuhr*, edited by D. B. Robertson (Louisville: Westminster John Knox, 1957), 59.

59. Warnock, *The Divided Mind*, 189.

60. Thanks to John Shelton for pointing us to this biblical connection.

CONCLUSION

1. Hunter, *To Change the World*, 109.

2. James Cone, *God of the Oppressed*, 69.

3. According to Gustavo Gutierrez, the gospel is inherently political, because "Jesus died at the hands of the political authorities, the oppressors of the Jewish people. According to the Roman custom, the title on the cross indicated the reason for the sentence; in the case of Jesus this title denoted political guilt: King of the Jews" (*A Theology of Liberation*, 132–33).

4. Wright, *How God Became King: The Forgotten Story of the Gospels* (New York: HarperOne, 2012), 187.

5. Yoder, *The Politics of Jesus*, 107.

6. Ibid., 106–7.

7. Willie James Jennings, *The Christian Imagination: Theology and the Origins of Race* (New Haven, CT: Yale University Press, 2010), 266.

8. Ibid., 274.

9. William Cavanaugh, *Theopolitical Imagination: Christian Practices of Space and Time* (London: T & T Clark, 2003), 86.

10. Bonhoeffer, "What is Church?" in *Dietrich Bonhoeffer Works vol. 12, Berlin: 1932–1933* (Minneapolis: Fortress, 2009), 265–66.

11. Bonhoeffer, *Life Together and Prayerbook of the Bible, Dietrich Bonhoeffer Works vol. 5* (Minneapolis: Fortress, 2004), 62.

12. Augustine, *City of God*, 15.21

13. Charles Marsh, *The Beloved Community*, 2. See also Marsh, "The Civil Rights Movement as Theological Drama," *Modern Theology* 18.2 (April 2002) 231–50.

14. King Jr., *Strength To Love* (Minneapolis: Fortress), 10.

15. King Jr., "Love, Law, and Civil Disobedience," *A Testament of Hope*, 51.

16. Dietrich Bonhoeffer, *Letters and Papers from Prison*, Eberhard Bethge, ed. (New York: Touchstone, 1997), 351, 382. Similarly, as Gutierrez puts it, the church finds its meaning in signaling the reality of the kingdom of God, which has begun in history (Gutierrez, *A Theology of Liberation*, 148).

17. King Jr., *Strength To Love*, 66.

Index of Selected
Subjects & Names

INDEX OF SELECTED SUBJECTS & NAMES